PICKING UP MY
SHATTERED PIECES

Bouncing Back When Life Throws You a Curve Ball

GINA PASTORE

with Mike Yorkey

Foreword by talk show host Dennis Prager

Afterword by Boston Red Sox pitcher Steven Wright

CORE.

Picking Up My Shattered Pieces:
Bouncing Back When Life Throws You a Curve Ball

For bulk purchases of *Picking Up My Shattered Pieces*, please contact Gina Pastore through her Facebook page: Gina Pastore Radio

To my children Frank and Christina, you are a legacy beyond words, and I'm deeply honored to be your mom.

Contents

Foreword

by Dennis Prager, host of the Dennis Prager Show

I am honored that Gina Pastore asked me to write the foreword to this remarkable, riveting, touching, tragic yet inspiring book.

I am honored because Gina is a great woman. And she was married to a great man.

Let me tell you a little about Frank Pastore. I saw Frank virtually every weekday of the year. We shared the same radio studio to broadcast our radio shows: my nationally syndicated radio talk show, broadcast weekday mornings; and Frank's enormously popular talk show heard weekday afternoons on KKLA 99.5 FM in Los Angeles.

Over the course of time, I came to realize that Frank was a very special man. I should emphasize that I'm not of the "everyone is very special" school of thought. Yes, we are all precious in God's eyes, but a few people stand out as truly unique and gifted. Frank was one of the finest minds in America.

But he was more than that. Frank didn't merely have a fine mind; he had the rarest of minds—an original mind. In every generation, it seems, God or nature gives us a few truly original minds. The number I have known can be counted on one hand.

I was so taken with both Frank's mind and his ability to clearly express his thoughts that I invited him to present videos arguing for God's existence on my non-profit educational website, PragerU. Because of PragerU's popularity—the website will surpass half a billion views this year—everyone we have ever invited has agreed to give a course. We have professors from Stanford, MIT, and Harvard, Pulitzer Prize winners, major theologians, philosophers, scientists, and former prime ministers. Yet who did I invite to give courses on God's existence?

Of all the theologians and philosophers in the world, I asked a former major league baseball player named Frank Pastore to do so. I even thought Frank would do this better than I would—and I have been arguing God's existence for over forty years.

Turns out I was right. The videos Frank made are brilliant, original, and delivered with his unique combination of charisma, energy, and charm. Frank's ability to apply faith and reason to global and personal issues alike was a gift that our increasingly godless and morally confused society badly needs.

Everyone who heard Frank was blessed to hear him, and by "everyone," I mean everyone of any faith or no faith. I am a religious Jew, and I loved listening to Frank.

This is why I am so touched by Gina's powerful book, which tells the "rest of the story." She was the love of Frank's life, and I know that because he would always light up when he mentioned her. When you read *Picking Up My Shattered Pieces*, you will understand why Frank and Gina were such a remarkable couple.

And you will understand why I began with what I did: "Gina is a great woman, and she was married to a great man."

pass around book

Karen Gilbert to Tina Muzikowski 4/15/22

1

Memories of a Weekend

I remember our last weekend together because we did nothing—and yet we did everything.

My husband, Frank Pastore, and I woke up that Saturday morning to moisture-laden clouds atop the San Gabriel Mountains a few miles from our home in Upland, California, located thirty-five miles east of downtown Los Angeles. Upland, a foothill community of 75,000, was my hometown, where I was born and raised.

Frank and I had dwelled in the same comfortable three-bedroom rancher for thirty-one years, building a life together and raising a son and a daughter who'd grown up, gotten college educations, and married wonderful Christian spouses. Our oldest child, Frank, Jr., and his wife, Jessica, had presented us with a grandchild, starting the cycle of life all over again.

Now we were in the latest chapter of this crazy thing called life: Frank was in his mid-fifties, and I had just celebrated my fiftieth birthday—childhood sweethearts traveling the open road, wherever God was leading us.

Frank was the host of the *Frank Pastore Show*, a radio talk show heard weekdays from 4-to-7 p.m. on KKLA 99.5 FM, the most-listened-to Christian radio station in the United States. According to listenership surveys, around a million people each week tuned in to hear Frank interview guests as well as engage listeners who called in to ask a question, stand on a soapbox, or vent their frustration and anger.

I was Frank's wife and a homemaker, twin titles I wore with great pride. Although Frank was in the public eye—and had been since *before* we got married thirty-four years earlier—we functioned like a well-practiced team. Frank, who was starting his tenth year at KKLA, was a much-in-demand speaker at churches in Southern California and occasionally out-of-state. The last thing Frank wanted to do was travel without me—like he did when he pitched eight seasons in major league baseball.

On many Saturday afternoons or Sunday mornings, we'd hop in our gold Ford Escape and drive to churches near and far, where Frank would share how he was a lifelong atheist whose life was shattered physically and emotionally until he discovered life's greatest treasures: faith and family. I loved being Frank's partner in ministry.

On this weekend leading up to the Thanksgiving holiday, however, Frank wasn't booked—a rare weekend off. Whenever that happened, our son Frankie and Jessica usually drove an hour from their home in Riverside County to visit us, which we encouraged. We loved seeing our only grandchild, Michael, who was in the midst of his energetic toddler years.

But Frankie and Jessica—who was five months pregnant and expecting another boy—had other plans that weekend. That was fine with us because we knew we'd be getting together a few days later when they would be hosting Thanksgiving dinner for us as well as our daughter, Christina, and her husband, Josh. Frank and I were looking forward to spending a long holiday weekend at Frankie and Jessica's home.

While we loved seeing our adult kids and their spouses, Frank often told me that he loved being alone with me on weekends. "I get my girlfriend all to myself!" he'd exclaim. Frank loved giving people close to him a nickname, a holdover from his time in baseball, I suppose. He cracked a big smile every time he called me his "girlfriend." This term of endearment was his way of keeping our relationship young. He never wanted our relationship to get old and stale.

When we got up that Saturday morning, I remember Frank stretching his large frame while he held a cup of coffee, mixed with 2 percent milk and sweetened with Splenda, and looking through our sliding glass doors at the dark clouds covering Mount Baldy beyond the backyard fence. "Gina, since it looks like a yucky day, what do you think of putting up the Christmas tree early?" he asked out of the blue.

"That's a great idea!" I couldn't recall ever putting up our Christmas tree before carving the turkey—we kept our fake tree in the attic eleven months a year—but the thought of getting ahead of the busy holiday season appealed to me.

We set ourselves to the task. Down came the artificial tree and boxes of ornaments—each with a priceless memory. We got the tree up with all the trimmings, as well as a green wreath with a gold bow on the front door. Then I sized up what Christmas 2012 was looking like in the Pastore house. To my eye, the holiday spirit needed some freshening up.

"I need to go to Hobby Lobby to get a few more decorations," I announced.

I didn't expect Frank to join me; he wasn't the type to frequent arts and crafts stores. But today was different. "I've never been to Hobby Lobby," he said, "so I'd like to see what all the fuss is about!"

We were both hungry, so before we left the house, I made Frank his favorite omelet with onion, tomatoes, and cheese, topped with ripe avocado.

Having the entire day to ourselves—unrushed, unhurried, and unfettered—felt like a treat because "just us" weekends didn't happen very often.

After I cleaned up the lunch dishes, we drove to a nearby Hobby Lobby. Walking past the model section, Frank spotted a kit for the *New Bedford Whaler*. Frank always had a thing for the great sailing ships of the 18th and 19th centuries with their intricate masts and billowing sails. There was a time early in our marriage when his off-season hobby was gluing and painting models of famous ships like the *USS Constitution* and *HMS Surprise*.

"I'm going to put this *New Bedford Whaler* model together with Michael," he said.

"But Michael is only three years old," I said, being practical.

"I know. But it's something we can do together."

I laughed because that was Frank being Frank—someone who loved making memories. Okay, maybe Michael was too young to build a model ship, but he'd be old enough one day, right?

We purchased the model ship and a few more Christmas decorations, and then drove home on damp streets. The weather had turned cool with intermittent showers, which Frank and I savored, since rainy afternoons were few and far between. After the raindrops eased up, he sat down next to our backyard fire pit, put his boots up, and looked out at the rugged San Gabriel Mountains.

"You want a coffee?" I asked from the kitchen, knowing what the answer would be. The slider doors were open to the patio and backyard.

"Sure. That would be great, honey."

I busied myself in the kitchen. I filled our Krups coffee maker with Starbucks coffee beans. Frank loved caffeine, but most of the time I mixed caffeinated and decaffeinated beans to take the edge off. Caffeinated coffee didn't bother Frank's sleep, but I'd stay up half the night if I drank the high-octane stuff.

Then I heard Frank talking to himself—loud enough that he *knew* I could hear him in the kitchen.

"I've had such a wonderful life," he said in a clearly audible voice to no one in particular. "I got to marry my girlfriend. We've had a great marriage. We got to have two children. Our kids married wonderful people. I'm so thankful. I really am."

I was touched hearing him utter these thoughts. Then he turned from the fire pit and looked in my direction. "Gina, come out and sit here!"

I looked up and smiled. "I will, honey. As soon as I finish making the coffee."

When I was done, I carried out his favorite white Starbucks mug and a cup of coffee for myself. I plunked myself into a patio chair and teased him a bit. "I heard what you were saying. Are you going to die or something?"

My husband smiled. All he said was, "I'm just so thankful for my life."

Frank changed the subject and asked me if I wanted to go out for dinner. After a busy day putting up the tree and shopping, a Saturday night without cooking sounded great to me.

"Sure. Where do you want to go?"

"How about The Heights?"

The Heights was a nicer Upland restaurant known for its burgers, steaks, ribs, and chops with a marvelous view of the gorgeous valley as well as generous portions—kind of like a Cheesecake Factory. I knew the real reason why Frank wanted to go to The Heights—to order the Macadamia Nut-Crusted Mahi-Mahi. I didn't like fish and never cooked mahi-mahi or salmon at home because the fishy smell did a number on my stomach.

I immediately said yes. During the short drive, big, white clouds filled the horizon, illuminated by a crescent moon, which made the evening feel romantic. We barely looked at the menus: Frank requested his nut-crusted mahi-mahi, and I ordered a Tuscany chicken dish with a glass of Pinot Grigio. Frank refrained from joining me in a glass of wine, however. He only drank occasionally, but he toasted us with a gleam in his eye, clinking his sweating water glass with my flute of light, fruity white wine.

We had a wonderful evening of conversation and relaxation, and I treasured our time together. When we got in the car for the drive home, he leaned over, cupped my face, and planted a tender kiss on my lips. "Look at the sky tonight," he said, and I did. Puffy white clouds still lit the evening sky—totally idyllic.

And when we got home and went to bed, we loved each other tenderly and warmly, as befitting such a special evening.

We woke up on Sunday morning with no agenda, which was another blessing. Ever since his autobiography, *Shattered*, had been released two years earlier, Frank said yes way too frequently to speaking requests at various churches throughout Southern California. Speaking on the weekend fatigued him because that meant no days off that week. Since we were free on this particular Sunday morning, however, we could attend Calvary Chapel Chino Valley, our church home for twenty-five years, and replenish our spiritual tanks.

Upon our arrival inside the sanctuary, we learned that our longtime pastor, David Rosales, wasn't going to be in the pulpit. Instead, a touring ministry known as Potter's Field would be demonstrating the power of the Gospel through a potter's wheel. While Mike Rozell worked a seventy-five-pound chunk of clay, his wife, Pam, sang uplifting songs, giving a powerful presentation of how God, the master potter, carefully molds our lives and transforms our character so that we can be His vessel.

We loved the Potter's Field ministry and knew it well. In fact, we'd seen them do their presentation live at least four times. When Frank realized that our regular pastor wasn't preaching that morning, he was disappointed. "I was hoping to hear Pastor David this morning," he said as we settled into our seats.

"Maybe the Lord wants us to hear this message again, Frank," I offered.

My husband thought a moment. "I suppose you're right."

We sat there, and as I expected, we were ministered to. Frank and I both teared up toward the end when Mike applied crimson red paint on top of the shaped vase. I quietly wondered what transformation God might have in store for my life.

When the 10:45 service was over, I grabbed my husband's right arm and led him out a side door. By and large, the several thousand people who attended the Sunday morning services were polite and didn't bug Frank. When well-meaning folks cornered Frank to "have a word" with him, however, our departure was stretched by a half hour to forty-five minutes. Frank was too polite to cut anyone off, but as the noon hour dragged on, we were famished. We only had a snack with our morning coffee.

"Whaddya say we go check out that new place on Foothill Boulevard—Sammy's Café?" Frank suggested.

I would have been happy going home and making another cheese-and-avocado omelet, but I could tell that he had his heart set on eating out.

Sammy's Café was a mom-and-pop diner with everything from sandwiches and salads to burritos and pasta—home-style meals but nothing fancy. Frank scanned the extensive menu and noticed the "senior citizen" specials for those fifty-five and older.

Frank had celebrated his "double-nickel" birthday a few months earlier in August, so maybe the fact that he qualified for a geezer discount amused him. "I've always wanted to order the senior bacon-and-eggs special," he said.

I looked at the menu description—two eggs cooked to order, two bacon strips, toast, choice of potatoes, and half waffle for only $5.99—and laughed.

"Frank, that sounds like a lot of food, but at that price, it won't be very big."

"I'll start with one, and if I'm still hungry, I'll order another one!" Frank said.

Frank paid attention to what he ate and was big on eating healthy, but he also had a weakness for comfort food—and could really pack it away if he put his mind to it. He was a big guy at 6 feet, 2 inches, and like many middle-aged men with a slower metabolism, he carried a generous girth that broadcast his 245 pounds. Frank had a standing rule: when he tipped the scales at 250 pounds, he limited himself to salads and veggies. Since Frank was nearing his self-imposed boundary, Sunday brunch in a diner would be a splurge.

Sure enough, when his order came out, Frank took one look at the "senior" portions and realized I was right. "You better bring me another bacon-and-eggs special," he informed our waitress. "And instead of the waffle, bring me the pancakes, please."

The waitress's eyebrows raised a notch, but that was typical Frank. He was always trying to squeeze the most fun out of life.

After lunch, we relaxed on the living room couch with NFL football. Frank hopped from game to game while I fiddled with my laptop computer. Frank didn't do much email, so I functioned as his personal secretary, answering emails that had come in the last couple of days. Frank received a lot of emotional messages from listeners, and many of them deserved some kind of a response. I handled those emails, as well as requests for outside speaking engagements. If people called Frank to book him, he let me handle that as well. Frank liked to have me involved in everything, which was good because then I had a good grip on his schedule and our family life. He was very much a family man with our kids and grandchild.

We stayed in on Sunday night. Frank barbecued steaks on the grill and we talked about the "short week" ahead since KKLA gave him Thanksgiving Day and "Black Friday" off and planned to bring in guest hosts to cover for him.

Frank mentioned that he had forgotten to tell me that he had a morning appointment with a show sponsor, Dr. John Shieh of Rejuva-You Medical Spa, a medical doctor who provides a holistic approach to minimally invasive skin and body rejuvenation medical procedures that make your skin look young. Dr. Shieh was a big fan of Christian radio and loved supporting Frank's show as a sponsor. The two agreed that doing an anti-aging procedure on Frank's face would give my husband a legitimate avenue for an honest on-the-air endorsement about the benefits of RejuvaYou.

Frank explained that he had a 9 o'clock appointment with Dr. Shieh in Pasadena, which wasn't far from the KKLA studios in Glendale, another fifteen minutes west of Pasadena on Interstate 134. To be in Pasadena by nine, that meant he had to leave the house by 8 a.m.—an early departure since Frank normally didn't get on the road until 11:30

a.m. It didn't make sense to drive back to Upland, so Frank said he'd just go in early for show prep and meetings with higher-ups at the KKLA studios.

I teased my big lug of a husband about his "spa" treatment with Dr. Shieh. The thought of him sitting back in a comfy chair and getting work done on his face made a funny picture in my mind.

When we retired to bed, I had no idea it would be the last time I would ever fall asleep next to my husband.

2

A Kiss Goodbye

Since we were empty nesters and Frank didn't have to be at KKLA until the early afternoon on most days, we never set an alarm. I automatically woke up at 7:30 a.m. while Frank "rested" until eight o'clock. Our morning routine was to have coffee together, and then Frank would make himself a delicious protein shake. I usually had a few sips while Frank scrolled through his favorite news sites and I caught up on email. We had dueling laptops at the kitchen counter: Frank sported his trusty Macbook Pro, and I loved my lighter Macbook Air.

Frank perused the Drudge Report, the Wall Street Journal, New York Times, Los Angeles Times, National Review, Fox News, and Christian Newswire as well as political junkie sites like Breitbart, Politico, and Real Clear Politics. Frank's talk show was driven by breaking news, and my husband was always looking for interesting topics to discuss. If the U.S. Supreme Court had issued an important ruling or a political figure said something controversial, Frank was thinking about whom he could interview on the subject. He saw his role as interpreting and disseminating the news with a Christian worldview.

On this particular morning, November 19, 2012, Frank set his alarm for 7 a.m. because of his nine o'clock appointment with Dr. Shieh in Pasadena. The alarm buzzer woke me out of a deep sleep; I had forgotten that Frank had set the alarm when we retired. I heard him tiptoe into the bathroom and take a shower—and I promptly fell back asleep.

I awoke again when he was dressing. Frank put on his usual "uniform"—a white button-down, long-sleeved Eddie Bauer dress shirt with a KKLA logo and classic Levi's 501 blue jeans—but when I saw him slipping his stocking feet into a pair of heavy black boots, I knew he was riding his motorcycle into Pasadena and Glendale that morning.

"Why don't you take the car?" I said. "You've got a long day ahead of you, and it's cold today." The wet weather system had blown to the east, leaving generally sunny skies but below-average temperatures in the low 60s. Don't laugh: we think that's cold in Southern California.

"What? And not wear my new jacket?"

I had forgotten about Frank's latest fashion accessory. Frank had recently purchased a heated black leather jacket, treating himself to an early Christmas present.

My husband *loved* riding his motorcycle. There was something visceral about being on a "bike," as he and all riders called their muscular machines: the sensation of speed coming from the wind pummeling their torsos; the thrill of passing pavement just inches from their feet; the adrenaline rush from leaning aggressively into corners; and the awareness of experiencing God's beauty while motoring through picturesque locales.

We were both mindful of the well-known dangers of motorcycle riding. Get too cocky on the road, drop your concentration just a bit, overcook a turn, or fail to practice awareness of every car around you, and you're destined to become a flower-covered cross on the side of the highway.

Frank hadn't always owned a motorcycle, although he had messed around with a dirt bike in his teen years and would talk about how much fun that was. When we got married, Frank *couldn't* ride a motorcycle because there was a clause in his baseball contract that forbid him from getting on a motorbike. He couldn't surf, skydive, or bungee jump either. Fortunately, Frank wasn't a beach boy nor interested in donning a parachute and jumping out of an airplane, and he had no desire to tether himself to a bungee cord and plunge off a bridge. But he sure wanted to ride a motorcycle in the worst way. He honored his contract, though.

When Frank retired from baseball, we were visiting some friends when Frank noticed a skinny Kawasaki parked in the driveway. "Hey, Joe, can I take your bike for a ride?"

As I recall, Frank didn't drive around the block. He was gone for a good hour, so he really took the Kawasaki for a spin. When he came back, all he could talk about was getting his own motorcycle someday soon.

I put my foot down. "No, no, no," I said. "We have small children. I don't want to raise them by myself."

When Frank and I continued the discussion at home, I compromised—a bit. "If you still want to ride when our children are grown, we can revisit the idea," I said.

And that's where we left things, although every time we saw a free-spirited dude with a bushy beard riding a Harley-Davidson chopper with "ape hangers," Frank would wistfully say, "Man, that looks like fun."

"When Christina's eighteen, then we can talk about it," I'd respond, secretly hoping that this overwhelming desire would pass.

"I don't think I can wait that long," he'd say.

The next time he raised the issue, I said, "The only people who should be on motorcycles are police officers," thinking that would end the discussion once and for all.

Frank had an answer for that. "Well, then I'll become a police officer."

I got a little worried. I didn't want him to become a motorcycle cop, either. At the time, Frank had gone into the ministry with Campus Crusade for Christ and its sports outreach known as Athletes in Action. Raising his own support was proving to be daunting, and we were having a tough time making ends meet. And then there was the ministry politics . . .

During this turbulent time, Frank sought out professional counseling, which changed his outlook considerably. He was able to explore issues that happened in his childhood that were still impacting him.

When Christina turned sixteen and got her driver's license in 2000, Frank pleaded with me to get his first motorcycle. During one session with a counselor, he recalled the time when he was seven years old and really, really wanted a purple Sting-Ray bike for Christmas. For weeks, he dreamed of finding that bike parked next to the tree on Christmas morning. When he received his prized bike, he thought he'd died and gone to heaven.

The next day, he rode his purple Sting-Ray to the local mall, where it was stolen—creating a monster-sized hole in his heart. The itch to have his own "bike" remained with him for decades.

Frank said when he described this emotional event to his counselor, she helped him connect the dots. By getting his own motorcycle, Frank could feel whole again.

Seeing how much this meant to him, I relented and allowed him to get his own two-wheeler. I joked to friends that Frank didn't have a midlife crisis in his forties; instead, he bought himself a black Yamaha, a comfortable bike that wasn't big at all. At the time, Frank was working on his master's degree in Philosophy and Ethics at the Talbot School of Theology at Biola University in La Mirada, thirty miles from our Upland home.

Money was so tight in those days that Frank's main source of income was giving private pitching lessons in our backyard. Area prospects would come to our backyard, where Frank would sit on a bucket and tutor teenage kids about curve balls and change-ups. While the $100 hourly rate was excellent, he only gave a half-dozen to a dozen lessons a week since kids weren't available until after school.

Making the sixty-mile round-trip commute to Talbot on a motorcycle saved us a lot of money, but friends would say to me, "Aren't you worried about him in all that traffic?"

"You know, he's a very safe rider," I'd say. "He doesn't do crazy things on the freeway. He's careful."

And that's not to say that every time Frank swung his leg over and got on his bike, fired up the engine, and roared off, I wasn't worried about the danger. But I knew he was vigilant on the road—and in his element.

After five years of riding his trusty black Yamaha, Frank wanted a bigger, better bike. By the mid-2000s, Frank had joined a small cadre of motorcycle riders—all Christians—for fun and fellowship on the road. His buddies rode Harley-Davidson motorcycles, the iconic brand with a distinctive "low-rider" design and engine exhaust note.

Even though there was peer pressure to upgrade to a Harley, Frank had his mind set on buying a Honda because he thought the Japanese import bested Harleys in price and performance. His riding friends gave him a hard time, but Frank didn't back down, teasing them by saying that Harley riders were knuckle-draggers focused solely on the characteristic sound and style of their machines. Frank ended up purchasing the highly regarded Honda VTX 1800—the 1800 standing for twin 900cc cylinder engines of sheer grunt. The Honda VTX was a beast of a bike with a muscular-looking body long and low to the ground.

After hearing about Frank's purple Sting-Ray bike and what that bike meant to him, does it surprise you that my husband chose a Honda VTX with a purple paint job?

Frank rode his motorcycle to KKLA every day—except when it was raining or showers were imminent. The big plus about riding a motorcycle on his commute was using the diamond lanes on Interstates 210 and 134. The high occupancy lanes were reserved for cars with two or more passengers or for motorcyclists. A diamond lane was usually considerably less crowded than the remaining three lanes of major Los Angeles freeways, which cut down Frank's commute time considerably.

When I told Frank that he should take the car on that Monday morning in November, he insisted that he would be fine. Eight a.m. was here before we knew it, and he barely had time for his morning coffee and smoothie. "Time to go," he said, gathering up his black Shoei helmet, thick gloves, and work satchel for the ride to Dr. Shieh's clinic in Pasadena. He leaned over and kissed me at the kitchen counter. "I love you," he said tenderly. No matter how many times he expressed his love for me, I knew he meant it. This wasn't something he did by rote.

"Love you, too," I replied. I watched him turn and tromp through our tiled hallway toward the garage, his heavy boots clicking with each step. He was wearing black leather chaps over his blue jeans.

Just before he stepped into the garage, he stopped and turned toward me. "Hey, I just remembered," he said. "Tonight is *Monday Night Football*. Can we watch the second half while we eat dinner? This Kaepernick kid is really supposed to be something."

The San Francisco 49ers were hosting the Chicago Bears on *Monday Night Football*. The game was being hyped by ESPN because second-year quarterback Colin Kaepernick was getting his first start due to an injury to first-stringer Alex Smith.

"Sure, I'll have dinner ready when you get home," I said. We both knew the drill: within ten minutes of signing off the *Frank Pastore Show* at 6:59 p.m., Frank had fired up his Honda VTX and was departing KKLA's studios in Glendale—located in the San Fernando Valley—and riding east on Interstate 134 until he merged with Interstate 210 to Upland. The thirty-five-mile commute took forty to fifty minutes, depending on traffic, which put his arrival between 7:55 and 8:05 p.m.—sometime during the third quarter of the NFL game.

I was sitting at the kitchen counter, looking at my computer screen, when a weird feeling came over me.

I didn't like the feeling. *Don't go there*, I said to myself.

Then I heard a voice in my soul say, *Get up and kiss him goodbye.*

No, this is crazy, I thought. I had already kissed him goodbye.

Get up and tell him you love him and kiss him goodbye.

I heard the Honda VTX start up in the garage and the purr of the twin engines. I jumped out of my chair and ran through the hallway to the garage. Frank was just about to back out and go, but when he saw me—perhaps a bit frantic—he stopped.

Frank lifted his visor. "What's up—"

"I want to kiss you goodbye," I explained.

"That's nice of you."

Frank had a start-of-the-art safety helmet that fit snugly around his face, so it wasn't the easiest thing to put on or take off. Since I couldn't kiss his lips, I settled for a peck on his nose while he sat on his bike. After delivering the unusual kiss, I tenderly said, "I love you."

"I love you, too," my husband replied, his eyes alive.

I stepped away. With a friendly wave, Frank left the driveway and cruised through the neighborhood, beeping at neighbors.

I stood and watched, trying to figure out what that weird feeling was all about and why it happened. When he exited our street and was out of view, I remained in the driveway and listened to the engine notes.

I could literally hear that powerful motorcycle blocks away—almost until he reached the westbound onramp of Interstate 210.

He was on his way.

3

Waiting for the Call

KKLA, 99.5 FM on the dial, is a Christian radio station that airs half-hour teaching programs featuring various pastors and ministries. Around the clock, you can hear preaching from pastors like John MacArthur, David Jeremiah, Charles Stanley, and Greg Laurie. Sprinkled among the teaching programs were topical marriage-and-parenting shows like *Focus on the Family* with James Daly and *Family Life Today* with Dennis Rainey.

The Frank Pastore Show was KKLA's only live show and only talk show—and the flagship program on the schedule. Billed as the "Intersection of Faith and Reason," the three-hour program aired during the all-important (at least for ratings) afternoon drive-time from 4-7 p.m. The *Frank Pastore Show* held up a mirror to the Christian community in Los Angeles—an aural gathering place where listeners could find out what was going on in the world and in their neighborhoods. Frank, as the host, had a folksy, entertaining style that kept his audience engaged—and he wasn't afraid to wade into controversial topics, including politics.

Frank occasionally wrote columns for Townhall.com, a conservative opinion website. One time he penned these words of reason that underscored his philosophical disposition: "The best way for me to love my neighbor is through those things I choose to do personally. The second-best way is through voting for candidates who support policies that I believe will promote the common good. Thus, I am political because I am loving, and I am loving because I am Christian. Therefore, I should argue—albeit in a God-glorifying manner—about politics."

And that's what Frank did, although please don't get the idea that his show had a heavy-handed political bent. Sure, he devoted plenty of airtime to the 2012 presidential election, bringing on journalists and experts while opening up the phones for listeners to air their opinions about the best direction for the country as well a forum to voice their complaints about politicians. That said, Frank was glad when the 2012 election cycle was over, which culminated with the re-election of President Barack Obama to his second term.

When Frank arrived at the KKLA studios following his "spa" treatment at Dr. Shieh's, he typed out a "run sheet" for that afternoon's program that was posted on KKLA's website.

Here's a description of the guests who'd be on the November 19, 2012 show:

- Melody Rossi, known as the "Mother of the Hood" for her work with Cloud and Fire Ministries in the San Fernando Valley, a faith-based outreach to low-income urban youth and their families. Frank loved turning the spotlight on well-deserving ministries and describing why they needed our prayers and financial support.
- Dr. Keith Matthews, a professor of Spiritual Formation and Contemporary Culture at Azusa Pacific University, a Christian college around fifteen miles west of our Upland home. Dr. Matthews had been a pastor for twenty years and recently co-wrote *The Divine Conspiracy Study Guide* with Dallas Willard, an American philosopher known for his writings on Christian spiritual formation.
- David Aikman, Frank's last guest, was an award-winning foreign affairs journalist for *Time* magazine from 1971-1994 and was currently a professor of history at Patrick Henry College.

Such a lineup was all in a day's work for Frank. At noontime, he dropped by the office of Vice President/General Manager Terry Fahy—his boss—to see if they could "do lunch."

"Yeah, good idea," Terry said. "Do you mind if Bob comes? I'm supposed to have lunch with him."

Bob was Bob Hastings, the sales manager at KKLA. The three of them walked a couple of blocks to Shakers, an old-school diner that had been around forever in Glendale.

During lunch, Terry and Bob sat across the table from Frank, talking shop and going over Frank's speaking schedule. They wanted to make sure their dates synced with Frank's bookings.

During their time together, Bob almost did a double-take looking at Frank. That afternoon, my husband's eyes were incredibly blue—practically azure in color. Frank's eyes were so blue that the sales manager wondered if he was wearing contacts, but my husband had never worn contacts in his life.

I wish I could have seen those bright blue eyes myself.

Frank usually called me to say hello and check on my day, but he didn't that afternoon. I didn't think much of it. His "power lunch" with Terry and Bob ran long, and I knew that in the last hour of show prep there were producers and technicians asking questions and looking for direction, and there were always a zillion phone calls between Frank and his guests and their assistants.

I always listened to *Frank Pastore Show* while I ran errands, and it wasn't because I was a captive audience in the car. I enjoyed hearing my husband deliver a fast-paced and entertaining radio show. While I often knew what Frank was going to say before he said it—we really could finish each other sentences—I immensely enjoyed how he pulled off the high-wire act of live radio, where there wasn't any safety net. Listen long enough, and anything and everything could happen and often did, especially when he took calls from his listening audience. There were some crazy callers over the years that gave us plenty to talk about over dinner after the show.

Speaking of dinner, I busied myself during the five o'clock hour with making one of Frank's favorite meals—Chicken Delicious. The recipe called for cut-up boneless chicken and sautéed mushrooms and green onions cooked in a sauce made with a can of condensed cream of mushroom soup, half-and-half cream, Pecorino cheese, and a splash of Marsala wine. Chicken Delicious wasn't terribly difficult to prepare, but Frank sure loved it. I wasn't going to cook any high-carbohydrate pasta, however, following the weekend indulgence. We'd have just the low-carb Chicken Delicious and a salad.

I did set out a bottle of South Coast Pinot Grigio that Frankie had given us. Perhaps this would be one of those evenings where Frank joined me with a glass of the white, fruity wine.

While I prepared dinner and puttered around the house, I listened to Frank's show on an old black radio in the kitchen with an old-fashioned antenna. That was the only way I could hear the show; the other radios in the house couldn't catch the signal due to interference from the mountains. Since I didn't have a smartphone—just a simple flip phone plus the landline—I couldn't play the iHeart radio app through wireless speakers. Having the latest technology at our fingertips wasn't our thing; we didn't even have a DVR in the house to record TV programs. That's why Frank knew he had to get moving if we were going to watch the second half of the 49er-Bears game together on *Monday Night Football*.

During the 5 o'clock hour, Frank was interviewing Dr. Keith Matthews, the professor at Azusa Pacific University. Frank ran a free-wheeling show. If something sounded interesting, he'd chase after that topic with a guest or a caller, just to see where the conversation led to. He knew that made for interesting radio. While tens of thousands of commuters listened in at any one time, Frank was also aware that the competition for listeners' ears in the L.A. market was just as intense as any pitcher-versus-batter match-up when he played for the Cincinnati Reds back in the 1980s. Frank's broadcast style kept things lively, energetic, and captivating.

Frank steered the discussion into the topic of life after death with Dr. Matthews and started waxing philosophical on the air. "Is there life after death? Are you more than just your brain?" my husband asked rhetorically. "Are angels real? If everything has a cause, who caused God?"

He and Dr. Matthews batted those questions around for a segment. When they returned from a commercial break, Frank was still animated when he turned the discussion toward a new show on the Science Channel called *Through the Wormhole*, hosted by actor Morgan Freeman. Then my husband said this:

> *Look, you guys know I ride a motorcycle, right? So, at any moment, especially with the idiot people who cross the diamond lane into my lane, all right, without any blinkers—not that I'm angry about it—at any minute I could be spread all over the 210. But that's my body part, and that key distinction undergirds the entire Christian worldview.*

I was cutting up chicken when I heard him say those words. I remember thinking, *I wish he wouldn't use that example*, but I wasn't upset by what he said. I knew my husband well enough to understand that he was speaking out of a philosophical bent.

Following his retirement from baseball, Frank had earned his master's degree in Philosophy and Ethics from Talbot and become a very good debater on the truthfulness of Christianity. He believed deeply that if people understood that they were more than a body—that they had souls, as well—then they would find it easier to believe in God. He was adamant that people understand that we were not just a physical system but also had real souls in our bodies.

When Frank and Dr. Matthews veered off on that tangent, it was natural for my husband to use himself as an example. It was like he was saying, "If I get killed tonight, you'll find my body parts on the freeway, but that's not who I am. I'll be with the Lord." His stark illustration was his way of pounding the point home. I knew he wasn't trying to predict anything.

At the same time, though, my ears had perked up because this was the *second* time I heard him say something about dying in the last few months. And then I recalled what he said from our patio fire pit on Saturday morning—about how thankful he was for the life God had given him.

Soon, though, my mind drifted elsewhere as I got the Chicken Delicious into the oven. I busied myself with clean-up. I was looking forward to my best friend coming home, giving him a big hug, taking dinner out of the oven, and serving a piping-hot meal with *Monday Night Football* in the background. Whenever we ate dinner with a game on, we sat at the kitchen bar. We could see the TV screen because we had an open-concept family room next to the kitchen.

Around 7:30, I called my sister, Marina, to chat and catch up. As time passed, I mentioned that it was strange that Frank hadn't arrived yet. Time got away from us, and when the call ended, I looked at the kitchen clock. The time was straight-up eight o'clock.

Frank will be here any minute, I thought. When another five, ten minutes passed without his arrival, I thought his last guest had kept up the chatter after Frank signed off. That didn't happen very often, but that would explain why he was running late.

Or maybe it was the famous Los Angeles traffic. The 210 was a busy corridor, and Frank was part of the mass exodus from the Pasadena/Arcadia area that traveled eastbound to cheaper housing in the Inland Empire in Riverside and San Bernardino counties. But even if traffic was stopped, Frank was able to "lane split" and ride between cars stuck in the diamond lane and the first lane. That could be dangerous, of course, and Frank didn't like to lane split, but riding at 30 mph was better than being at a standstill.

It was 8:15. Frank *had* to be arriving at any moment. If he had stopped at a gas station after he got off the freeway, he would have called out of courtesy. So I called his cell phone—Frank had an iPhone—that immediately went to voice mail.

"Hi, honey. I'm just checking in to see where you are," I said.

Frank was tethered to his iPhone. That was one part of modern technology he had embraced, so if he was standing at a gas pump, he would have called me back immediately.

After leaving a message, I took dinner out of the oven and the green salad out of the refrigerator. I didn't open the bottle of wine because I wasn't sure if Frank would want a glass. I twiddled my thumbs, anxious for him to step in the house at any minute.

At 8:30, dinner was getting cold—and I was famished. I scooped a helping of Chicken Delicious onto my plate with a bit of salad and started eating. A few more minutes passed, and I knew Frank had never been this late without at least calling me with a head's up.

Between bites, I called Josh Jacobs, Frank's producer on the radio show.

"Hey, J.J., it's Gina," I said, employing the nickname Frank had given him.

"Hi, Gina."

"Frank's not home yet. I know it's not super late, but I was wondering if he got hung up with his last guest."

J.J. immediately responded. "No, Frank was out of here by 7:10, 7:15, his usual time."

"Oh." I know my voice sounded deflated. I was trying to process why he would be so late.

"Maybe he stopped for gas or something," J.J. remarked, trying to help.

"I already thought of that. But he'd be home by now if he stopped for gas."

"Tell you what," J.J. said. "I'll go down to the parking garage and see if the bike is there."

"That would be very nice of you." I was grateful that he'd go to that trouble for me since the KKLA studios were situated in a high-rise commercial building and the parking garage was a hundred yards away from the front entrance.

"I'll call you right back," he promised.

Ten minutes later, about a quarter to nine, I heard from J.J. "The bike is gone, so I called the Traffic Center," he said, referring to the service that KKLA and every major Los Angeles radio station subscribed to for their freeway traffic reports. "They're reporting a motorcycle accident on the 210."

Hearing the words *motorcycle accident* sent a shiver through my body. "Where?" I asked.

"At Buena Vista in Duarte, eastbound," he said matter-of-factly.

I was ready to panic. I immediately pictured the Buena Vista Drive exit, just west of Azusa, in my mind. I had driven that stretch of the 210 thousands of times over the years.

Call it a wife's intuition, but a heavy sense of doom filled my heart.

"Do you know when the accident happened?"

"The CHP said 7:35 p.m."

That was *exactly* the time Frank and his Honda motorcycle would have been passing through Duarte. At that moment, I *knew* Frank had been involved in a crash. My body immediately experienced shock and fear that I had never known before.

"I can't believe this is happening . . ."

J.J., sensing the fear in my shaky voice, tried to lift my spirits. "Let me make a phone call. Then I'll call you right back."

"Thanks, J.J."

I ended the call, but alarm and anxiety that I'd never felt in my life engulfed me.

A single thought came to mind: *Gina, don't let yourself go there.*

But as they say, you can't unring a bell.

4

Hope Against Hope

Frank had been in a motorcycle accident on a busy Los Angeles freeway. That was the only explanation for his tardiness.

Panic threatened to swallow me whole. And then shock settled in, a feeling like I'd never experienced before. I literally felt like I was leaving my body.

I looked around the kitchen to get my bearings. All sorts of thoughts about Frank rushed through my brain: *He was knocked out. He suffered bumps and bruises. He can't call because he's unconscious. He's going to be okay.*

Then my thoughts turned darker: *He could be dead.*

At one time, I studied to be a nurse, so I imagined doctors and nurses working like busy bees in an emergency room, stabilizing Frank or embarking on a life-saving operation. I knew that when helmeted motorcyclists tangled with 3,500-pound cars, their bodies had little to no protection between them and hard steel, shiny aluminum, glass windshields, and freeway concrete. What I didn't know was that every single day in California, a motorcyclist loses his or her life.

My cell phone rang again, and I recognized J.J.'s number.

He got to the point immediately. "Gina, I just talked to the CHP," referring to the California Highway Patrol, "and I inquired about the 7:35 p.m. accident. They asked if I was a family member."

Now my heart was in my throat.

"What did you say?"

"I said no, I wasn't. They told me to have a family member call. I have the call-back number for you."

I looked around the kitchen countertop for a piece of paper and something to write with, but I could barely move my arms or legs. The out-of-body experience had returned, and everything felt strange.

"Hold on . . ." I said into the phone.

When I was ready, J.J. dictated the number. I immediately dialed the CHP number with a pounding heart.

When I got to a live voice, I blurted, "This is Gina Pastore, and I'm trying to find out if my husband, Frank Pastore, was involved in an accident."

"Just a minute," I heard a male voice say.

After putting me on hold, the CHP officer returned and started asking routine questions, but I didn't have time for that.

I raised my voice. "I NEED TO KNOW IF MY HUSBAND, FRANK PASTORE, HAS BEEN IN AN ACCIDENT!"

I wasn't screaming, but the CHP officer needed to know that I meant business.

I heard a shuffling of papers. "Yeah, well, on this report there's a Frank Pastore here. He's been airlifted to the USC Medical Center."

Airlifted? Oh . . . my . . . God.

I didn't scream, but I wanted to.

That's all the information the CHP officer had. He urged me to call the University of Southern California Medical Center, which was Los Angeles County's biggest hospital and major trauma center. He gave me a number to call and wished me all the best.

My first thought was, *Why hasn't anyone at the USC Medical Center called me? How many hours were they going to wait to notify a family member?*

I dialed the number. When I finally reached a live voice, I breathlessly said, "This is Gina Pastore calling about Frank Pastore. He's been airlifted to the Medical Center. How is he?"

"Just a minute, ma'am."

I must have repeated this three or four times as I was patched through to different departments. Finally, a female voice came on the line. After identifying myself, she said, "Where are you?" She spoke with a snooty manner.

"What do you mean, *Where am I?* I was told to call this number!"

"Well, you need to get here!"

"I NEED TO KNOW WHAT'S HAPPENED TO MY HUSBAND!"

"Just one minute."

Another female voice came on the line. She identified herself as a doctor.

"What happened to my husband? I need you to tell me right now." This time, I was calmer.

"I'm sorry, but I can't tell you over the phone. You need to come here. Where do you live?"

"I'm in Upland. I'm far away. Can you tell me what happened? What's going on?"

"He's here."

"I need to know—"

She relented a tad. "We've stabilized him. He was resuscitated."

I knew what *resuscitation* meant from my interest in nursing. Frank had been knocked out to the point where his heart had stopped. He had been brought back to life.

The doctor continued. "I can't tell you about his injuries over the phone, Mrs. Pastore, but if you can get here as fast as you can, we'll explain everything to you."

"Thank you. I will get there as soon as possible."

I hung up and immediately called my sister, Marina, older by nine years. She and her husband, Don Gardner, had recently moved back to Upland, so that was in my favor.

I kept my composure as I relayed the information that Frank had been in an accident and airlifted to the USC Medical Center. I heard the shock and fear in Marina's voice as I outlined what little information I knew.

"We'll be right there," Marina said with no hesitation.

I hung up and ran to our bedroom, where I opened our closet and grabbed a light jacket. I was dressed in jogging pants and couldn't care less how I looked. Then I heard a car horn. Marina and Don had arrived in a matter of minutes. I ran outside and jumped in the back seat of their Infiniti SUV.

Marina turned around. She'd been crying. "Oh, Gina, I'm so scared," she said.

Meanwhile, Don was typing "USC Medical Center" into his GPS but was having trouble nailing down the best route to take. It looked like the most direct way was to take surface streets to Interstate 10 and follow that main artery into downtown Los Angeles. The 600-bed hospital was located at the busy intersection of the Interstate 10 and Interstate 5.

I leaned back in my seat, shaking from nervousness of the unknown and shivering because of the damp cold.

"I think I got it," Don said. "Traffic looks good. We should be there in forty-five minutes."

Marina chimed in. "I'm calling Andrea. Maybe she can find out something."

Andrea was Don and Marina's thirty-six-year-old daughter. She worked as a freelance investigative reporter and would know which website to check or whom to call to get more information.

Marina reached Andrea and explained the situation, then hung up. A few minutes later, my niece called back. First, Andrea went to the CHP website, which had a running list of all the freeway incidents throughout the day. She found the 7:35 accident on the 210 eastbound at Duarte, which said a motorcycle was down. The report also noted that a man was standing at the accident scene. Andrea then called the CHP directly, who confirmed that the motorcyclist was airlifted to the USC Medical Center.

When my niece called with the news that a man was standing at the accident scene, my heart quickened. If that was Frank, there was a good chance that he'd be all right.

I realize now that shock kept me from thinking clearly. There was no way Frank could have stood on the side of a freeway with serious injuries, but I grasped onto the report of a man standing on the freeway like a drowning swimmer hung onto a life preserver.

And then freeway traffic came to a standstill. It was probably 10 p.m., the time when Caltrans begins maintenance and repair work. As anyone who's driven on Los Angeles freeways knows, there are an amazing number of cars on the road in the middle of the night. Shutting down two lanes created a huge bottleneck.

Don slammed the steering wheel in frustration. I remained stoic in the back seat since there was nothing I could do. Marina was holding back tears as she said, "You need to call the kids."

I had thought about that. I knew Frankie and Jessica were either going to bed or in bed. Frankie went to work early—he was a family dentist and had a busy patient schedule. As for our daughter, Christina, who lived in Newport Beach in Orange County, she didn't have any children and stayed up later, but I knew it was late . . .

I dreaded calling my kids. I was aware that this terrible news would devastate them, so I procrastinated for a few moments. Marina softly urged me to phone them anyway, saying that what had happened to their father was too serious *not* to call.

I felt I should try to reach our oldest child first, so I dialed Frankie. He wasn't asleep when he answered, but I could tell he was tired. I sputtered in a frantic voice, "Dad's been in an accident."

"Oh, no. How bad?" Frankie asked.

"He was coming home when the accident happened near Duarte. He was airlifted to the USC Medical Center. The CHP report said a man was standing after the accident, so there's hope."

"We're coming out!" Frankie immediately responded.

From Frankie and Jessica's home, that would be a two- or three-hour trip to downtown L.A. in the middle of the night. "No, Frankie. It's too far and too late."

"We're coming anyway!" Frankie exclaimed.

That was typical of my son, but too much was unknown and the distance was too great. Besides, Jessica was five months pregnant and having problems with varicose veins, and waking up a three-year-old in the middle of the night wouldn't have been a good idea.

"Don't come, Frankie. They're doing road construction on Interstate 10, and it will take you forever to get here."

Reaching Christina proved to be more difficult. I didn't know until later that her phone was dead—and she and Josh had gone to bed. I decided to text her as well as Josh to call me as soon as possible on my cell, saying it was urgent. Neither replied right away, however.

How could I reach Christina? Then I remembered that a close family friend had a daughter who lived nearby. A couple of phone calls later, and my friend's daughter was pounding on Josh and Christina's front door. Their bulldog, named Sherlock, barked like crazy, waking everyone up. When Josh and Christina answered the door, they received the startling information that Frank had been in an accident and they needed to call me on my cell.

When Christina reached me, tears flowed as I described what I knew. She was upset by the news and said she and Josh were getting in a car immediately and would meet us at the USC Medical Center. This time, I didn't discourage her because their family situation was different than Frankie and Jessica's, plus they were only forty-five minutes away.

I sensed that I needed family around me for whatever the future brought.

A GPS, as everyone knows, has its limitations.

As we neared the USC campus near downtown Los Angeles, we drove in circles trying to find the right building, which left us frazzled. There were blocks and blocks of hospital buildings; the medical center was massive. We weren't sure where to go.

"I'm parking the car," said Don, frustrated like all of us.

He turned into a parking garage and we started walking. It was after 11 p.m. We asked security guards for directions; each one pointed us in the right direction, but it wasn't easy finding the right Intensive Care Unit building. After being misdirected a couple of times, we were all so tired and frustrated, and I just wanted to get to my husband. I felt like I was in a bad dream—trapped and frantic, feeling unable to run or move.

We finally found the right ICU for brain injuries and the right floor. Upon reaching the reception, we were directed to a nearby waiting room, which was deserted at this late hour.

We didn't have to wait too long for a young neurosurgeon to walk out in blue scrubs. I almost jumped out of my chair.

"Are you Mrs. Pastore?" he asked.

"Yes."

"We've been waiting for you."

"Yes, I know. We live in Upland, but nobody called me. I didn't know anything until my husband's colleague told us that Frank had been in a motorcycle accident."

"I don't know what happened, but I apologize," he said.

I noticed that the neurosurgeon was avoiding eye contact with me. I started to cry.

"What's my husband's condition?" I asked through the tears.

"Well, he's got two broken legs and a fractured wrist. We think he may have a broken shoulder, but we'll have to wait until the morning to run X-rays on him. Of course, the most serious injury, and the one we're really concerned about, is his traumatic brain injury. Do you understand what that is?"

I nodded for him to continue, but I could feel shock setting in even more. My head was absorbing all this horrible information, but my heart was saying, *No, this can't be happening!* My initial reaction as a happily married woman was to always go to Frank. I knew he'd comfort me and give me his reasoned opinion, but I was becoming increasingly aware that I would be facing this trial alone.

The neurosurgeon continued to look down at his notes. "With the brain, there's no way of knowing exactly the severity of the injury. We won't know how serious the injury is until and if he wakes up."

If he wakes up?

"Do you think he's going to make it?"

"I can't answer that question, but I have seen people come in here in bad shape and walk out. I've seen people in here with lesser injuries and pass away—and everything in between. We'll know more in three days. Right now, we're monitoring the swelling in your husband's brain, and we have not had to release the pressure. But within three days, that should peak and we may have to go in and break his skull and release the pressure building up in his brain."

I exhaled as I considered the ramifications of what I just heard.

"Would you like to see him?" he asked.

"Yes."

I followed the doctor into the ICU unit with Marina and Don close behind.

As we walked down a long corridor, I was in shock and feeling like I was part of a bad dream. The strong smell of disinfectant and rubbing alcohol nearly overwhelmed me. I glanced in several rooms along the way and saw patients in very bad shape. Then we reached the nurses' station, where Frank was lying on his back, eyes closed and oblivious to the world. (I would later learn that the most critical patients are always next to the nurses' station.)

As we drew close, I could see that a breathing tube was inserted into his mouth. All sorts of monitors surrounded him, connected by tubes and wires. What surprised me was that his face looked perfect: no bruises, contusions, or unusual swelling. There were no casts. His legs were bandaged and splinted, and ace bandages were wrapped around both arms. Frank looked a lot better than I expected.

At that moment, I wanted to jump in his hospital bed, wake him up, and say, "Frank, let's get out of here and go home." I was still in this weird stage of shock and disbelief. At the same time, though, these thoughts came to the forefront: *Oh, my gosh, I don't think my husband can survive this. This is really, really bad.*

I wondered if Marina and Don were carrying the same thoughts. Marina was silently crying, while Don looked like he had seen a ghost. I stood frozen, unsure if I could or should touch him because he was so wounded and injured. Right at that moment, a nurse came in and moved Frank's left arm.

"Please don't do that," I said. I had a sense that I needed to protect my husband, who could not speak. I didn't want him to feel any more pain that he was already in.

About fifteen minutes passed by. A nurse approached and said she needed to take Frank for some type of CAT scan, a signal that we needed to leave the ICU. As the nurse walked us down the corridor, I had a question.

"Can I stay here tonight?"

"Oh, honey, there's nowhere for you to sleep. You can't stay in the ICU with him. You saw all the monitors. But we can't stop you from staying in the waiting room all night or sleeping on the floor."

I didn't want to leave Frank—not when he needed me so badly—so as far as I was concerned, I'd stay in the waiting room and visit him as often as I could.

Marina excused herself to find a restroom When she returned, she looked sick as a dog and told me that she had just thrown up. I felt a bit nauseous as well, but I was too numb to vomit.

It was past midnight. A nurse came out of the ICU holding a clipboard with a paper attached.

"Mrs. Pastore, we'd like to do a test on your husband," she said, holding a pen.

When I asked for more details, the nurse explained that the USC Medical Center was doing an experimental clinical trial with a new hormone therapy that could help the brain rejuvenate. "We'd like to do this test on him, so if that meets with your approval, I need you to sign these papers."

"No, I won't sign."

Don inserted himself into the discussion. "Gina, it can't hurt to try."

"Okay, tell me more," I said to the nurse.

Satisfied that this experimental hormone therapy could help my husband, I signed the consent form.

Twenty minutes later, the female French-Canadian doctor that I had spoken to on the phone walked into the waiting room.

I probably asked her "Is he going to make it" three times. On each occasion, she said, "We don't know."

Christina and Josh arrived around 1:30 a.m. The ICU nurses insisted that only two could visit Frank at a time—they let the three of us slide during the first visit—so my daughter and her husband saw Frank without me. When they returned to the waiting room, they looked devastated and were crying. Josh kept rubbing his thick brown hair in anguish. They had brought blankets with them, and they said they were staying.

The vigil continued. At 4:30 a.m., I asked to see Frank again. It looked like he hadn't moved a muscle since our first visit. I felt grieved.

On the way back to the waiting room, a new nurse pulled me aside. "You really need to go home and get some rest. I've worked here many years, and when you're dealing with patients in comas, it's going to be a roller-coaster ride. So you're going to be here a lot. I don't recommend sleeping on the waiting room floor. Why don't you go home, rest up, and come back later?"

In my fatigued state, she made sense. I've always had a bad neck, so there was no way I could sleep on the floor anyway—or in a chair.

Feeling helpless and exhausted, I realized that I was in for the ride of my life. I turned to Marina and Don and said, "Let's go home." Somehow, a part of me was already groping for parts of my husband's existence, and our home was our sanctuary. Maybe a couple of hours of sleep and a shower would invigorate me.

When the three of us stood to leave, Christina and Josh insisted they weren't going anywhere. "I'm staying here until Dad wakes up," my daughter announced.

My heart melted. I remember looking at her and thinking as a mother, *I hope he does wake up, but I'm not sure he will.* But I didn't voice that thought to Christina.

We arrived in Upland at 5:30. It was still dark since sunrise was an hour away. After Don and Marina dropped me off at the house, I took a shower and fell into bed. But I couldn't sleep. Instead, I laid there and stared at the ceiling, my heart beating out of my chest. And then I heard a key rattling and our front door opening. Marina had returned with my mother, Ann Pignotti. She lived in a condominium complex less than a mile from me. My father, John, had died six years earlier.

Both Mom and Marina were crying as they entered the master

bedroom. Both sat on the edge of my bed, but Mom was crying hysterically. I leaned close and hugged her.

I jumped out of bed. "I'm getting dressed, and we're going back to the hospital," I announced.

Marina said she had spoken with Veronica Roggemann, one of our good friends. "She's forming a team. Somebody is going to be with you all the time. You're not going to the hospital by yourself today. You're going with Veronica."

Hearing that I would be cared for was comforting. I jumped out of bed to start getting dressed. Marina had brought over a box of muffins.

"I'm not hungry," I said. How could I eat? I felt like I had been punched in the stomach. "Let's go. I just want to get to the hospital."

We left around nine o'clock and swung by Chino to pick up Veronica. When we arrived at the USC Medical Center, I received another shock: probably twenty people were in the waiting room, standing and milling about.

Frankie and Jessica had arrived; they had taken our grandson Michael to her parents. Christina and Josh hadn't gone anywhere. Frank's boss from KKLA, Terry Fahy, was there with Bob Hastings, the sales manager. When they told me they had eaten lunch with Frank less than twenty-four hours ago, the surreal reality of the situation hit me again.

I recognized everyone, including a couple of pastors, Steve Wilburn and Dudley Rutherford. I saw Don and Kristi Kase with their daughter Melissa in the waiting room. I was accepting hug after hug when a nurse approached and asked me to accompany her—not to see Frank but to meet Rosa Saca, the public relations director for the USC Medical Center.

I was escorted to her office, and the door was shut behind me.

"Thank you for meeting with me, Mrs. Pastore, under what must be the most trying of circumstances. I'm sorry to hear about your husband."

"Thank you," I replied.

"The reason I asked to see you is because we have been receiving a high volume of calls from the media as well as personal inquiries regarding your husband's condition. Because of this, we are putting Frank under an alias here at the medical center, for his protection and yours, and we will not be releasing any information about his condition unless you have approved it."

Another surreal moment. "Why—why are you doing this?"

"Because, Mrs. Pastore, your husband is famous."

5

Back to the Beginning

Frank would have laughed if he heard that the USC Medical Center had registered him under an alias because he was "famous."

That was so opposite of the life my husband wanted to live. Oh, sure, there was a time when Frank wanted to be "rich and famous"—like during his days of playing professional baseball—but when he gave his life to Christ toward the end of his career, he surrendered that look-who-I-am persona and wanted to be known as a "normal guy." He didn't like it when people treated him deferentially or referred to him as a VIP.

I witnessed the transition of a professional ballplayer seeking fame and fortune to someone who was comfortable leaving all that celebrity stuff behind. I can say that because I had known Frank a long time, having met him when I was an eleven-year-old sixth-grader on the cusp of puberty. On that occasion, Frank was fifteen years old, a high school junior with peach fuzz on his cherubic face. There was quite an age and maturity gap between us, but I'm getting ahead of the story.

Describing our family's backgrounds will help you understand how Frank and I came together. First of all, we both have Italian heritage and are proud of that. Frank's father was his namesake, Frank Pastore—pronounced *Pas-store-eh* with an Italian lilt—but his mother, Elma, was a "regular" American from Birmingham, Alabama.

On my side were the Pignotti and Neroni families, both 100 percent Italian. All four of my grandparents immigrated through Ellis Island in the late 1920s. My parents, John and Ann Pignotti, were raised in Italian-speaking homes in the Chicago area, but they grew up fluent in English because of school and neighborhood friends.

John and Ann were introduced to each other by a cousin named Olivo Angellotti when my mother was sixteen and my father was twenty-one. The story goes that when Ann walked down a staircase in a purple bathing suit, she caught the eye of handsome John Pignotti. This happened in the early 1950s, just before my father was drafted into the U.S. Army and was about to be shipped off to fight in the Korean War.

Dad spent most of the war hunkered down in foxholes, firing away at the enemy. During one firefight, my father was hit with shrapnel and given a Purple Heart and a one-way ticket home. (Dad always said the TV show *M*A*S*H* was a "bunch of bologna.")

Back in Chicago, my mother's cousin Olivo had a question for him: "You want to get together with Ann?"

Dad's memory was good, and he said, "Sure." Their re-introduction ignited a whirlwind romance between a worldly and war-hardened twenty-three-year-old man and an innocent, eighteen-year-old high school debutante. Their relationship blossomed quickly; they were married three months later. The fast trip to the altar meant they didn't know each other very well, and that would set the stage for a volatile relationship in the years to come.

They settled down in California after their wedding. Dad's family had moved out west while my father and his brothers were fighting in Korea. Dad and Mom joined my grandparents, Vincent and Maria, in Montebello, a Los Angeles suburb packed with Italian immigrant families.

With construction booming in California, my father sought work as a carpenter. He was a sturdy six feet tall with matinee good looks; friends often said he looked like movie star James Garner. His huge hands and strong back made him perfect for the construction trade.

Not long after they moved to California, a cousin invited them to visit Upland, a small town filled with lemon groves at the base of the gorgeous San Gabriel Mountains. Dad took one look at the beautiful surroundings and said, "This is where we're going to live—Upland!"

Dad bought a lot on a quiet street and built our house with a small crew. Then he and Mom started filling the house with children. I was born at Upland's San Antonio Community Hospital, the third of four children: my sister, Marina, is nine years older; Johnny is five years older; then came me; and Nick is twenty-two months younger.

In many ways, we were the typical American suburban family, but there's also another word to describe my family: we were LOUD.

A lot of my friends said my father reminded them of Fred Flintstone of the cartoon series, *The Flintstones:* the roaring, bigger-than-life character who never tiptoed around anything. Our TV was always blaring, especially if a Los Angeles Dodgers game was on. (In later years, my dad also bore a resemblance to longtime Dodgers manager Tommy Lasorda, known for his colorful personality and obscenity-laden outbursts that brought out his Italian upbringing.)

If the TV wasn't on high volume, then our record player was booming Italian operas at full blast—or the melodious voices of Frank Sinatra and Tony Bennett (both of Italian heritage, of course). Today, all I have to do is hear Sinatra singing "The Summer Wind," "Something Stupid," or "Fly Me to the Moon," and I'm transported back to our living room.

As a young kid, though, I didn't like all the noise and commotion, so I spent most of my time in the bedroom I shared with Marina. (We had a three-bedroom house, so the two girls and two boys each shared a bedroom.) Everyone thought I was a sweet, quiet, and shy girl, content to play with her Barbie dolls and do homework in our bedroom. Up until sixth grade, they were right, although Mom and I fought continuously about my hair. There was friction between us because she didn't want to mess with my hair, so she cut it very short—Gidget length for those of you who remember the surfing, boy-crazy character from popular teen movies during the 1960s.

We were an Italian family in every way, living large. My parents drove us around in a block-long Cadillac, and my father would always tell us how superior the Italian language was, which, looking back, is interesting since he and Mom didn't teach us to speak *Italiano* growing up. (I wish they had.) Back in those days, second-generation Italians (and other ethnic groups) didn't pass along their maternal language; that was considered un-American at the time. Sure, we learned all the swear words, but whenever Dad and Mom wanted to talk about something important, they whispered to each other in *sotto voce.*

And if you're part of an Italian family, that means you're Catholic. Not only did we go to Mass every Sunday morning, but my parents enrolled us kids at St. Joseph's, a Catholic parochial school staffed by nuns in black habits who were quick to whack your fingers with a wooden pointer for the slightest infraction of classroom rules.

Those punishments were meted out by the Sisters of the Presentation of the Blessed Virgin Mary, an order founded in Cork, Ireland. I remember their strong Irish accents as well as their strict demeanor. As the good girl who didn't raise her hand many times, I felt intimidated each day that I stepped into the classroom. I was afraid to draw attention to myself or send notes to friends, lest I receive a stinging thwack on the back of my hand.

Everything changed when I was in sixth grade. We had a young nun fresh from Ireland—Sister Leoni, who didn't wear a long black habit or a white coif that covered most of her face and all of her hair. She wore a shorter black habit with stylish black leather pumps and a smaller coif that allowed her bangs to show. Sister Leoni was not only fun, but she also helped me come out of my shell. It all started when Sister, who loved playing the piano and was very theatrical, announced one day that she would be directing the class play, which was *Jesus Christ Superstar*.

When she asked for volunteers to try out, my hand shot into the air—that's how much confidence Sister Leoni gave me. During rehearsals, Sister Leoni chose me to be understudy for the part of Mary Magdalene, whose role included singing *Jesus Christ Superstar's* big torch song—"I Don't Know How to Love Him." This was huge for a shy girl who didn't like drawing attention to herself. I must say that I worked my tail off, honing my acting and singing skills. That hard work paid off when Sister Leoni picked me for the lead part in our next production, *The Story of Christmas*. I belted out my first solo, surprising not only my former teachers but pretty much everyone in the auditorium. The person I surprised the most, however, was myself.

Sixth grade was also the year when I told Mom that I didn't want my hair to be short anymore. We fought for a long time until she relented. My hair grew out really fast until my tresses reached past my waist. Kids at school were shocked by the change in my appearance.

Sixth grade, as I mentioned, was also the school year when I met Frank for the first time. It all happened because of baseball. My dad had grown up a Chicago Cubs fan, thanks to his mother Maria, who loved taking my father to Wrigley Field. They were part of the "Bleacher

Bums" who sat in the grandstands behind Wrigley's ivy-covered outfield walls.

When my father wasn't cheering on the Cubbies, he was playing sandlot baseball until he turned thirteen, when he had to spend his summers working as a caddy at Olympia Fields Country Club in Chicago Heights to contribute to the family income. When Dad reached high school, he played the outfield on the varsity team, but that was as far as his baseball career went since he was drafted into the U.S. Army following high school graduation.

After Dad married Mom and they settled in Upland, he coached Little League baseball when my older brother Johnny started playing organized ball. Their father-son coaching relationship continued into Pony League as well as amateur city leagues that scheduled games nearly year-round in Southern California. Johnny proved to be a stud on the diamond—a great-hitting catcher and team leader who everyone admired.

When Johnny graduated from St. Joseph's in eighth grade, he moved on to Damien High School, an all-boys Catholic high school in nearby La Verne. One of Johnny's teammates was a flame-throwing pitcher named Frank Pastore, who'd moved to Upland a couple of years earlier. They were both fifteen years old.

One spring night, I was doing my homework after dinner in the family room. Our front door was always open—just a screen door to keep the flies out—so there were always random kids walking in and out of the house. I didn't pay much attention to the commotion until I heard some guy say from the kitchen, "Hey, Johnny! I drove my mom's car here!"

I perked my ears to overhear the conversation, which went something like this:

Johnny: "What if she finds out?"

Male voice: "So? It's no big deal. I've got my learner's permit."

Johnny: "You're crazy, man."

Then my brother and his friend strode into the family room, where I sat cross-legged on the couch working on a book report.

"Oh, my God, Johnny, who's that?" his friend asked.

"That's my little sister Gina," Johnny said.

"Oh, my goodness, she's gorgeous!" exclaimed his friend, as if I wasn't there. "You didn't tell me you had a little sister."

By now, I was sinking further into the soft couch, just dying of embarrassment. At the age of eleven, I wasn't hormonal or romantically inclined—I was still a girl. I put my head down, totally mortified.

My brother's friend leaned in closer to me. "Hi," he said, trying to make eye contact.

I continued to ignore him because I was so self-conscious.

Then he stepped closer and extended his right hand. "Hi, I'm Frank Pastore."

I shook his hand but felt too frozen to say anything.

"You are just beautiful!" he declared with a beaming smile. Then turning to my brother, he said, "Piggy, I can't believe you have such a cute sister and never told me about her."

I didn't know how to handle that remark, so I gathered up my homework and scooted to my bedroom, where I shut the door to the outside world.

But, from our brief interaction, Frank Pastore seemed like a fascinating guy.

I'd never met someone like him before. He was so self-assured and comfortable in his skin. He smiled easily and spoke with command. At eleven years of age, I was drawn to him in a way that I had no words for.

Frank shared his unusual and complicated upbringing in his autobiography, *Shattered*. The *Cliffs Notes* version of Frank's autobiography is that Frank's dad, also named Frank, was a semipro baseball player in the 1930s and 1940s who got his ribs busted in a barroom brawl on the eve of a professional tryout, which effectively ended his baseball dreams.

Frank Sr. was an ironworker by trade who moved from job to job—even working in Saudi Arabia and Morocco—before settling in Los Angeles. A lifelong bachelor, content to bend steel on weekdays and play in union baseball leagues on weekends, Frank Sr. was forty-two years old when he met Elma Jean Bates. She had recently dumped Husband No. 2 and was looking for someone else to help pay the rent when she brought Frank Sr. into her web of intrigue. Elma ended up getting pregnant, but she probably did so on purpose because she was always finagling relationships and thought Frank Sr. had money.

Frank Sr. took the news that he was becoming a father very seriously. He did the right thing and married Elma, providing a home for her and their newborn son, named Frank, born on August 21, 1957, in Alhambra, an East L.A. suburb between Pasadena and Montebello. Since Frank Sr. was forty-three years old at the time of Frank's birth, people thought the guy with gray sideburns was Frank's grandfather.

A steady home proved to be a challenge. For one reason or another—usually an aversion to paying their bills—there was always more month than there was money. Often behind in their rent or trying to stay one step ahead of bill collectors, Frank's family moved twelve times before he graduated from elementary school.

Frank's father coached him in Little League ball, too, pitching to him in batting practice and schooling him on how to pitch a breaking ball and a moving fastball. Frank and his family moved to Upland because of baseball; there happened to be a lot of good ballplayers coming out of my hometown, and Frank needed an upgrade in competition.

The Pastores, however, lived on the other side of the tracks. In Upland, that meant living south of Foothill Boulevard in the cookie-cutter tract homes and threadbare apartments where lower middle-class white and Latino families resided. We lived north of Foothill in a lily-white, pristine neighborhood with tended lawns and maturing trees.

When Frank was in eighth grade, his baseball team happened to crush a "Chicano" team, as Mexican-Americans called themselves in the early 1970s. After the game, Frank stepped into the bathroom behind the snack bar only to be jumped by four Latino ballplayers who beat the heck out of his pitching arm, pummeling his upper arm and shoulder black and blue and threatening to break it the next time he pitched against them. They also left a message: *We'll be watching out for you next year at Upland High.*

Frank's parents freaked out when they heard about the menacing threats and saw what happened to Frank's arm. Since the public schools were racial cauldrons in the early 1970s, they began to look at their options.

Frank had played against several kids who were enrolling at Damien High, the private boys' Catholic high school that had a great reputation for athletics as well as academics. One of those ballplayers was Johnny "Piggy" Pignotti, my older brother.

One day, Frank Pastore, Sr. called my dad and described how Frankie had got beaten up by Latino kids and would have to constantly look over his shoulder at Upland High. "We're looking at options," Frank Sr. said. "What about Damien?"

"One of the top private high schools around," my father boomed. "Great academics and athletics. Your son will love it there. Plus Johnny can be his catcher."

"But we're not Catholics," Frank Sr. interjected.

"Not a problem," my father promised. "Frank just has to take the same religion classes like everyone else."

I don't know how the Pastores could afford Damien, given their checkered financial history, but when Elma Pastore heard that tuition was a couple of hundred dollars cheaper if they were members of the Catholic Church, she informed Frank, "We're Catholics now."

That was Mrs. Pastore, always working the system when she swore allegiance to the Pope and Catholic doctrine, but that was the way she went through life—one turmoil-filled day at a time. That's probably why Frank was drawn to our "normal" family and became good friends with Johnny and his baseball buddies.

There was always an extra seat at our dinner table for any of Johnny's friends—"the boys," as my father liked to call them. I can remember Frank joining us for dinner a couple of times a week since his mother slogged through long days at Bond's Men's Clothing and wasn't around at dinner time. As for Frank's dad, he was usually bending rebar at a far-flung construction job that involved a long commute.

We loved having Frank around, and he soon became part of the family. Mom always covered the dinner table with a massive Italian spread, and we ate family style, passing around heaping platters filled with veal cutlets, barbecued steak, linguini pasta, robust salads, and homemade bread. Frank loved to eat, and Dad loved to feed him.

I can still hear my dad hollering, "Frankie, you gotta try this!" while holding a plate of salad with lots of radicchio, an Italian leaf known for its chicory taste. Everyone called him "Frankie" in those days.

"What's that, Mr. Pignotti?"

"It's radicchio! Our best lettuce!"

Frank sampled a forkful, but the pungent aftertaste didn't agree with him.

"Ah, you don't know what's good!" my dad said. Then he sort of slapped Frank on the head, which was more of a love tap than a smack. "*Mangia*, Frankie. Everything's good for you," he ordered.

Frank would smile each time something like that happened. He loved the male attention and affirmation, as any teen boy would.

Dad was also known for his generosity. He'd do trade-outs with friends—a backyard patio for a car repair or a piece of furniture—but always got the short end of the deal because he looked out for the welfare of others first. That made my mom upset, but Dad didn't care.

One time when I was in junior high, Mom flew to Chicago to visit family. That *never* happened before. Mom was a homebody.

As soon as we dropped Mom off at LAX, Dad made an announcement to the kids: "We're going to Disneyland!" That day, we had the run of the park, riding the Matterhorn bobsleds and the Pirates of the Caribbean until Disneyland closed late that night.

The following morning at breakfast, Dad announced, "We're going to the Dodgers game tonight!"

I'd seen plenty of baseball games over the years, but never a major league game in person. My eyes were as big as saucers when we found our seats at Dodgers Stadium. Dad jerked his head toward the broadcaster's booth and pointed out Vin Scully, the golden voice of the Dodgers whose play-by-play descriptions filled our living room from April to September—or longer if the Dodgers made the playoffs.

As soon as we found our loge seats, Dad announced that he'd be right back with our Dodger Dogs, the ten-inch frankfurters made by one of the Dodgers' biggest sponsors, Farmer John. I had heard so much about Dodger Dogs that I couldn't wait to bite into my first one.

Twenty minutes later, Dad's arms were filled with a big carton carrier of frankfurters (my brother Johnny's best friend Mark Caraway had joined us) along with Cokes and peanuts. Dad nearly lost the prized Dodger Dogs as he trampled through our row to reach us.

As he was handing out hot dogs, Cokes, and peanuts, a Hispanic family sat down in front of us. Four or five young boys turned around and stared at our Dodger Dogs. Their parents told them no, they couldn't have a Dodger Dog, which Dad understood because of the similarities between Italian and Spanish.

Next thing I knew, Dad was collecting our Dodger Dogs and snacks and handing them to the Hispanic family, turning frowns to smiles.

My father then made a beeline for the concession stand again to buy a second round of Dodger Dogs and snacks for us.

That was my father, generous to a fault. He always wanted to make sure everyone had a good time. Every time he got paid for a big job, he'd take us out for dinner in Upland. Before Mom could stop him, he'd buy a meal for two cops or tip our waitress really well. "I know what it was like to be a caddy, relying on tips," he'd explain.

Back in the car, on the way home, Mom would confront him. "We're scrapping by, and you're giving people money we don't have!"

That would set off an argument. My parents also fought about the evenings that Dad spent hanging out at friends' homes, smoking cigars and dealing cards during all-night poker games. The following morning, Mom would lay into him again. "You should be home with the kids!" she would say in a raised voice.

"Yeah, yeah," he'd reply. Maybe Dad was gone too much or had too many poker nights, but I remember him as a hands-on father who regularly shopped for groceries, made our school lunches, enjoyed helping out my mother in the kitchen with the preparation of Italian specialties, attended almost all of our extracurricular school activities, coached my brothers' baseball teams, and attended our school plays and parent-teacher meetings. I can still remember waking up Saturday mornings, hearing his thunderous voice yell out, "French toast or pancakes?" My old friends who spent the night in our home still laugh about this.

My father is gone now, and I still miss him.

My first interactions with Frank started when he'd "drop in" around dinner time, knowing there was always room for one more around our large table. My parents loved on him so much—and filled his bottomless-pit stomach—that Frank started calling my parents "Dad" and "Mom."

After dinner, Dad and Frank would watch Dodgers games on TV, with my father pointing out the cat-and-mouse game between pitcher and batter—how pitchers were setting up hitters when they were ahead in the count or what they were thinking on 2-and-0 or 3-and-1 pitches. My father would point out when the pitcher needed a strikeout or an inning-ending double play, which called for different types of pitches and locations.

I liked it when Frank hung out at our house. In fact, I developed a major league crush on him—a schoolgirl infatuation with a high school ballplayer four years and three months older than me.

One evening, when Frank was saying goodbye and giving my mom a hug and a kiss, I announced my intentions.

"One day, I'm going to marry you, Frankie Pastore!" I said in front of my entire family.

Of course, there was a lot of good-natured laughing and kidding around. I giggled and turned red as a sugar beet.

But at eleven years of age, I knew I had found my knight in shining armor.

6

Turning Heads

The summer between sixth and seventh grade is when I blossomed. I sprouted five inches to my present height of five feet, seven inches and slimmed out, although I was never chubby as a young child. I weighed 110 pounds at my new height and parted my long brown hair in the middle. The winsome hippie look was still going strong in the mid-'70s.

Suddenly, I was turning heads and hearing wolf whistles. My dad ran a construction company out of our home, so his subs—carpenters, plumbers, and painters—were constantly coming and going. They'd say things like, "Hey, John, look-a what we got here. Little Gina's growing up!" or "Wow, that daughter of yours is a knockout!" Then they'd give each other one of those raised-eyebrow, you-know-what-I-mean looks. My father would pretend to act indignantly, to protect my honor. "Hey, watch your eyes!" he'd mildly protest.

I felt lanky and uncomfortable with my new body, and my clothes no longer fit my string-bean physique. I didn't have that many clothes anyway since I wore a school uniform at St. Joseph's, but I still needed some "play clothes" and something nice to wear to church and social occasions.

Mom sized up the situation and announced that she was taking me on a special shopping trip—to the Broadway department store. I beamed with pride when she led me to the Junior Miss department, leaving behind the Children's section forever. This being 1975, polyester long-sleeved shirts were in fashion as well as corduroy bell-bottom pants. We bought several pairs of each, and I felt like I was growing up—a very special moment for me.

The start of my seventh-grade year was a bit scary, though, since I had changed so much over the summer. I had nothing to fear:

I soon learned that I was one of the popular kids. How did I know that? Because the popular girls wanted to sit next to me at Mass every morning. I was still soft-spoken, but I was no longer extremely shy. I auditioned for the Scripture reading at morning Mass . . . and won the coveted job. An added bonus was discovering that I liked speaking in public. My new persona, coupled with my maturing body, drew welcome attention from my peers—especially the boys.

Jim was the first boy who liked me. He was cute with white blond hair and green eyes, but he was shorter than me since he hadn't hit his growth spurt yet and had some catching up to do. It seemed that one of my girlfriends liked him, so when we were in the library, Christina entrusted me to give him notes from her. Passing handwritten notes is how we communicated in those awkward junior high days long before texting was an option.

One afternoon, I delivered a note to Jim from his "girlfriend." He looked at the note and then me. "I don't like her," he said. "I like you."

I was too stunned to put together a coherent sentence, so I mumbled something like, "That's nice." And then I hightailed it back to my girl-friend and told her everything that happened. Christina wasn't upset at all. In fact, she looked relieved. "I don't like him anymore," she said.

Well, as you can imagine, it didn't take long for the entire class to find out that Jim liked me and not Christina. Typical junior high drama!

With a path cleared, Jim put a big move on me, and I had my first Official Boyfriend. What does that mean in the seventh grade? Well, neither of us were allowed to date, so "going steady" meant that we saw each other at the lockers between classes, sat next to each other at lunch, and exchanged notes during and between classes. I also made sure I was invited to spend the night with a girlfriend who lived across the street from Jim. We could talk out in the street after dinner.

Then one day I received a note from Jim that sent my heart flutter-ing. *Hey, wanna meet me behind the lockers after school?*

Even someone as innocent as me knew what he meant: he wanted to kiss me.

I'd never kissed a boy before, so I asked my girlfriends for advice.

Me: What should I do?

My girlfriends (in unison): Oh, you have to go!

I might as well have broadcast my first kiss over the school intercom since news of Gina's first kiss swept through the grounds of St. Joseph's like a Santa Ana wildfire. I don't think I'd ever been teased as much in my life. Then I heard a rumor that he'd been practicing, which only raised my anxiety level.

My heart was thumping when the school bell rang. I tried to ditch my girlfriends, but they insisted on discreetly following me as I walked toward the lockers. Jim, with a big grin on his face, was waiting for me.

"Ah, nice to see you," he said.

I ran a hand through my hair and wondered if my face was red from embarrassment. I'm sure my cheeks were on fire.

"Ah, good to see you, too."

Jim wasn't into talking. He took my hand, led me behind the lockers, and leaned in close with lips puckered. Our lips locked . . . I felt excited by the touch. What a sweet kiss!

"Hey, you're good at this," he said. "You sure this was your first time?"

"Well, yeah," I said.

After kissing Jim, the boyfriend/girlfriend thing tapered off. I decided that I wasn't at all attracted to Jim and liked him as a friend. The guy who caught my eye now was Bobby. I'd heard through the grapevine that he liked me. So, in typical junior high fashion, I plotted a way out of my predicament. I had heard that one my girlfriends named Laurie had eyes for Jim, so there was my out. I sent Jim a note saying that we were breaking up, which made me available for Bobby.

Arguably the most popular boy in the class, Bobby was smart as a whip, the class leader, and very handsome. During a school walk-a-thon, Bobby and I held hands while strolling along scenic Euclid Boulevard, which earned me a reprimand from Sister Celestine the next day. After English class, Sister pulled me aside and said in her Irish brogue, "Gina Pignotti! What is happening to you? You are pretty and smart, and you need to keep yourself devoted to God and the spiritual life!"

I felt ashamed. I had never disappointed the nuns—my life mentors—before.

I got over the shame rather quickly. A couple weeks later, Bobby and I met up at a nearby schoolyard with a few other classmates to "make out." I'll be honest here: I thought kissing was fun! Some classmates were graduating to what we called "second base." I was seriously giving this some thought, which shows you how boy-crazy I was getting.

As much as I liked kissing, Bobby didn't last any longer than Jim as my boyfriend, and the reason why is because there was another emotion swirling in my heart: I couldn't shake my attraction to Frank Pastore.

There was just one problem. Okay, make that a huge problem: Frank was a sophisticated and worldly senior at Damien High School, and I was a measly seventh-grader barely out of training bras. He was shaving the stubble on his face, and the only reason I was shaving my legs was because I begged Mom to let me start.

My heart skipped a beat every time Frank dropped by the house, which was still fairly often—usually at dinnertime since there was always room at the table for him. I'd secretly steal glances at him as he would dig into a plate heaped high with an Italian dish like *spaghetti Bolognese.*

One Saturday afternoon he was hanging out with my brother Johnny. I was in my bedroom getting ready to meet some friends. I put on a cute halter top and white shorts, and when I walked through the living room, Frank's eyes left me and turned toward my brother.

"Hey, Johnny, in a couple of years, you're going to have fight off the guys," he said. "Your sister's looking mighty fine, yes, siree."

I was mortified. I kept walking right out the front door. As soon as the coast was clear, I exhaled and breathed a sigh of relief.

Frankie Pastore had noticed me.

Johnny was a high school senior, so I knew he didn't want to waste too much time talking to his pipsqueak sister. One afternoon, when I felt the time was right, I asked him several questions:

"What's Frank like?"

"What do people think of him?"

"Is he dating anyone?"

Like most guys, Johnny was economical in his replies. "He's really popular, the senior class president, and a great baseball player. I like him, but some people think he's too cocky."

"Why do they say that?"

"Because when he walks in the room, he takes charge," my brother replied. "He says things people wouldn't say."

Well, I like that, I thought, and this was long before the term "political correctness" came into vogue. But now I needed my brother to dish.

"But who is he dating?" I asked.

I already knew that Frank was dating one of the cheerleaders—one of Johnny's friends clued me in—but I wanted to hear that bit of information directly from my brother. He confirmed that Frank had a "hot romance going."

My source also said the rumor going around school was that Frank wanted to marry her. I couldn't bear the thought of losing him. I mean, my heart longed, really *longed* to be with Frank. I had a major crush on him, but even at the immature age of thirteen, I knew that six-foot, two-inch, 185-pound high school seniors weren't romantically interested in waif-like seventh-graders. But that didn't mean I couldn't like him, so I took every chance I got to go watch him pitch.

During his senior year, Frank was drawing twenty to thirty scouts every time he took the mound, whether he was playing American Legion ball in the fall and winter or pitching for Damien High during the spring baseball season. Frank had a special skill—throwing a baseball *really fast*. He was striking out cowering batters left and right, and Dad told me that Frank had a good chance of getting drafted in the first round of the major league draft held every June.

I remember being at an American Legion game before the start of the high school season and seeing Dad nearly hyperventilate.

"What is it, Dad?" I asked. "Is something wrong?"

"Tommy La—"

Dad couldn't spit out his name because he was so excited.

"Tommy Lasorda! He's here!" my father blurted.

Tommy was still a year away from being named the Los Angeles Dodgers' manager for the next twenty seasons, but he was the third base coach and the heir apparent to longtime Dodgers manager Walt Alston. Like my dad's family, Tommy's father had emigrated from Italy through Ellis Island at the turn of the century, so Lasorda was a hero to my father.

Tommy Lasorda wasn't the only baseball celebrity to make the trek to the San Gabriel Valley to see Frank take the mound. Dodgers legend Sandy Koufax and the Yankees' Whitey Ford, both brilliant Hall of Fame lefthanders, wanted to see Frank pitch.

College coaches filled the grandstands as well. The big baseball schools in California and Arizona wanted him badly—USC, UCLA, Cal Berkeley, Arizona State, and the University of Arizona. Stanford came knocking, too.

After the winter American Legion season finished, however, Frank decided that he would keep his options open by signing a national letter of intent to attend Stanford University. Think about it: one of the most prestigious and expensive universities in the country had offered him a full-ride athletic scholarship—room, board, and tuition. He couldn't pass up that offer!

Dad wasn't surprised Stanford offered him a full ride and said he was one of the best high school pitchers in the country. A glowing article in the local paper, the *Progress Bulletin*, noted that Frank had started throwing from the mound when he was two years old and had tossed twenty-six no-hitters in youth baseball prior to enrolling at Damien.

The feature story then went on to say this:

> *Although he is noted for his best pitch, an overhand fast ball, Pastore also rates, in order, an overhand curve screwball (against lefties), a slurve (a ¾ breaking pitch), and a butterfly. "I learned the butterfly when I was 12," Pastore recalls.*

The knuckleball was called a "butterfly" pitch back in the day because of the way the ball darted and danced on its slow, convoluted trip from the pitcher's hand to the catcher's mitt.

Frank wasn't a knuckleball pitcher. Even I knew that. He threw BBs, as I heard my dad say, and blew batters away with his heater—a fastball that hit in the 90s. That's awfully fast for the high school level.

But the *Progress Bulletin* story also reported that Frank didn't "eat and sleep" baseball, noting that he was senior class president at Damien (which meant he was popular and respected), carried a 3.8 grade-point average (Damien was known for its academics), and was part of *Who's Who Among American High School Students* (I had no idea how he was chosen).

While Frank liked sitting around our backyard patio with my brother, Dan Monroe, and Steve Schiro—a quartet that had been playing on the same baseball teams since age twelve—I also knew from Johnny that Frank spent time and socialized with two of the class nerds: George de la Flor and Jorge Gomez.

George and Jorge didn't have plastic pocket protectors on their white, button-down shirts, but they wore the classic black horn-rimmed glasses. They were part of the debate team, and believe it or not, debating was a big deal at Damien. Everyone in Los Angeles County knew that Damien fielded one of the best debate teams.

Consider Frank's situation in the spring of 1975 as he was tearing through lineups with his blazing fastball: in terms of baseball talent, there was no getting around that he was one of the best. He was good enough to get drafted early and make a lot of money from a signing bonus. But there was another side of him that thought about pursuing an academic career while still pitching college ball.

Frank took philosophy classes at Damien with George and Jorge. Mr. Steck was their teacher, and Frank adored him. Mr. Steck, who also taught history, encouraged Frank to read the *Great Books of the Western World* series, which covered categories such as natural science, drama, history, politics, religion, economics, ethics, and philosophy. I don't think Frank finished all fifty-four books in the series, but I know those volumes rounded out his education.

So, during this senior year, Frank planted his feet in two camps at Damien: the jocks and the brainy nerds. Thinking big thoughts about the universe was as important to him as pondering how to pitch to the No. 3 hitter with the bases loaded and two outs.

His closest friend was my brother Johnny, who was also Frank's catcher. In baseball terms, Frank and Johnny were a "battery," meaning they had the most important working relationship on the ball diamond. There has to be a lot of trust and cooperation between a pitcher and catcher.

The catcher gives signs to the pitcher on what type of pitch he should throw—fastball, curve, slider, change-up, slurve, butterfly—whatever. The pitcher has the right to "shake off" a certain pitch called for by the catcher (for instance, changing from a fastball to a slider), but when the chemistry is right and the catcher is calling for the same pitch that the pitcher believes is right for the situation, then the pitcher and catcher are said to be on the "same page."

Frank and Johnny, after five years of playing together on the same teams, could read each other's minds. They'd spent a lot of time practicing in our backyard, where Johnny had built a mound in an area big enough to fit a 60-foot, 6-inch gap between the pitching mound and home plate. They'd go out back after dinner, and Johnny would get into his crouch and imitate the mannerisms of his idol, Johnny Bench of the Cincinnati Reds. Frank, who idolized Tom Seaver of the New York Mets, would rock into his windup and start firing away.

Johnny was a much better, more well-rounded athlete than Frank—and Frank knew it. Johnny was a great tennis player, a star of the Damien basketball team, and was called the Warren Beatty of Damien High after the current Hollywood heartthrob. The girls had major crushes on him, and Johnny dated a lot of cute classmates.

Frank knew he wasn't as charismatic as my brother, or as good-looking, but he had one skill that few possessed: he could throw a baseball 92 miles per hour with pinpoint accuracy, and that was his ticket to the future.

A future that I hoped included me.

7

A Glimpse into the Future

I was thirteen during Frank's final year of high school, so I was all hormonal and romantically inclined. Every time Frank came over to the house, I had to suck in my breath to hide my excitement. I really liked him.

One warm spring day—a Sunday—white fluffy clouds drifted lazily across the electric blue sky toward the San Gabriel Mountains. Dad was watching the Masters golf tournament in the family room. Mom was making a giant pot of spaghetti sauce: the aroma of onions, garlic, parsley, and tomato sauce filled the air. She knew to have extra on hand in case Frank and other strays showed up at the front door at six o'clock, ravishingly hungry.

The house was quieter than usual. I looked out of the family room window, and nobody was in the backyard. I decided to head out and try an intriguing new way to pray that a visitation nun had talked about in my 9 a.m. religion class.

"The topic today is prayer," she had said a few days earlier, and I was expecting her to describe the importance of praying to the saints or the Virgin Mary as our intercessors, the sort of teaching consistent with Catholic dogma. Instead, she took a more nuanced, theological route.

"Prayer is going into a deep time with God the Father, His Son Jesus Christ, and the Holy Spirit—the triune being," she began. "You want to pour out your heart to God. He already knows all about you because He's omniscient and all-powerful. After you pray, you want to listen to what the Holy Spirit tells you. Sometimes He'll talk to you, sometimes He won't say a thing. But you'll never hear His voice unless you pray."

That spring afternoon, I needed to pray to God about Frank. My inner heart was desiring him, but deep inside, I knew he was way too old for me. I wanted to talk to someone about my situation, and who better than God Almighty to discuss this with?

I grabbed a beach towel and headed for the back door. That's when I heard the booming voice of my father yell out, "Gina, where are you going?"

I had an answer all prepared.

"I'm just going to lay out for a while and get a tan," I said.

I laid my towel on the prickly green grass and plopped down on my backside so that my face and body were in the direction of the sun. It felt good to feel the warmth of the sun on my skin.

I closed my eyes and began pouring out my heart to God. This was true confession time as I knew God was all-knowing, so there was nothing to hide from Him.

I started off by saying, "Okay, Lord, you know how I feel about Frankie Pastore. You know our age difference, but I think I'm falling in love with him and I'm only thirteen. I don't want to fall in love with him unless he loves me back. If he loves me back, then I want to marry him someday. So God, I guess what I'm asking you is this: Could he love me back? Then could I marry him someday? Oh, and one more thing, God. Could he be loved by a lot of people . . . like hundreds, maybe thousands?"

The last prayer came from what my brother had told me about Frank—that some people thought he was cocky. This was important for me because I saw the tender heart in Frank. I saw past his boldness and recognized the confident, intelligent, and good-hearted man that he would mature into.

After pouring out my heart, I laid still and waited to hear from God. I remember the warm sun penetrating my skin, a gentle breeze blowing, and the sound of the big tree in our backyard softly bristling.

Suddenly, I heard God's voice, not audibly, but His words traveled straight into my soul. The Lord of the Universe said, "Gina, you can be with Frank, but he is going to die young."

I sat straight up. I was shocked and horrified. I thought, *Wait a minute. I'm not supposed to hear this! This is very strange!*

I sat there for a few minutes trying to make sense of this bizarre moment. I decided to lay back down on my beach towel and enter into this exchange again and listen for a response. Once again, I asked God for these things about Frank.

With my eyes closed, I gently heard Him say, "I hear you, Gina, but

Frank is going to die fairly young. Do you still want to marry him?"

I responded "Yes, Lord. Yes, I do! I would like to have children with him, if that's possible. At least two or three."

This is where our conversation stopped. My time with God Almighty seemed to fade away. I sat up and realized I could never share this with anyone. What had just happened was between God and me.

For the next thirty-five years, I buried His words deeply in my heart.

Not long after this supernatural event, I saw Frank at St. Joseph's Catholic Church one Sunday morning. Despite his mom's declaration of fidelity to the Catholic Church, Frank wasn't much of a Roman Catholic. Frank was interested in classes in philosophy and discussing what makes the world go round, but *The Baltimore Catechism*? Not so interested.

The reason Frank was going to Sunday Mass was so that he could see his new flame—a senior sweetie at Pomona Catholic, an all-girls high school. Her brother was my classmate. Apparently, Frank had broken up with the cheerleader he was rumored to be marrying.

After Mass that morning, I was walking in the parking lot with some of my girlfriends. Frank, from afar and all alone, made eye contact with me—easy to do since I couldn't keep my eyes off of him.

Without prompting, he cupped his hands and yelled, "What a fox!" from across the parking lot. I turned bright red, and my girlfriends laughed.

Those light moments, however, turned into tears on Friday, April 25, 1975, when Damien High's other undefeated pitching ace, Vince Garcia, was killed in a tragic automobile accident. The Damien baseball team and community were grieved beyond belief. I can still recall the somberness in our house.

After the long and sad funeral, life slowly resumed to normal. Frank ended the season with a 6-0 record and a 1.11 earned-run average in the San Antonio League. He set a California Interscholastic Federation (CIF) record by striking out 16 batters in a seven-inning game.

Frank pitched so well his senior year that major league scouts were telling him that he could go in the first round. Stanford baseball coach Ray Young told the *Stanford Daily* that Frank was "one of the top two or three prospects in Southern California" but that he was still hopeful that Frank was coming to The Farm.

I remember Dad having a lot of phone calls with Mr. Pastore during this time about what Frankie should do. The two fathers were peas in a pod: both agreed that "Frankie needs to play ball!"—meaning he should turn pro. Perhaps Vince Garcia's sudden death was a reminder that life was short and came with no guarantees.

Frank Sr. was calling Dad a lot because Mrs. Pastore wanted Frank to go to college and accept the golden scholarship offer from Stanford. Frank Sr., who felt like he missed his shot at pro baseball, had lived with that regret for twenty-five years and didn't want Frankie to make the same mistake.

I didn't tell anyone, but secretly I hoped Frank would go to Stanford. Staying in school and playing baseball seemed a lot more familiar to me than him being on his own playing professional baseball.

When Frank's senior year came to an end, he graduated near the top of his class, which numbered 123 students at Damien High. My brother Johnny asked my parents if we could host a graduation party, and they agreed. Not all 123 kids came, but our house was a zoo that evening.

Mom made a huge pot of sloppy joe mix and set out a platter of buns plus a spread of Italian sandwiches, chips, dips, and soda pop. Oh, and there was a beer keg getting a workout in the backyard. Mom and Dad invited several sets of Damien parents to join them as chaperones, and I don't recall things getting too out of hand. (Pretty amazing they would allow underage teens to drink and drive, don't you think?) The adults sat out in the patio, smoking their cigarettes, while boisterous high school kids streamed in and out of the house.

My brother set up our stereo and speakers in the patio to blast out hits like "Taking Care of Business" by Bachman Turner Overdrive, "Bennie and the Jets" by Elton John, "Love Will Keep Us Together" by Captain and Tennille, and "Band on the Run" by Paul McCartney and Wings.

I wore my new pair of rust-colored corduroy bell bottoms and a long-sleeved green-and-rust top. I still had the hippie look going, but I dolled myself up with makeup and mascara in hopes that Frank would stop by. I figured he would, but there were other graduation parties going on.

I was on the lookout for him and stayed close to the door that led into the garage. Dad always kept the garage door up, and kids were used to coming into our house through the garage and not the front door, which was deemed "too formal."

I saw him get out of the car and make his way to the garage, his shoulders hunched. His hair was wet as if he had just jumped out of the shower. He was dressed nicely.

I stood on the top step of the stairway that led into the house. "Hi, Frank," I said.

Frank looked up. His eyes quickly looked me over, and his smile signaled that he approved. "Hi, Gina," he said. "Hey, you look great!"

Frank skipped up the steps and stopped to give me a friendly peck on the cheek—an innocent exchange of affection from someone who considered himself to be part of the family.

Frank leaned close . . . and my heart stopped. Instead of holding my head straight, I turned my head and found his lips. I kissed him . . . and then he not only accepted my kiss, but he returned the physical touch between our lips with just as much . . . well . . . passion.

I guess all that practice with Jim and Bobby paid off.

I could tell Frank was shocked—and pleasantly surprised—by my boldness, and we let the moment linger. When he broke away, our eyes met. There was something different in the way Frank looked at me, and I'm sure my eyes signaled something had changed as well. But we both knew that something *hadn't* changed—our difference in age. He was a high school graduate, and I was going into the eighth grade in the fall.

Frank was the first to break the silence. "Ah, I hope I didn't do anything—"

Before I could answer, one of his classmates came out of the shadows to pass through the door and exit the garage. He acted like he hadn't seen a thing.

Our touching moment together was broken by the interruption. "Ah, I better go," he said.

Frank wasn't embarrassed, but I could tell that he was startled by what happened between us and needed some space to figure out what had just happened.

"See you," I said.

I was happy. I had kissed Frankie Pastore!

Wait until the girls hear about this!

A week after graduation was the 1975 Major League Baseball Draft. Frank didn't go in the first round as he had hoped, but the Cincinnati Reds picked him in the second round, which was great news. The club was nicknamed the "Big Red Machine" for its exploits between 1970 and 1976, when Cincinnati would win five National League West Division titles, four National League pennants, and two World Series titles. This was a club coached by George "Sparky" Anderson and filled with a murderous lineup featuring Pete Rose, Joe Morgan, Tony Perez, and my brother's idol, Johnny Bench.

After Frank got the phone call from the Reds organization that they had selected him, two scouts descended upon the Pastore home in Upland. They knew they had some work to do: get Frank to turn his back on Stanford and cast his lot with pro baseball. Once Frank signed a contract, he could never play amateur baseball again, meaning he could never pitch in college.

There was a lot riding on his decision, although his parents had some say-so since Frank was still seventeen years old and couldn't enter into a legally binding contract until his eighteenth birthday in August. At least one of his parents would have to sign off when Frank inked a professional baseball contract.

Mrs. Pastore was the only parent around when the two Cincinnati Reds scouts came knocking. Frank Sr. was working that day at a plant near downtown L.A. It's mind-boggling to think Frank and his mom had no agent—no bulldog like Scott Boras—representing them, but that was the norm back then. They were on their own.

The negotiations started in earnest. "You're our bonus baby," one of the scouts said with enthusiasm. "We're offering you $42,000 to sign."

In today's dollars, that would be $190,000—an astronomical amount, especially for a seventeen-year-old teenager. (Second-rounders typically get $800,000 to $900,000 today.)

"You're getting top dollar for a second-round pick," the scout declared, "and we think you have a bright future with the Reds' organization." After the pitch, he and his partner settled into the Pastores' well-worn living room couches. They were there for the long haul.

The Reds' offer was awfully enticing. All parties knew that signing bonuses were non-refundable. If Frank tripped on the dugout steps and permanently injured himself or couldn't cut it in the minor leagues, he'd get to keep all the money.

Mrs. Pastore—dressed in a garish muumuu and chain-smoking a pack of Camels—was adamant that Frank receive a college education.

"You're going to Stanford if it's over my dead body," she harrumphed. "There's no way I'm signing that contract."

Frank, who'd been sitting on the fence about what to do, now felt his mother was meddling in the most important decision of his life—a decision that was *his* to make.

Frank called his father at work, brought him up to date, and then handed the phone to his mother. His parents proceeded to argue vehemently about Frank's future while the scouts watched and wondered whose opinion would win in the end. Frank Sr. was just as adamant that Frankie sign the contract and get his baseball career started.

Nothing was resolved. The scouts, sensing that they might lose Frank, upped the ante. "We're prepared to offer you a $50,000 bonus," one scout said. "That's as high as we're authorized to go."

Nonetheless, the stalemate continued. Because they were getting nowhere fast, Frank asked if he could be excused for a moment. He went into his bedroom and called my dad.

This was the biggest decision in his life, and he trusted my father for wise counsel. After explaining the situation, Frank said, "The Reds just offered me $50,000. They said that's twice what Johnny Bench got. They also said take it or leave it."

"That's a lot of money," Dad said, stating the obvious. (In today's dollars, that would be $226,000.) "You know, if you go to Stanford and get hurt, then your career is over. This is a bird in the hand. I think you should go for it."

Frank really leaned on Dad as a father figure. "You really think so?" he asked.

Dad didn't equivocate. "Frankie, I think you should sign. You can always go to college later."

Keep in mind that Dad never went beyond high school, and the importance of a college education wasn't as stark as it is today.

Now Frank was really in a quandary. Deep down, in his heart of hearts, he wanted to stay in school and attend one of the top universities in the country—on their nickel! He could play three seasons for the Stanford baseball team and then get drafted at the end of his junior year. In three years, he'd have a body of work and perhaps command a bigger signing bonus.

Perhaps . . . but life was a crapshoot, right?

"Frankie, you're a really good pitcher. You can make it to the big leagues. I know you can," Dad said. "Take their offer."

I'll admit that I was eavesdropping from the living room couch as I listened to Dad speak with Frank.

Johnny was there, too, hanging on every word.

And then Dad hung up.

"So, what's Frankie going to do, Dad?" my brother asked.

Dad ran a hand through his slicked-back hair. "Beats me," he said. "I think his mother is having too much influence."

Mrs. Pastore was still refusing to sign the contract. Her obstinacy, however, tipped the scales—at least in Frank's mind—toward turning pro. His mother had always made major decisions on the fly, without thinking through the ramifications for all sides. This time Frank was caught in her web of intrigue and wanted no part of it. Plus, the Cincinnati Reds, one of the best franchises in baseball, were giving him 50,000 reasons to say no to Stanford.

"Come on," he said to the stunned scouts, waving them to follow him. "We'll go find my dad."

Frank and the pair of Reds scouts jumped into their rental car and hopped on Interstate 10 for the drive into downtown L.A. When they arrived at the plant, Frank walked in and brought his dad back out to the parking lot. Handshakes were exchanged, and then a standard boilerplate contract was pulled out of a folder. A $50,000 figure was inserted, and the contract was placed on the griddle-hot hood of the rental car. Frank signed his name, followed by his father, who dabbed at the tears filling his eyes. Frank Sr. was so proud that his son was a professional baseball player that he could not speak.

The scouts said that Frank would start at the lowest rung of the Reds' farm system in Billings, Montana, in the Pioneer League. This was a rookie league for players who had just been signed out of high school.

The die had been cast. Frank had turned pro, and there was no turning back. On the way back to Upland, the scouts swung by the Rawlings warehouse, where Frank picked out a couple of gloves and three pairs of baseball cleats.

When Frank got home, he immediately called my father to deliver the news. My father was overcome with emotion as well and energized to hear that Frank would get a shot at playing in the major leagues. Over and over, he reminded Frank that very few got this chance. He also congratulated Frank and told him that he wouldn't regret his decision.

From my perch on the living room couch, I had this thought when I heard the news: *Oh, he's going off to play baseball. That's it; he's leaving me forever. I'm never going to see him again.*

If I did ever did see him again, it would be because he was pitching for the Cincinnati Reds on TV.

8

Back in Town

I'm sure I moped around like a love-struck teenybopper when Frank went off to play professional baseball. After all, I was just an eighth-grader when Frank signed a contract with the Cincinnati Reds. My head was telling me to forget about him, but my heart was "all in," and my ears perked up whenever family members mentioned his name. I told myself to focus on my life: school, friends, and sports. I even became the lead pitcher on my eighth-grade softball team. Keeping myself busy, I didn't skip a beat during my junior high years.

I picked up bits and pieces about Frank's first season in the minor leagues from overhearing conversations between Johnny and his friends. They would carry on in the living room while a Dodgers game blared away in the background, never knowing that I was listening from the hallway.

I hear Frank is quite the ladies' man up there in Montana . . .

Yeah, there's more action off the field than between the white lines.

I bet you Frank is beating back the girls with a Louisville Slugger . . .

And then they'd dissolve into laughter. Another time, Mr. Pastore dropped by to see Dad, and he bragged about Frank's bachelor life and how he wasn't lacking for feminine attention. I'd been around enough baseball games to know that there were plenty of girls who threw themselves at ballplayers. These groupies were known as "baseball Annies," and the way Johnny and his friends talked, it sounded like Frank was hitting a home run every night.

I'll admit that I couldn't relate to that world. It was over my head. I was too young, too removed.

The next time I saw Frank was in September, when he drove up to our house in a spanking new Datsun 280Z, a low-slung, two-seat sports car that announced its arrival ahead of time with a throaty engine whine.

My brothers oohed and aahed over the persimmon-colored coupe.

"I paid seventy-five hundred cash for this baby," he said, which set off another round of atta-boys. Frank couldn't have been prouder of his new wheels, which he purchased from his $50,000 signing bonus.

Dad came out for a look and whistled his appreciation. "Hey, Frankie," he bellowed. "Don't think you're getting out of here without staying for dinner."

"Dad, only if you insist."

"I insist."

I'd heard this face-saving back-and-forth between Dad and Frank a zillion times. That night, around a dinner table filled with plates of pasta and leafy salads, Frank painted a picture of minor league ball that wasn't a glamorous one. He couldn't afford an apartment, so he checked into the Northern Hotel for five bucks a night and shared a room with three other guys. Just one problem: there were only two twin beds, so two players had to sleep on the floor. When Frank was pitching the next day, he was eligible for a twin bed. They subsisted on breakfast cereal, lunch at McDonald's, and peanut-butter-and-jelly sandwiches in the clubhouse. Frank didn't mention his active social life since he was in mixed company, which was just as well.

Beneath the good-humored smile, Frank didn't look that happy. I could tell that he missed seeing his friends, who were embarking on the next rite of passage—going off to college.

Perhaps that's why Frank decided to enroll at Stanford at the last minute after returning from Billings, Montana. After all, Stanford had accepted him, so he could go, right? A few weeks into the fall semester in Palo Alto, Frank was dealing with crazy dorm life, the haze of marijuana smoke, stereos at full blast at 2 a.m., liberal professors, 200 people in lecture-style classes taught by teaching assistants . . . college life wasn't what he expected.

Then an invoice landed in his dorm mailbox for the *full* tuition since Frank wasn't eligible to play on the Stanford baseball team. That's when Frank decided that maybe he didn't want to go to college during the off-season after all.

When Frank showed up at the house after dropping out of Stanford, he looked like a wet puppy with its tail between its legs. I didn't see him that much, but when he did come over, we remained friendly and enjoyed talking to each other. Before we knew it, he was off in early

February for spring training.

When I graduated eighth grade from St. Joseph's, my parents were debating where I would go to high school. The options were enrolling at St. Lucy's Priory High School in Glendora, an all-girls college prep school overseen by Benedictine nuns, or staying local and attending Upland High School, the public school. I was torn between St. Lucy's and Upland High since I had friends going to each school. I passed St. Lucy's entrance exam and had the grades to get in, but I really didn't want to go there because I'd have to take a forty-five-minute bus ride back and forth from Upland to Glendora, which didn't sound like a lot of fun. Plus I liked going to school with boys.

Dad, however, had started a building company with two partners called PG&P Construction, and times were good. Since my parents had the money, they wanted me to get a good private school education, so St. Lucy's was decided for me. For the next four years, I'd be wearing the same uniform each day to school: a navy-blue skirt, a white button-down, short-sleeved blouse, a navy-blue cardigan with my class number, and black-and-white saddle shoes.

And riding that stupid bus every day.

On a late October afternoon, the St. Lucy's yellow school bus dropped me off at Euclid Avenue in Upland and chugged away in a puff of black smoke.

When the air cleared, the beautiful San Gabriel Mountains sparkled in the warm sun. I had a mile walk ahead of me—around twenty minutes. I carried my books in a backpack and adjusted my navy-blue skirt, which I had rolled up at the waist—after school—to make the hem shorter. The nuns were sticklers about us wearing knee-length skirts.

Then I heard a distinctive noise—a 280Z bearing down on me. I turned and immediately recognized the persimmon-colored sports car coming my way.

I kept walking as the 280Z pulled up alongside me. A window rolled down from the moving car.

"Wow, is that you, Gina?"

"Oh . . . hi, Frank," I replied as nonchalantly as I could.

"See you in a minute." Frank smiled and then hit the gas pedal and sped off, turning a corner and driving straight to our house.

He had done it again: my heart was fluttering. No matter how little I saw him, or how much older he was, or how many "girlfriends" he had, the candle still burned brightly.

I was nervous when I strode up the walkway and through our front door, which was open and protected by a screen door. I could hear the loud voices of my father and Frank greeting each other in the living room. When I slipped into the hallway on the right, neither acknowledged me as I passed by. They continued conversing.

"Frankie, how's the off season treatin' ya, huh?" my dad said. "You wanna eat? Let me fix you something good . . . ."

Frank had a different agenda other than filling his tummy with our yummy food.

"Dad, I want to take Gina on her first date. She's turning fifteen next month. Can I?"

I imagine Dad frowning when he heard that. "We'll have to see, Frankie. We told her she can't date until she's sixteen, so I'm going to have to talk to the Missus."

Then Frank called for me. "Gina, can you come out here?"

I came out of my bedroom with a big smile. I was glad to see Frank. We hugged, but not in a romantic way. He grabbed my hand and walked me over to the family room couch, next to Dad's comfortable recliner.

We sat and talked with my dad. I had secretly hoped that I wouldn't see Frank again because I was attracted to him in such a powerful way. Now, here he was in our living room, showing an interest in me!

"How long are you in town for?" Dad asked.

"I'll be in and out," he replied. "I got instructional ball coming up in Florida, then a break from Thanksgiving to Christmas, and then spring training in February. So, with your permission, Dad, I'd like to be the first person to take Gina out on a date."

My father thought for a long moment. "We'll see, we'll see," he said, not promising anything.

This conversation happened when I was still fourteen years old and barely a freshman at St. Lucy's. Football season was in full swing, we had dances with the boys at Damien, our "sister school," and many weekends I had sleepovers with my girlfriends.

The thought of me going out with a nineteen-year-old guy—a worldly one at that—felt like I could be getting in over my head. But another side of me was *excited* about the prospect of going on a real, romantic date with someone I'd always had a crush on.

A few weeks passed, and I was in torture wondering what my parents would decide. I didn't see Frank during this time. Meanwhile, my fifteenth birthday was rapidly approaching. The date fell on a Thursday—November 25—which also happened to be Thanksgiving Day.

The Saturday before Thanksgiving, I went to my first dance at St. Lucy's. The Damien boys had been invited.

My older brother Johnny was dating a new girl who had a freshman brother at Damien. She thought Brett (not his real name) would make a great dance partner for me. As an enticement, I was told that Brett was a hunk: six feet, two inches tall with dark hair.

The night before the big dance, Johnny cornered me. "I want you to promise that you'll dance and talk with Brett," he said.

I blushed from the attention. "Okay, I'll dance with him," I said.

I'll admit that I was excited and nervous as I got ready for the big dance. I curled my hair with hot curlers and applied make-up. I put on a new pair of rust-colored dress pants and a rust sweater, which were in fashion that fall. My friend Mia invited me to ride with her, saying her mom would drive us there and pick us up.

When Mia and I entered the beautiful, outdoor amphitheater at St. Lucy's, a whole new world opened up for me. I saw the popular upper classmen on the dance floor, laughing and having fun. I'll admit to feeling a bit out of place as a freshman.

Mia and I decided to walk up to the second level of the high school building, where we could overlook the dance and check everyone out.

Wait a minute. What's Frank Pastore doing down there, cutting up a rug?

I was still trying to figure out why a guy eighteen months removed from his high school graduation was at our dance when I received a tap on the shoulder.

"Are you Gina, Johnny's sister?" asked a tall, gangly freshman with dark hair. He had to be Brett.

"Yes, I am. It's Brett, right?"

"Yeah. Would you like to dance?"

Brett extended his hand like a gentleman.

I accepted and allowed him to lead me downstairs to the dance floor. We separated and started boogying to the beat. Then, out of the corner of my eye, I could see Frank moving rhythmically while he stared at me.

Within minutes, Frank cut in.

"Sorry, Brett," I said as Frank led me by the hand to another part of the dance floor. We grooved to the beat, and then the band moved into a slow song. Frank drew me in close and took my right hand with his left and placed his other hand on my waist.

"I still want to take you on your first date," he said. "I'm going to stop at your house tomorrow and see if your dad says it's okay."

I really wasn't sure what to make of this "first date thing," but Frank sure seemed to have his mind set on making it happen.

And that was fine with me.

It's pretty neat when a national holiday like Thanksgiving coincides with your birthday. My fifteenth birthday felt doubly special because my parents had said they would grant me permission to go out on an official date with Frank. I never asked them why they relaxed their standards or changed their minds, but they did.

On Thanksgiving, Mom outdid herself as more than a dozen family members and Frank gathered around the dinner table for turkey and all the trimmings—plus a birthday cake along with the pumpkin pie. About a half hour after the last serving of dessert, Frank figured that an appropriate amount had time had passed. He excused us from the dinner table, which prompted a few "a-hems" and nervous twitters around the table. Nonetheless, we bade everyone goodbye. I was dressed in a brand-new, brown-colored jumpsuit, which was popular at the time.

Frank swiftly opened the passenger door to his spiffy 280Z, and I slipped in, holding a handbag. Then Frank took the wheel.

"Well, what do you want to do? Do the movies sound good?"

I wasn't sure what I was supposed to say. This was a first-time experience for me. I took the safe route.

"Sure, that sounds like fun," I said cheerfully, trying my best to act older and more sophisticated.

We headed down to the Montclair Plaza, which had a three-screen Cineplex. The movies on the marquee were: *Bambi, Shampoo*, and a third movie I can't remember.

Bambi was the G-rated tale of a white-tailed fawn whose mother was shot and killed by a deer hunter. The Disney animated film was re-released to theaters every half-dozen years or so in those pre-DVD days. Kiddie fare.

Shampoo, on the other hand, was a racy R-rated flick starring Warren Beatty as a Beverly Hills hairdresser who has sex with any woman he can, as often as he can. I didn't know the plot line in any great detail, but I was aware of the general gist of the movie because my parents had seen *Shampoo* at home on the Z Channel, one of the first pay TV channels available in Southern California in those pre-cable days. I had heard my parents talking about *Shampoo* with a few friends, so I wanted to see what the hoopla was all about.

Frank, understanding that he was taking an innocent high school freshman out to a movie, steered us toward the safe choice. "I guess we'll see *Bambi*," he said, digging into his pocket for some cash.

I immediately squashed that idea. I wanted to act sophisticated with this older guy. "No, let's see *Shampoo*!"

"Really? Won't your parents—"

"They already saw the movie on the Z Channel. I say we go."

Frank shrugged his shoulders and reluctantly purchased two tickets. We walked into the dark theater, holding hands, and found our seats. I remember feeling so comfortable with Frank—his strong hands, his warm smile, and the wonderful smell of his cologne.

The movie started, and honestly, I watched it, but I couldn't stop thinking about Frank and how much I liked him. He held my hand throughout most of the movie. Looking back, there really were some adult situations in that movie, but I didn't catch on to them at the time. When the movie ended and we walked out, Frank said, "Wanna get some coffee?"

"Sure!"

Frank drove us to Alfie's Diner in Upland. We sat and talked and talked and talked. Each minute we were together, I was falling in love.

So what if I was only fifteen years old? I knew Frank was falling for me.

But as we continued to see each other—either on dates or when he came over to the house—it was becoming more and more apparent that our age difference *was* an issue. After all, he was used to being with young women much more mature in every way, especially in the sexual arena.

That Christmas, he slowed down the train. "Maybe when I come home next year, we'll date again," he said. "However, I'm not sure I'll return to Upland. I'm going to see how the season goes."

Alarm bells went off in my mind, but I maintained a poker face. While we continued to see each other every now and then until Frank left for spring training, I did my best *not* to get attached to this guy by busying myself with school and "getting into" the social scene at St. Lucy's. That spring, I even invited a Damien boy to our annual Sadie Hawkins dance—a girl-asks-boy affair.

What kept my hopes flickering for Frank was that he called the house several times during the baseball season. After speaking with Dad or Johnny, he always asked if I was available. I enjoyed our conversations as well as the few postcards he mailed me.

When his second minor league season was over—compiling a mediocre 10-11 pitching record for the Tampa Tarpons and the Trois-Rivières Aigles in French-speaking Quebec—Frank had a change of heart. He returned to Upland as I was starting my sophomore year at St. Lucy's in the fall of 1977.

Little did I know that our lives were about to intertwine and become crazy.

Really crazy.

Once again, Frank dropped by the house and asked Dad if he could date me again. I was still fifteen years old but would reach "sweet sixteen" status at Thanksgiving time.

Inwardly, I squealed with delight. Frank still liked me . . . liked me enough to ask me to go out with him. And it wasn't just one date. Seemed like every Friday and Saturday night we were going out for a bite to eat, having coffee, or going to a movie—things that dating couples do. Back in the day, they called this "going steady."

Our budding romance didn't escape the eyes of my mother.

In chronological terms, a twenty-year-old male was dating a fifteen-but-soon-to-be-sixteen-year-old female. In reality terms, there was a maturity gap the size of the Grand Canyon between a guy who should have been in his junior year at college and a high school sophomore.

At least, that's how my mother saw things shaping up. Suddenly, I heard her muttering things like, "He's way too old for her" and "I don't like him coming around here." Since she was aware of Frank's reputation for "playing the field" while pitching in the minor leagues, she was worried that Frank had one thing on his mind—getting me into bed.

Dad played the role of the peacemaker. One evening, he knocked and came into my bedroom while I was doing homework. "Gina, you gotta slow things down with Frankie. Your mother is flipping out," he said. "We gotta change things between you two."

Dad said I could only go out with Frank once a week, but what happened was that he'd come over for dinner on Friday night and after dessert, we'd go have coffee at Alfie's Diner. On Saturday night we'd have our "official" date by going to the movies, but we still had a 10 o'clock curfew. Sunday morning, Frank would join us at St. Joseph's for the 9 a.m. Mass, holding my hand as we entered the vestibule. Of course, there's no way that we could not invite Frank to our big Sunday sit-down meal around the family dinner table.

I think the point-of-no-return moment came when I asked Frank to escort me to St. Lucy's Christmas Formal just before our two-week holiday break. He agreed, which thrilled me. The Christmas Formal was like a debutante ball—we would be announcing our romance to the world and making our relationship very official. Mom got upset when she heard the news because she recognized the stakes: Frankie and Gina were getting serious.

I bought myself a pretty red dress for the occasion. On the day of the formal, I spent a lot of time getting ready: curling my hair, applying makeup, and putting on my gorgeous new long red dress.

Frank came by the house in his 280Z to pick me up, and while there was some tension in the living room as he presented me with a corsage, my parents wished us a good time. We met several couples at the Ruddy Duck, a fancy steak house in Upland.

When we left the restaurant, the pitch-black sky released a downpour of rain that came down in sheets as we drove to St. Lucy's. We parked the car and made a mad dash to the gymnasium. What happened next was right out of a cheesy Hallmark Channel movie: my red dress got soaked, my shoes were drenched, my curly hair was a mess, and my makeup was ruined. Frank's gray woolen suit was doused as well.

I was almost in tears, but Frank kept saying, "You look beautiful!"

Then Frank looked at the arms of his wool suit. His wet sleeves were creeping up his arms, which made us crack up. It wasn't the perfect night, but we had a great time, rain and all. We were falling madly in love.

A few weeks later, Frank asked my dad if he could pick me up from school on a Friday afternoon and take me for a drive. My father agreed. Frank and I headed off to a hillside area known as Etiwanda, about a half-hour east of Upland. Etiwanda was out in the sticks. When we stopped to walk around the rural landscape, Frank told me that his dream was to buy some land here and build a log cabin someday.

I was rather surprised to hear this, but excited since I could tell that he was using me as a sounding board. As we hopped in the car for the return trip, Frank asked me, "Do you want to have children someday?"

"Of course!" I exclaimed. "Two or three!"

"Me, too!"

I smiled. We were on the same page in so many things.

"Hey, I'm hungry," he said. "Whaddya say we get something to eat?"

I was up for that. Frank drove us to Tiffany's, a greasy spoon on the way back to Upland.

I can't remember what I ordered, but I do remember—as I was taking a bite—hearing Frank blurt, "Gina, I love you!"

I nearly dropped my fork. I sat there looking at him, not saying anything. I was speechless for one of the few times in my life.

He wasn't finished. "I want to spend my life with you," he added.

I understood and wanted that, too.

But I was only sixteen years old.

9

A Different Kind of Proposal

After Frank told me that he loved me and wanted to spend the rest of his life with me, our relationship became serious—as in *really* serious. Frank hadn't actually said, "Will you marry me?", but he might as well have proposed.

What went unspoken were the realities staring us in the face: Frank was leaving in six weeks for spring training in Tampa, Florida, and would be gone until September, and I still had two-and-a-half years of high school left. It made sense to both of us that if we were to get married, I should at least be a high school graduate.

Then I had an idea: What if I transferred to Upland High and graduated a year early? St. Lucy's was a college prep school with the senior year devoted to AP (advanced placement) classes and Catholic training. With all my core classes out of the way plus the summer school credits I had earned, I could graduate from Upland High in eighteen months and start my life with Frank a year early. Plus, I wouldn't have to ride a bus for an hour-and-a-half a day. Upland High was less than a mile from our house.

Frank thought that was a great idea, so the both of us approached my father—knowing that he was more in our corner than Mom—and asked him what he thought about me transferring to Upland High. We gathered in the living room while Mom was making dinner.

When Dad heard my idea to switch schools, he immediately sensed where this was going, even though we hadn't mentioned getting married following my graduation.

"Gina, just hold on and finish at St. Lucy's," he said. "If this is meant to be, it'll happen."

"Dad, we don't want to wait," I said, tucking my arm into Frank's for emphasis.

Dad sighed. "You know I have to speak with your mother on this."

"I know."

Dad got up from his recliner and entered the kitchen. Half a minute later, we heard my mother yell, "ABSOLUTELY NOT!"

Then Mom marched into the living room, drying her hands on her apron.

"Forget it, you two," she said in a raised voice. Then, looking at me with an angry face, she said, "You're way too young. You're just trying to speed this up by transferring to Upland High."

Tears welled up. "But, Mom, I love—"

"I don't want to hear it! It's not going to happen!" With that, Mom stomped off to the kitchen to resume dinner preparations.

During Christmas break, Frank was feeling conflicted because he thought that being with him meant I would be cheating myself out of the carefree days of high school: school lunches, dances, proms, and dating other guys.

"If you never experience another relationship, you might regret that down the road," he said.

"I'll never regret being with you," I assured him.

When Frank wasn't around, my mother would bombard me with her unsolicited opinions about our relationship. She would burst into my room and just attack me. "You're way too young to be thinking about marriage!" she'd yell.

"No, I'm not!" I'd yell back.

Then Dad, hearing the fighting, would come investigate, and then *he'd* get caught up in the quarrel. With Mom and I fighting and Dad and Mom arguing with each other, it felt like chaos. My parents both tried to convince me that all men wanted was sex, but hearing them say that was incredibly hurtful.

"Frank is in love with me, and I'm in love with him!" I shouted back.

Finally, Dad put his foot down. "We're gonna knock this off!" he yelled.

"You're making a huge mistake!" my mom added, at which time Dad spoke to her *en italiano* while guiding her out of my bedroom. *Calmati* . . . take it easy.

Mom wouldn't let it go. Her attacks were nonstop. Dinner time was the worst. Mom would start digging into me with the same old arguments . . . *You're making a big mistake* . . . *You're not old enough to get married* . . . and I'd slam my napkin on the table and storm to my room, shut the door, and not come out. I stopped eating dinner with my parents most of the time. The experience was too stressful.

In reflection, my poor mother was trying hard to break Frank and I apart. Her over-the-top reaction, however, brought us closer together. It was her against us. We were a modern-day Romeo and Juliet . . . two star-crossed lovers against the world.

I remember coming home from a date one night and before we exchanged a good night kiss, I checked to see if the coast was clear. Sure enough, the living room curtains parted and Mom's eagle eyes were staring at us through the window. This happened on several occasions.

My mother and I basically stopped speaking to each other and did our best to stay out of one another's way. Dad, caught in the middle, knocked on my bedroom door one evening to have a father-daughter chat.

"Look, your mother's pretty upset. You're young. You have your whole lives ahead of you. You just have to find a way to slow this down."

"But, Dad, I love Frank . . ."

"Just wait until you graduate. Then we'll do you a wedding," he said.

In two-and-a-half years? At sixteen years of age, that seemed like an eternity. I couldn't wait that long. With a November birthday, I was one of the oldest students in my class. I would be eighteen years and nine months old if we waited until I graduated from St. Lucy's. That's why I wanted to transfer to Upland High so badly.

Speaking of not being able to wait . . . the sexual tension was super high. But I was committed to the morals of my Catholic upbringing, so we didn't go much past first base . . . well, make that second base. Whenever we "parked" in Frank's 280Z overlooking the shimmering lights of San Gabriel Valley, we'd have some intense make-out sessions. We both felt the heat.

I remember my older brother Johnny coming into my room one night after Frank dropped me off at the 10 p.m. curfew. "Gene, what are you guys doing? You better not get pregnant!"

"So that's what you're worried about," I said, collecting all the indignation I could muster. "I have everything under control."

"You do, huh? I sure hope so," Johnny said.

Johnny must have said something to Dad because one afternoon in January, my father had a talk with Frank. It happened before I arrived home from St. Lucy's. Dad asked Frank to have a seat in the living room and immediately cut to the chase.

"Look, Anna's putting a lot of pressure on me. You better not be having sex with my daughter because if you are, I'll break-a your legs," he declared in his best Mafioso accent. Marlon Brando as the God-father couldn't have said it any better.

Frank immediately backpedaled. "Don't worry, Dad! We're not going to do that. I promise."

"Yeah, yeah," my father said. "You just make sure no funny stuff happens, because if it does . . ."

Dad didn't finish his threat. But it was clear to him and everyone around us that we were madly in love when Frank left for spring training in the middle of February.

I knew I wouldn't see Frank until the end of the 1978 baseball season, seven or eight months away. How could we stay in touch? We could talk on the phone, but long-distance phone calls—remember those?—were expensive. We had to limit ourselves to a twenty-minute phone call on Sunday nights (when rates were the cheapest). Otherwise, we sent each other long handwritten letters in those pre-computer times.

The phone calls were the best since I could hear Frank's voice and have instant communication with him. We had three phones in the house: one in the family room, one in my dad's office, and another in my parents' bedroom. When Frank would call on Sunday night—in those days baseball teams always played day games on Sundays—I'd sit on the floor next to my parents' bed and speak with Frank. I wasn't allowed to shut the master bedroom door, so I was never sure if my conversation was private. Sure enough, one evening I peeked from behind the bed and saw a shadow in the hallway. Mom was listening in.

I wrote Frank the next day with this message: *Mom is being real nosy. I think she might try to open your letters, so be careful about what you're writing.*

We got into a rhythm of mailing each other two letters a week. What Frank did was keep a daily journal of what was happening around him and then after three or four days, he'd tear out the pages and stuff them into an envelope that he sent to me in Upland. I hid his letters in my dresser drawer at the start, but then I took them to school with me in my book bag.

The good news is that Frank had been put on the 40-man roster of the Cincinnati Reds, which meant that he was eligible to be added to the 25-man active roster. Now that the Reds organization considered Frank to be a major league prospect, he trained alongside legendary players like Johnny Bench—my brother's idol!—and Pete Rose, known as Charlie Hustle. The Reds had added a new pitcher to the rotation during the off-season: Tom Seaver, the former New York Met and Frank's hero growing up. Frank felt like he had died and gone to baseball heaven.

Frank wrote about the latest Robert Ludlum novel he was reading—he loved thrillers and intrigue—and shared anecdotes from the baseball field. One of them happened on the first day of training camp when he was warming up with a game of catch. As Frank described it, his errant throw sailed over a player's head and struck Reds' manager Sparky Anderson in the calf, earning Frank a not-so-welcoming glare.

In a subsequent letter, Frank shared something more serious: his father had driven from Los Angeles to see him in Tampa because he had been booted out of the house when Elma Pastore said their marriage was over and she was filing for divorce. Frank Sr. had nowhere else to go, which complicated life for his son.

Early in the season, Frank phoned on a Sunday night. Everyone knew who was calling. I was running from the living room to my parents' bedroom when my father intercepted the call in his office.

"Hi, Dad!" Frank said cheerfully.

"Frankie, how ya doin'?" he said in his usual shooting-the-breeze manner.

Frank gulped. He hadn't expected to speak with my father, but now seemed as appropriate a moment as ever. Frank missed me terribly, and seeing his teammates being warmly greeted outside the clubhouse door by gorgeous wives and girlfriends reminded him that we were separated by 3,000 miles and wouldn't see each other for more than a half a year.

"Dad, I, uh, need to talk to you about something important."

"Do you need help?" my father asked. "Because if something happened—"

"No, I'm fine. I want to talk to you about Gina and me."

Oh, that. "Whatcha thinkin'?"

"Well, I want to marry Gina."

"Oh, Frankie," he responded. "I knew that. You'll have plenty of time to get married later. Right now you need to focus on baseball."

"But, Dad, we love each other! I love her, and I'm asking your permission for us to be engaged."

"Frankie! She's only sixteen years old! And how old are you? Twenty or twenty-one? No. She's too young. Focus on the baseball now, and you can get together all you want when the season's over."

"But, Dad—"

"Wait, Frankie. Wait."

My father then cupped his hand over the receiver and yelled, "GEEE-NAH! It's for you!"

"Thanks, Dad. I got it!" I yelled out. I ran from my room to my parents' bedroom and picked up.

"Hi, baby," he said in a soothing voice. "I just asked your father if we could get engaged, but he told me to concentrate on baseball. But I can't focus on my pitching when I'm thinking about you all the time. Gina, I love you, and I love you more than anything. Being apart is killing me. I can't wait two more years or however long it is. I don't even want to wait one year. Sweetheart, let's elope as soon as the season is over."

Eloping? Wow, the idea sounded intriguing. I was struck by how much Frank wanted to be with me. And, goodness knows, I wanted to be with him. In a strange way, it all made sense. I was worn down with fighting my parents. Frank and I were truly in love and committed to each other, and deep down I knew my parents would forgive me. The constant turmoil was hard on all of us. Perhaps running away to get married would alleviate the tension.

"You really think that's a good idea?" I had to be careful with what I said since the walls had ears. I certainly wasn't going to say the word *elope* in our house.

"Yeah, let's do it after the season's over. Let's be together."

"Ooh, Frank. You're the best."

Our discussion turned to other things—school, baseball, and what my brothers were doing.

When our twenty minutes were up, I said goodbye and set the phone back in its cradle. I leaned back against the side of my parents' bed and closed my eyes. I loved the idea of eloping.

Let's see Mom and Dad stop this!

Frank was assigned to the Nashville Sounds, the Reds' Double A affiliate that had country singers like Conway Twitty and Barbara Mandrell as part owners. Throughout the spring, he wrote about the vibrant nightlife in Music City and the celebrities who threw out the first pitches. He shared an apartment with two pitchers, Joe Price and Rick O'Keeffe, and the good news was that this time around he had his own bed. Besides that, Frank said that he was miserable without me. We continued to talk about eloping during our weekly phone calls, but nothing could be done until the baseball season was over.

When my sophomore year finished in late May, my brother Johnny told me at dinner one night, "Gene, you need to get a job." Since I couldn't see Frank, Johnny sensed that I needed to do something to occupy my time. His girlfriend, a knockout named Staci Isles, had gotten a job at the Claremont Tennis Club just a few miles from Upland. She was working in the snack shop.

"Staci said they need some help," Johnny said. "Tell you what. Let me drive you over there and you can check it out."

I got my first job. That summer, I worked alongside Staci making turkey sandwiches and protein shakes. It had become pretty clear to me that Johnny, who was attending nearby Claremont Men's College and playing on the basketball and baseball teams, was smitten with Staci, and the feeling was mutual. We had a lot of interesting discussions about our beaus that summer. (Staci turned out to be my future sister-in-law. She and Johnny have been married for more than thirty-seven years and have two daughters.)

I liked working at the Claremont Club because that meant I didn't have to be around my mother. Every time Frank called or another letter arrived in our mailbox, my relationship with Mom declined a bit more. I looked for ways to stay out of the house. In fact, I spent most weekends at friends' homes or with my older sister Marina, who was married and lived in a nearby suburb. Marina had recently given birth to my niece Andrea, who I adored.

Meanwhile, Frank and I continued to plot our elopement. Like any baseball player, Frank had a lot of dead time on his hands. He didn't have to be at the ballpark until 3 p.m. for a night game, and there are long road trips with interminable bus rides or red-eye flights.

Frank used that time to fashion a scenario that would allow the two of us to elope without my parents and/or the authorities stopping us before a justice of the peace pronounced us husband and wife. He was putting all the spy tradecraft he had picked up in the Ludlum novels to good use.

First off, we couldn't tell anyone about our plans, not even my closest friend, Donna Pastorelle—interesting how her last name was so close to Frank's—who Frank and I would meet with for coffee and chats. If either us breathed a word to anyone we knew, a secret like that would get back to my parents.

As far as logistics and timing went, Frank suggested that we elope in early September after the season finished. On the day of the elopement, Frank would pick me up in the morning, making it look like he was driving me to St. Lucy's. But instead of hopping on the freeway to Glendora, we'd make our getaway. On the way to the justice of the peace, I'd have to change out of my school uniform since a twenty-one-year old guy marrying a teen girl dressed in a St. Lucy's cardigan sweater, blouse, and skirt might raise questions. I would carry a change of clothes in a brown paper bag since a suitcase would be a dead-give-away. I would purchase new clothes, shoes, makeup, toiletries, and a curling iron during the honeymoon.

But I was still sixteen, considered a minor by the law. That meant I needed my parents' permission to get married. Frank had a solution: he'd forge my baptismal certificate. Would a local courthouse accept that form of identification? We didn't know; we'd have to hope for the best. Frank was confident he could falsify my baptismal certificate since he'd forged fake IDs for himself and his friends back in the Damien days.

Frank did some research and said the best place for us to get married would be the San Bernardino County Courthouse in Colton, a blue-collar community thirty miles east of Upland known for being one of the smoggiest places in Los Angeles because of its proximity to the Kaiser Steel mill. In other words, not a garden spot. Then we'd make our getaway, being careful not to break any traffic laws or do anything to draw undue attention.

In case there was a manhunt, we'd book three flights from Ontario

International Airport, a regional airport that was a fifteen-minute drive from our Upland home. Flight reservations would be made using aliases to three different popular honeymoon spots: Acapulco, Hawaii, and Orlando.

Meanwhile, the *real* reservation would be on a nonstop flight from Los Angeles International (LAX) to Nashville, Tennessee, where Frank left his car and his belongings at the apartment he shared with two teammates.

Frank believed that we would really fool everybody because they would be *expecting* us to fly out of nearby Ontario Airport instead of LAX, which was a good ninety minutes from the San Gabriel Valley.

"No one will be looking for us at LAX," Frank said.

I had to admit that he was very clever.

Hearing the excitement in Frank's voice made *me* excited, but he wasn't finished explaining his plan on a Sunday night when my parents weren't home.

"After we get to Nashville, we'll drive up to Birmingham, where my mom's living. She bought a house with some of my bonus money. We'll stay off the radar screen for a few weeks until the start of Instructional League at the end of September. That's in Tampa."

My head was spinning. I kind of knew where Tampa was in Florida, but I wasn't so sure about Birmingham. The only place I'd traveled to out of state was Chicago to see relatives.

"Where's Birmingham?

"In Alabama, around two hundred miles north of Nashville. It's not too far," Frank said. "So what do you think? Are you sure you want to go through with this?"

"I'm more sure than ever!" I exclaimed. I was ready to elope because I was sick and tired of fighting with my mother. She was constantly threatening to send me to a convent in Italy—as if becoming a nun like Maria in *The Sound of Music* would change everything. Mom had married Dad when she was eighteen, and their marriage wasn't exactly like Captain von Trapp and Maria. Perhaps she saw too much of herself in my situation, which is why she was so hard on me.

Frank's plan sounded exhilarating—and foolproof as well. I knew once I eloped, however, that my life would never be the same. It would be like jumping off a cliff; there would be no turning back.

But I wasn't enjoying high school. I was tired of dealing with Mom,

and the only thing I wanted to do was be with Frank.
That could happen—if we eloped.

10

The Craziest Story Ever

Frank was a pretty good hitter for a pitcher, so he wasn't a stranger to the base paths.

During a late season, mid-August game with the Nashville Sounds, Frank hit a gapper toward the right field wall and decided to try for two. After rounding first base and speeding toward second, he dove headfirst into the bag.

"Safe!" yelled the ump.

Frank immediately jumped to his feet and grimaced. His pitching hand hurt!

Frank had to come out of the game, and X-rays determined that he had broken the middle finger, which was taped to a splint. His teammates teased him about the eternal middle finger "salute," but it was clear to everyone that Frank's season was over. When he called me on a hot summer afternoon to inform me that he'd be coming home in a few days, I was overjoyed. And then Frank repeated the question that was uppermost in our minds: "Are you sure you want to go through with this?"

"Yes, I'm certain," I replied, careful to keep my voice low in my parents' bedroom.

After saying goodbye to Frank, I ran out to the front yard, where I found Dad talking with a neighbor. I waited patiently until I could have his undivided attention.

"Dad, Frank's coming home early. He injured his pitching hand sliding into a base," I said breathlessly.

Dad was happy for me. "I'm sure you're excited to see Frankie again. Tell you what," he said, drawing closer so that Mom couldn't overhear us from the house.

"Gina, you're gonna be a junior and turning seventeen soon. Things are gonna change—the curfew, the rules. You know, you'll have more freedom with Frankie. You'll see."

What Dad was doing was extending an olive branch and trying to lower the thermostat of tension surrounding Mom and me. In many ways, though, his overture was too little, too late. Our secret plan to elope hadn't diminished one bit in the last five or six months. In fact, like a missile launch, we were ready to light this candle!

What happened next is so crazy, so unbelievable, but so true—and I want Frank to share in telling it with me. He described how we tried to elope in his autobiography *Shattered*, and I'd like to weave his story in with mine as we go along. This will give you a glimpse of what a fun, creative, and memorable character Frank was. He really was one-in-a-million.

So, without further ado, we'll start the story with Frank's words:

> *I injured a finger on my pitching hand, and that circumstance allowed me to the leave the team before the season ended. In late August, I flew from Nashville to LAX. We planned the Elopement Day for Thursday, August 31, 1978.*
>
> *It was Gina's first day of her junior year in high school. I rolled up to the house about 6:45 a.m. and walked into the kitchen to find Dad in his chair at the kitchen table reading the paper and making breakfast for the family.*
>
> *"Geee-nahhh," he bellowed, suspecting nothing. "Frankie's here!"*
>
> *Gina came down the hall dressed in her school uniform, carrying a brown paper bag.*
>
> *"What's in the bag?" Dad asked.*
>
> *"My PE clothes," said my lovely bride-to-be.*

I was about to leave the only world I had known and launch into the unknown. I was prepared to leave behind my family, school life and my friends, my niece Andrea who I adored, and everything that was familiar to me. The reason I could take this step was because I was certain that I loved Frank and would never regret this decision.

The "gym clothes" inside my brown paper bag were really my wedding outfit—a light brown silk blouse, a champagne-colored silk skirt, a pair of tan-colored Candies high-heeled shoes, plus some undergarments, a nightgown, a toothbrush, a small tube of toothpaste, and lip gloss. I wasn't taking a whole lot of material things with me into this new world. In a sense, I was placing my whole self into my new life with Frank Pastore from this moment forward.

My goodness, I was nervous. What if our grand plan went haywire? How would this all turn out? I had no idea what was about to unfold.

We hopped into my dad's Riviera—he had returned to L.A. following the divorce—and headed to his apartment so Gina could change out of her Catholic school uniform. I grabbed my already packed suitcase.

We wanted to be the first in line to pick up our marriage license at the county office in Upland. With all the documentation in hand, including our three-day-wait blood test and Gina's forged baptismal certificate, we were at the window when it slid open at eight o'clock.

Like a counterfeiter passing bad bills, I may have looked calm, cool, and collected on the outside, but inside, my heart was racing. The license fee was $7.50. I handed the clerk a $20 bill, accepted her congratulations, and then we raced off to the county offices in Colton to get married by a justice of the peace.

Frank and I plotted that we would need my birth certificate to attain a marriage license, but after doing some research, we learned that a baptismal record would suffice. This saved us a trip to the county recorder's office because I knew a copy of my baptismal certificate was in a bookcase where my parents stored important documents.

It was a hot morning—in the triple digits already—and the light brown classic Riviera, circa 1965, that belonged to Frank's dad didn't have air conditioning. I was very nervous, and the heat wasn't helping.

We were on a tight schedule. Our flight would leave LAX at 12:40 p.m. We arrived at the little courthouse in Colton a few minutes before nine. When the doors opened, there were just four of us there—Gina and me and the judge and his assistant. The judge was friendly, chatty, and genuinely interested in this young couple who wanted to get married with no witnesses in the middle of nowhere.

What Frank didn't mention is that we were so far out in the sticks that we drove up a dirt road to a little building that was on a farming property. When we walked into the building, however, the receptionist—with a coy smile—immediately asked, "Are you Frank and Gina?"

My heart sank. *How did she know our names?* I was obviously paranoid.

Thankfully, the receptionist answered my question before either of us could fashion a reply. "The gal from the marriage license office called and told us you were heading here. I'll go and get the judge."

A man appeared, looking much younger than what I expected a judge to look like. He was dark haired, had a wry smile on his face, and appeared excited to perform the ceremony.

"Now tell me: Why are you two getting married?" he asked in a breezy manner that was a bit too familiar.

Frank was ready. "I'm a baseball player, and we'll be heading to winter ball in Florida soon, so we want to get married now and have a family reception during the off-season," he said.

The judge cocked an ear. "You play baseball? What team do you play for?"

"I pitch for the Cincinnati Reds organization," Frank answered, and then they talked baseball for a couple of minutes. I remember Frank saying something about hoping to get to pitch in the major leagues someday but that hadn't happened yet.

Frank picked up the story in this way:

We didn't want to slip up and reveal too much, so I told the judge that we had a flight to catch and needed to get this show on the road.

The judge grinned, handed the paperwork to the secretary, and escorted us outside to a grassy place beneath a big oak tree about ninety feet from the county offices. Gina and I were dying with nerves, excitement, fear, and the thrill of our newfound calling to the world of espionage. We stood under the tree holding hands.

The judge got started with the ceremony, and just before he got to the part about, "Frank, do you take Gina to be your lawfully wedded wife?" his secretary emerged from his office.

"Judge," she called out, "may I speak with you for a moment?"

He was such a nice guy. "Excuse me," he called to her. "Now is not a good time. Could it just wait a few minutes, please?"

"No," she responded. "You need to take this call right now."

My heart was in my throat, but I played it cool. "You go ahead, Judge."

The judge excused himself and walked over to the secretary. They spoke in whispers. I instantly knew what she was telling him and began to cry.

The judge thanked his secretary and walked over to us. "Frank . . . Gina," he began, looking at my husband-to-be and then me. "I just learned that Gina's only sixteen."

Frank's face turned red, and sweat formed on his forehead. "Judge, can you please marry us anyway?"

The judge shook his head. "I'm afraid I can't do that," he said. "How about the two of you coming back to my chambers and we'll talk about this."

We both felt defeated as we followed the judge back into his office. Here's how Frank described how we had been found out:

Our perfect plan had been foiled by the dear lady at the county office in Upland, where we got our marriage license. I had left her window without taking the change from my $20 bill. I hadn't left any local phone numbers for her, so she grabbed *a phone book and looked up our last names. She called the only Pignotti in the book, and sure enough, she'd gotten Gina's father on the phone.*

Ring . . . ring.

"Hello?"

"Excuse me for calling," the nice lady said, "but is this the Pignotti residence?"

"Yes," said Dad.

"Do you have a daughter named Gina?"

"Yes," said Dad.

"Well," Nice Lady went on, "this morning when Gina was here to get her license, they left their change, and we have $12.50 for them. Would you like me to mail it to you, or will someone be coming by to pick it up?"

Bless her heart.

"What?" Dad said. "I don't understand, Gina already has her driver's license, and besides, she's at school."

"Oh, no, sir," Nice Lady chuckled. "It not her driver's license. It's her marriage license."

Nuclear explosion.

I wouldn't find out about Dad going ballistic until later, but sitting in the judge's office, I knew the recent turn of events wasn't going to turn out good. Too bad I didn't have a common last name like Smith.

The judge also let us know that there was an all-points-bulletin on Frank's Riviera, so we wouldn't get very far anyway.

"I sense you two really want to get married," the judge said. "Gina, can I ask . . . are you pregnant?"

I dropped my head and started to cry. "No," I sniffled.

"Then why are you two eloping?" he asked gently.

Frank began to explain the whole situation, and when he was done, the judge leaned back in his chair with his hands clasped behind his head.

"Tell you what," he said. "I'm going to call Gina's dad and have him and your mother come over here, and we'll talk things through like adults. You don't have a thing to worry about. I'm here for you."

I felt differently. I *knew* I had a lot to worry about.

The judge picked up the black rotary dial phone on his desk and turned to me. "Shall we call your father, Gina?"

I nodded and dictated the number: 982-0268.

I held my breath, and then heard the judge identify himself and say, "Mr. Pignotti. I'm sitting here with your beautiful daughter, and—"

"ARREST HIM!"

I could hear my father over the line as clear as day.

The judge deflected the directive. "Mr. Pignotti, perhaps if you came to the county courthouse, we could all sit down and talk this through."

Once again, my dad's booming voice was audible. "ARREST HIM! Don't let him out of your sight because when I get that son of a @#$%, I'm gonna break his legs, okay?"

"Surely, Mr. Pignotti, we can reasonable—"

Then I heard my father say, "On second thought, she does this. He can have her!"

The exasperated judge cupped his hand over the handset. "Does your father have a bad temper?"

You have to ask that?

I nodded—when suddenly the judge winced. My father had hung up on him.

The judge looked at his watch. "Darn—I have an important appointment I have to get to, but I'll be back in an hour. You two stay right there, and we'll get this handled."

With that, the judge grabbed his black briefcase and hustled out of his chambers, leaving Frank and me alone in our silence. Here's what Frank said in *Shattered*:

It was an obvious stall ploy. I had read it a hundred times in

Ludlum's novels. The spy was trying to detain the target long enough for the sniper to get into position to take the shot. We had to get out of there.

We looked at each other like Bonnie and Clyde with the long arm of the law closing in.

"Let's run for it!" we said to each other at the same time.

Hand in hand, we ran out of the office, passing the secretary, who tried to stop us. "The judge said you have to wait!"

We didn't care. We made a mad dash for the Riviera, jumped in, and sped down the dirt road, leaving a trail of dust—just like in the movies. Because we knew there was an APB on such a distinctive car, Frank didn't jump on nearby Interstate 10 but headed south on surface streets to catch the 60 freeway—an east-west freeway that ran parallel to Interstate 10. He hewed to the speed limit, lest he draw any attention from traffic cops. He also told me "Get down!" whenever I lifted my head to see where we were going.

I slunk down on the floorboard, drenched in sweat since the temperature was 108 degrees and we didn't have air conditioning.

"What are we going to do?" I asked Frank as he merged onto the 60.

"We have to go to Plan B," Frank said. "Remember how I told you that you only have to be sixteen to get married in Tennessee?"

There were so many moving parts to our elopement that I had forgotten that Frank said I could legally get married at sixteen without a parent's approval in Tennessee.

"Oh, yeah," I said, suddenly remembering. "So, can we still get married?"

"We can! We'll drive to LAX and get on that Delta flight for Nashville, pick up my car and the rest of my stuff at my apartment, and then tomorrow morning, we'll find the nearest courthouse. It's all going to work out!"

I felt the Riviera slowing as Frank exited the freeway.

"Is something wrong?"

"We have to stop at my bank," he said. "I'm low on cash. We're going to need some."

Back in the late 1970s, credit cards weren't ubiquitous like they are today. I didn't have one and Frank didn't either. ATM machines were still to come.

Frank pulled into the parking lot of Chino Valley Bank, where he had deposited his $50,000 bonus check. I became even more nervous because Chino Valley Bank was where my dad got his construction loans. The bank owners, the Borbas, were friends of my parents.

"Do you think word has gotten out about us?" I asked Frank from the floorboard, which was soiling my dress.

"Let's hope not," he replied. "I'll be right back."

Frank hustled inside, where he ran into the bank manager.

"Frank, good to see you," the bank manager said. "How did your season go?"

Frank acted like he didn't have a care in the world. "Oh, just fine, although I busted my finger a couple of weeks ago . . . ." Frank held up the right hand with the splint on the middle finger. "But I'm in a hurry to get some cash, so if you'll excuse me—"

I was relieved when Frank returned, patting the seat of his pants where he had stashed his cash-filled billfold. Once again, we were back on the 60, and I feared that any minute we'd be stopped, detained, imprisoned, and yes, even shot! I was scared to death, but like I said, there was no turning back for me. That's why everything felt surreal and real at the same time.

It took every bit of ninety minutes to reach Los Angeles International Airport, which had Frank looking at his watch every five minutes. "This is going to be tight," he said as he steered the Riviera into one of the parking garages inside the "ring"—the same multi-story parking garage his dad had used when he picked up Frank. "I'll tell Dad that he can pick up his car here," Frank explained.

We ran into the terminal and approached the Delta counter. Imagine how hot and sweaty we were and the smudges of floorboard dirt on my dress.

The uniformed woman behind the counter, who'd probably seen it all, asked for our tickets.

"We have reservations for the Nashville flight, ma'am," Frank said.

The reservations agent shook her head. "Sorry," she said. "The flight left ten minutes ago."

"Shoot," Frank said. "How about Birmingham? We have reservations for that flight, too."

Frank had told me on the way to LAX that if we didn't make it in time for the Nashville flight, he had a back-up to our back-up plan:

flying to Birmingham and staying at his mom's place and then driving to Nashville to get married and pick up his stuff.

The Delta agent consulted a sheaf of papers. "You're in luck. The flight leaves for Birmingham in thirty minutes. Names?"

"Richard Wright. And this is my wife, Stephanie Wright."

Frank had reminded me in the car that we would fly using aliases. He chose "Richard Wright" because he saw the name on a matchbook cover, he said. In those pre-computer days, nobody stopped you from flying while using an alias.

"And how will you be paying today?" the Delta agent asked.

"With a check."

If Frank had been a real spy, he would have had enough green money on hand, but my husband-to-be didn't want to spend all his ready cash on plane tickets, so he reached for his checkbook and wrote out a check with his real name, Frank Pastore, imprinted on the upper left-hand corner.

"I'm sorry, but didn't you say your name was Richard Wright? The check is from a Frank Pastore, so there appears to be a discrepancy."

"Oh, that!" Frank leaned forward. "Actually, Frank Pastore is my real name," he said conspiratorially. "I'm a famous baseball player, so when I travel, I need to fly incognito, if you catch my drift. Makes it easier on everyone."

With that, Frank reached for his wallet and pulled out his Cincinnati Red's ID card.

"Wow, you play for the Reds? I'm from Ohio," she said. "Let me get these tickets finished for you. And then can I get your autograph?"

Frank blushed as if that had been the first time someone asked him for his signature. After Frank signed a piece of paper, the Delta rep said, "You're lucky you're not checking any luggage. You better hurry. You have only a few minutes to catch your flight."

We dashed off for the gate—no security check in those days! Both of us were perspiring like long-distance joggers as we ran through the long, narrow corridors from the check-in area to the departure gates. Frank's shirt was wet, and I was holding my possessions in my brown paper bag. I was aware of people staring at us as we rushed past them.

I had to run in my pair of high-heeled Candies. Suddenly, one of my heels broke.

"Wait, Frank."

"Take 'em off," he said.

Now I was running to the gate barefoot, with shoes in hand, which prompted more open jaws. We arrived just as the gate agent was making the final boarding call for Birmingham, Alabama.

Frank stopped us. "Wait, I've got to find a pay phone to call Dad so I can tell him where I parked his car! You get on the plane and hold it until I get there."

Frank had the right idea. I could ask one of the pretty stewardesses to hold the plane until Frank arrived. The last time I had flown was when I was seven years old on a flight to Chicago, so I was sure that my request was reasonable.

I ran down the jet bridge in my bare feet, holding my brown paper bag. Up ahead, I saw a stewardess shutting the cabin door.

"Wait! Please wait!"

The stewardess looked up, but I stopped and didn't board the plane.

"Miss, you need to board immediately. The plane is getting ready to leave!" she barked.

I literally took half a step into the plane to stop the stewardess from closing the cabin door.

"What are you doing, Miss?"

"I'm waiting for my fiancé. He'll be here any moment."

"We can't wait. So if you will take your—"

"No, we have to wait for him!"

We went back and forth for a minute or two—long enough for one of the pilots to come out of the cockpit and demand an explanation for the delay.

"Miss, we will not hold the flight, so please make up your mind."

"You see, sir, my fiancé will be here any second—"

On cue, Frank arrived, out of breath. We hugged and were let on board.

Romeo and Juliet had made their getaway.

11

On the Lam

I magine how nervous I felt as Frank and I settled into our tight seats in the rear of the economy section. With eyes locked on the cabin door, I expected a pair of LAPD cops to board the aircraft and lead us away in handcuffs as the other passengers stared at us with dropped jaws.

The minutes passed by excruciatingly slow. I glanced at Frank, whose normally fine hair had become drenched and stringy, matting to his forehead. Sweat dripped down the side of his face like he was pitching in muggy New York City during the heat of a pennant race. We were both terribly anxious and tried to occupy ourselves with small talk, but it wasn't working. Just when I thought I couldn't take the suspense any longer, a Delta flight attendant closed the cabin door and the plane was pushed out to the tarmac.

At any moment, I expected the pilot to announce that we were going back to the gate . . . *All routine, ladies and gentlemen, and then we'll be on our way.* We'd be led off the plane by a pair of cops. Waiting for us would be my father—cradling a shotgun and doing his best to restrain himself from breaking Frank's legs.

When the plane started moving forward, I exhaled a heavy sigh of relief. I could feel excitement building as we taxied to the end of LAX's north departure runway. We would soon be on our way to Birmingham.

"Flight attendants, prepare for takeoff," the captain said, as he lined up the Delta 727 for a routine departure into the sunlit western sky.

I reached for Frank's hand as the jet engines whined to high pitch, and the pilot released the air brake. We started the takeoff roll. Frank and I glanced out of the window as the aircraft quickly accelerated. What stood out was a dark blue, four-door Ford sedan racing alongside us on a service road between the runaway and the passenger terminals. A blue light on the car's roof rotated quickly.

Oh, no . . .

And just as suddenly, the engine whine diminished and our takeoff speed decreased rapidly. This could only mean one thing: we had been found out.

The captain came back on the PA system. "Ladies and gentlemen, there is nothing to be alarmed about. I anticipate a momentary interruption, and then we will be on our way. When we come to a stop, please remain in your seats."

I buried my head into Frank's shoulder, never so frightened in my life. I was sure that newspaper racks the following morning would be filled with copies of the *Los Angeles Times* trumpeting a front-page photo of a young couple, arms clasped behind their backs in handcuffs, being led off a passenger jet at LAX.

The Delta jet taxied toward one of the terminals, but instead of returning to a gate, we stopped at a remote holding area. The dark blue Ford pulled up, and a truck with a passenger staircase positioned itself next to the front cabin door, which flung open. Two men in dark suits and dark glasses stepped inside the plane, where they flashed gold badges to the pilot who greeted them onboard.

We were busted now.

One of the Men in Black showed a photo to the pilot, who nodded and beckoned him and his partner to search the aircraft. I watched mesmerized as the pair worked their way down the aisle, patiently looking into passengers' faces and comparing what they saw to a photograph cupped in one of the agent's hands.

"Act like you're reading," Frank hissed.

Neither of us had brought any books, so we grabbed inflight magazines from the seat-back pockets. I thought my heart was going to shoot out of my chest. When the leading G-man reached our row, I feigned boredom as best as I could. I quickly looked up and then away. I could feel his eyes examining my nose and face. From the corner of my eye, I saw him refer to the photo and look at me, then at Frank.

I was expecting to hear him say, "Ma'am, if you and the young man could come with me" at any moment, but he didn't say a thing. After a final look, he and his partner moved on to the next row.

My face remained frozen as a mask. I was afraid to look at Frank, as if any expression between us would betray our true intentions. To the front, people's heads popped up like whack-a-moles. To the back, the two agents made a ruckus as they peered inside the lavatories. No one was inside, of course.

The G-men turned on their heels, walked up the aisle, had a word or two with the captain, and double-timed their way down the passenger staircase. Within ten minutes, we were wheels up for Birmingham.

As the Boeing 727 banked into a right-handed turn for its four-hour journey east, I looked over to Frank. He looked lost in thought and would later tell me that the FBI or whoever those guys were in the shades and dark suits were just confirming that I was on board and would take us into custody upon our arrival in Birmingham. Something about taking a minor across state lines would nab him a longer jail sentence. It was all part of my father's plan to punish Frank to the furthest extent of the law.

Frank didn't share those dark thoughts with me, which is just as well. I had difficulty relaxing as it was while the passenger jet settled into cruising altitude. Was it really possible that I had left my home—and my childhood forever—when I hopped into Frank Sr.'s golden Riviera earlier that morning? I recalled the drama with the justice of the peace—only to be foiled by my father's phone call and having to run for it like a pair of bank robbers. Now I found myself on a flight to Birmingham, traveling under an assumed name and speeding toward an entirely new life, which left me feeling overwhelmed and scared for my future.

Any doubts about eloping were left behind in Southern California. I wasn't turning back if my life depended on it. I was forging ahead and "all in" with Frank—and ready for wherever this adventure took me.

We landed in Birmingham as the last embers of orange flitted above the western horizon. I was glad to have my feet back on the ground—actually my bare feet since one of my heels had broken off at LAX. As we filed off the aircraft and entered the terminal, I expected a phalanx of policemen to be waiting for us, but there was no greeting party.

Frank's eyes warily looked side to side as we made our way to the first bank of pay phones. Fortunately, Mrs. Pastore was home when

Frank called. She had no idea we were eloping, of course—she couldn't be trusted with that information—but I'm sure she was surprised to learn that I was in Frank's company nearly 2,000 miles away from my home. She was well aware of my father's volcanic personality as well as his protective spirit for his daughters, the flowers of his life. So when Frank asked his mother to give us a ride, she didn't exactly jump up and down with excitement.

"Take a cab," she said as if she didn't have a care in the world.

In these pre-Uber days, taxi fares were sky high—probably $100, which was money we didn't have.

"Mom, you get your butt down here right now!" Frank yelled into the phone. My beau could talk to her that way because he had paid for her car—a Riviera, too!—as well as the house she was living in. Frank had told me that he had lent his mom $20,000 of his bonus money for the down payment and put the house in his name since his capital financed the purchase. She was supposed to pay him back any time.

Mrs. Pastore got the message loud and clear—but she took her sweet time coming out to the airport. I'd say that we didn't see her for a good hour while we fidgeted on a bench outside baggage claim and waited for her arrival.

When she pulled up to the curb, it was past 9 p.m. We were both hungry enough to take down a smorgasbord, having eaten only cheese and crackers during the long flight.

"Let's go to Shoney's," Frank said to his mom.

Like an obedient chauffeur, she drove us to one of the ubiquitous red-roofed restaurants similar to a Denny's or Waffle House. We sat in a booth with a Formica table and watched waitresses with beehive hairdos sling hubcap-sized plates heaped high with comfort food to the after-hours crowd. Frank quickly brought his mother up to speed on what happened while she watched us devour hamburgers and fries like it was our last meal.

"I'm not so sure about this," she allowed. Mrs. Pastore then turned toward me. "And I shudder to think how your dad's going to react the next time he sees—"

"Mom, we thought this all through," Frank interjected. "Her father wanted us to wait until Gina graduated from high school, but we can't wait that long. That's almost two years from now!"

"Well, you're making your own bed."

We were exhausted by the time the check arrived, so a bed sounded like heaven. Mrs. Pastore suddenly developed rigor mortis as the bill sat in a plastic receipt holder. Frank slapped a few bills down, and we were off.

We arrived at Mrs. Pastore's place, where she generously offered us the master bedroom. We weren't married yet, but she wasn't concerned about our virtue. After all, her latest live-in lover, a freeloader named Buddy (not his real name), had just moved out.

Clutching my brown paper bag with my nightgown and toiletries, I showered. Then Frank did the same. We were exhausted when we slipped under the covers of the king-sized bed. Frank reached over and turned off the lamp on the nightstand. We embraced and kissed each other, tenderly stroking each other. Sheer fatigue set in from what seemed like the longest day of our young lives, and within minutes we were fast asleep in each other's arms. We clung to each other through-out the first night of sleep together, as if to say, "I'll never let you go!" The reason we didn't go any further is because we both knew we would be married very soon and could wait a little longer.

We woke up bright and early on Friday, September 1. The plan, as Frank had outlined it to me, was to drive to Nashville to pick up his car and belongings at his old apartment as well as his last paycheck from the Nashville Sounds, who'd finished their season in Double A ball the previous night. Then we'd find the nearest justice of the peace and get married.

We drove the Riviera straight to the Sounds ballpark. Herschel Greer Stadium looked almost big league to me. Beyond the outfield wall, I spotted a guitar-shaped scoreboard, which was unusual for a baseball venue, but fit in an urban municipality known as "Music City." Frank found an open parking spot in front of the team offices.

"I'll be right back." Frank left me in the Riviera and walked inside, where secretaries did their best to hide knowing smirks.

"Is Larry in?" Frank stood in front of the secretary perched outside the office of Larry Schmittou, the Sounds' general manager.

"Sure," she replied, barely keeping a straight face. "I bet he's not too busy to see you."

Larry nearly jumped out from behind his desk when Frank walked in. I know this because I could see through a window right into Larry's office.

"Frank! Everybody's been looking for you! The big honchos in Cincinnati are wondering where you are. Something to do with your girlfriend. She's only sixteen. Is everything okay?"

"Everything's going great. She's outside in the car. See her?"

Frank pointed toward me sitting in the passenger seat. I noticed Larry's head swivel in my direction. I didn't know who he was, but I figured he was someone important. I gamely waved to him, and he gestured back.

Larry hitched his pants. "Whoa, Frank. You really stepped into it this time. You better call the Reds. You're in big trouble."

"I'll do that," Frank promised.

After collecting his final paycheck, we drove to the apartment complex where Frank shared a unit with three other pitchers. They were packing when we arrived and looked at Frank like he was a walking ghost. "You're really eloping?" asked Joe Price, a fellow hurler who got the good news that he was a September call-up with the parent club in Cincinnati.

"Yeah, we are," Frank said. "We ran into a roadblock yesterday, but we'll get everything straightened out. We're going over to the courthouse right now to see if they can marry us today."

Since the marrying age was sixteen in Tennessee, we thought that all we needed to do was present our California driver's licenses and our blood tests and we'd be saying "I do" in a New York minute. The courthouse clerk squashed that idea when she did not accept our out-of-state blood tests. We were informed that we would have to get new tests done, which would take three business days to complete. That was a huge disappointment.

It was getting late on Friday afternoon. "Where do we go?" Frank asked the clerk.

She handed Frank a slip with the address of a local hospital. We raced out the door but by the time we reached the hospital, the Office of Blood Work was closed for the weekend. We'd have to come back Monday to have blood drawn. Disappointment number two.

We caravanned back to Birmingham since we had picked up Frank's car at the apartment. Frank led the way in his light gray Ford LTD filled with his belongings, which weren't much—just a couple of suitcases filled with clothes and a few books. (He had sold his "bonus baby" 280Z sports car the previous year and purchased more sensible transportation.)

Upon our arrival, Mrs. Pastore had some bad news. "Gina, your dad called, looking for you," she said.

Dread filled my heart.

"What did you say?"

"I told him that you hadn't showed up yet but promised to keep an eye out for you two lovebirds."

I had to smile. Mrs. Pastore had always been a pretty good liar.

Dad was persistent and called back later that night—at 2 a.m. local time! The loud jangling of the phone stirred us all out of bed.

Mrs. Pastore picked up in the living room and ran interference. "John, I haven't heard hide nor hair of them, but if they do come here, I'll have Gina call you the minute she steps—"

"You put my daughter on the phone right now, or I'll have you arrested!" my father retorted.

"Okay, okay," she said. "Don't have a cow about it."

With that, Mrs. Pastore handed me the phone.

"Hi, Dad. It's me," I said sheepishly.

"Thank God I found you." Dad's tone ratcheted down several notches. "Your mother and I have been worried sick about you."

My father sounded defeated, which surprised me. I expected bluster and a good tongue lashing in English and Italian, but he spoke again in a conciliatory tone.

"Is this what you want? If so, I'll give you my blessing."

My heart melted. I could tell my father loved me and wanted to make peace. "Yes, Daddy, I would like that. You know I love Frank with all of my heart."

"I wish you hadn't done it this way, but you're my daughter, and I love you no matter what."

I burst into tears and thanked my father. When I hung up, I realized that we could stop running and start building a life together.

My father thought we were married. I didn't dissuade him of that notion. We had gotten *this close* to being officially hitched, so mentally I was Mrs. Frank Pastore. Legally, I wasn't there yet, but that would happen.

Getting married, however, proved to be a greater challenge than I thought.

We slept in on Saturday morning and then headed to a nearby mall to do some clothes shopping. I needed blouses, pants, shoes, toiletries—everything! A purse, a wallet, and hot curlers, too.

When we headed back to the house after a long day in mall stores, I half-expected baked mostaccioli to be heating up in the oven with a loaf of parmesan bread, lathered with butter and garlic and wrapped in aluminum foil—a substantial, hearty Italian meal like I got at home every night.

I soon found out that Mrs. Pastore knew how to make only one thing for dinner—reservations. Frank had told me that he and his family went out to Shoney's-type places six days a week when he was growing up. His mom did try her hand at some type of meat-and-potato dish on Sunday nights, but that was the limit of her cooking prowess. She had neither the attitude nor aptitude for being in the kitchen.

I didn't mind pinch-hitting for Mrs. Pastore, but I didn't know how to cook! You'd think that my parents, who loved to whip up *italiano* specialties from the Old Country and derived great pleasure from watching others enjoy their food, would have taught me a few things, but they didn't allow me in the kitchen. I guess they thought I was too young or they would have time to teach me a few basics before my college years. Since they shooed me away from the kitchen, I didn't even know how to slice an onion or make a carbonara sauce.

So we ended up at Shoney's again, but on Sunday morning, I decided that I would tackle the kitchen even though I was panicking from the idea of producing a hot breakfast. Wait a minute . . . I'd seen my dad make scrambled eggs countless times growing up. I recalled those memories and gave it a try. I took the egg carton out of the refrigerator, broke a half-dozen or so Grade A eggs into a bowl, stirred them up, threw some butter into a sauce pan, poured in the beaten eggs, added a dash of salt and pepper . . . and kept them from burning with frequent stirring.

I popped a couple pieces of sourdough bread in the toaster, and *mangiamo* . . . I served my husband-to-be a hearty American breakfast. He ate with great gusto and complimented me to the hills. I think he was tired of cold breakfast cereal and Pop-Tarts.

We headed out Monday morning on a mission. We drove back to

Nashville and got blood drawn at the right hospital, and then we started the three-hour return trip to Birmingham. We didn't mind all the driving: we were so head over heels for each other that being in the same car was the greatest thing ever. I snuggled up to my future husband and dozed off with my head on his shoulder. I was in dreamland when I was startled by a loud blast that shattered the front windshield and left a huge spider web gash in front of the driver's side.

"What happened?" I suddenly straightened up.

"We got hit from something that flew off that truck!" Frank steered the car to the shoulder and parked behind an eighteen-wheeler that had pulled off to the side of northbound Interstate 65 as well.

A sweaty truck driver, dressed in jeans and a dirty wife-beater tank top, jumped out of his cab and came running back to us.

"Are you all right?" he yelled, panting from exertion.

"I . . . think so," Frank replied, taking stock of the damage to front windshield of his car.

A large sheet of plate glass flew off the truck, hung in the air for a long moment, and then crashed into our car. We could have been killed.

Contact information was exchanged, but it was apparent that we couldn't go far. Since Frank couldn't see anything through the shattered glass, he leaned out of the driver's side window and pulled off the first exit and found a gas station. The kid at the Exxon station let him borrow a hammer, which Frank used to punch out a hole in the windshield, but that wasn't going to work. The next thing I knew, Frank was swinging the hammer like Hank Aaron and totally blew up the windshield into little pieces that sprayed everywhere. Frank and the attendant then swept up the broken glass.

So, picture the scene: Frank and I tooled back to Birmingham with no windshield to break the wind and wore sunglasses to protect us from the leftover glass fragments flying through the air.

Little did I know that our near-serious accident on the road would later become a metaphor for the sudden shattering of my life into little pieces.

12

Will Somebody Finally Marry Us?

This was turning out to be the longest elopement on record.

A week after I left my Upland house dressed in my St. Lucy's uniform and carrying a brown paper bag with a few things, I still wasn't married. But on the morning of Friday, September 8, 1978, on our way from Birmingham to Nashville, we believed this would be our wedding day.

The previous day was frustrating: we had made the long trip to Nashville, thinking we were all set only to be told that our blood work wasn't finished. Frank was ready to pop a blood vessel when he heard about the delay, but the courthouse clerk assured us that when we came back in the morning, nothing would stand in the way of getting married.

We arrived in Nashville at 11:30 a.m. following another three-hour drive from Birmingham. When we arrived at the courthouse, located downtown in a large brick building, the clerk's face lit up in recognition when we walked in. She quickly found the Pastore file.

"Good news. Everything's in order," she said. "I'll tell the judge you're here."

I fidgeted with the same silk shirt and blouse I had worn on the day we made our getaway in Los Angeles. Thank goodness they were washed and clean. I wore new Candies shoes since my other ones broke while running for the gate at LAX. Frank wore a white dress shirt and brown dress pants—no tie.

"How y'all doin' this morning?"

I looked up to see the judge, a tall Southern gentleman who looked like he stepped out of a Nicholas Sparks novel. Dressed in a plaid suit and a cowboy hat, Hollywood couldn't have cast him better. His Southern drawl practically dripped with honey.

"Fine," Frank replied. I nodded in agreement, my eyes wide open with anticipation. His presence meant we really were going to get married.

The judge looked down at our file. "Pastore's the name. Son, are you one of our Nashville Sounds?"

"Yes, sir," Frank replied. My husband-to-be-in-five-minutes wasn't a "Yes, sir," "No, ma'am" type, but he adapted to the situation.

"Well, I'll be. A real live ballplayer in our midst. Whatcha play, son?"

"I'm a pitcher. Now if we can—"

"I thought so. I seen you on the mound. You smoke that horsehide. And who's this pretty little lady? You a Soundette, honey?"

I giggled. The judge thought I was one of the baseball versions of a cheerleader—a cute young thing dressed in a team jersey and hot pants who followed the team mascot around the ballpark and tossed out free T-shirts during the seventh-inning stretch. I'm sure he was also thinking I was part of one of those ballplayer/star-struck teen romances that heated up during the Sounds' season like a fast-moving forest fire.

"No, sir," I said, falling into the Southern way of addressing elders.

"Well, well," he said. "And now you two kids want to get married. Tell you what. I'm awful hungry. I'm supposed to meet some friends at Tavern on the Row, and I don't want to be late. You sure you don't want to wait until after lunch?"

"*No, sir!*"

Frank and I spoke in unison, which cracked us up and had a way of loosening the tension.

"That's okay, Judge," Frank interjected. "We don't need a long ceremony or anything. A quickie will be good. We're going to have a church ceremony later."

His Honor backpedaled. "Well, okie-dokie. A quickie it will be. We'll make it fast!"

We followed the judge to his wood-paneled courtroom that smelled of polished pine. A couple of bailiffs were inside, keeping their eyes on two guys sitting at the defense table, bound in handcuffs and leg shackles. We would later learn that they were waiting to be arraigned for the armed robbery of a liquor store the previous night. Their soiled clothes and body odor lent a certain smell to the cavernous courtroom.

"Don't mind them," the judge said as he escorted us to the bench. He walked around to his chair and found the volume he needed as well as his reading glasses. Then he returned and stood before us, holding the book open to the right page.

He reviewed his notes and stopped.

"Well, I'll be dadgum . . . we need some witnesses." The judge peered over his glasses to the accused armed robbers and then to us.

"Whaddya say we ask Willie and Leroy to do the honors," he said like he was shooting the breeze.

Frank looked at me. I looked at him, and we shrugged. We apparently needed witnesses, and the prisoners were the only ones available.

"Fine with us, Judge," Frank said. We both wanted to get this show on the road.

The courtly judge nodded toward one of the bailiffs. Willie and Leroy, who had probably been waiting a while for something to happen, grinned their approval. They rose to their feet as a bailiff watched over them and then hobbled their way to the bench, chains clanging on the wood floor.

The thought hit me that this wasn't exactly how I envisioned my wedding day, but after the events of the last week, nothing could faze me now.

"All right," the judge said. "We can start."

Frank and I straightened our shoulders as the judge began the ceremony.

"Ladies and gentlemen, we are gathered here today to celebrate the marriage of Frank Pastore and Gina Pignotti. Does anyone have any reason that these two should not be united?"

All eyes turned toward Willie and Leroy, bound and shackled. They lowered their gazes and were quiet as church mice.

"Very good," the judge intoned. "Frank, do you take Gina to be your lawfully wedded wife?"

"I do!" Frank beamed.

"And Gina, do you take Frank to be your lawfully wedded husband?"

"I do." And I meant it.

"Awright," the judge said, as if the issue had been in doubt. "Then, by the power vested in me by the State of Tennessee, I now pronounce you man and wife. Congratulations. You may kiss the bride."

That was short and sweet.

Frank drew me close and leaned in for a long kiss. I heard Willie and Leroy clapping and jangling their chains, but I didn't mind. We had finally done it—we were married!

We were also famished like the judge. We collected our marriage license and walked across the street to an Arby's restaurant, where we dined on roast beef sandwiches and toasted each other with Cokes. The roast beef wasn't real, but we couldn't afford anything fancier than dollar sandwiches.

Frank apologized a half-dozen times for celebrating our marriage at a fast-food joint, but it didn't matter. I had no big expectations anyway. I was so happy to finally be with him that I didn't care about minor stuff like what restaurant we ate at. I joked that we would live off love.

As the miles passed by on the drive back to Birmingham—and after what seemed like the longest week of my young life—I was simply glad to be officially married. I was now Mrs. Frank Pastore. Sure, I had always dreamed that I'd one day have a traditional wedding: the bride wearing a gorgeous white dress with a long train; an over-the-top reception with family and friends celebrating with Italian foods; a series of teary toasts and speeches, including one from my father describing how the family wasn't losing a daughter but gaining a son; and my husband and I feeding each other rum wedding cake.

Frank and I had taken a whole different route. There was no wedding gown, no bridesmaids or groomsmen, no church filled with friends and family smiling and tearing up, no reception and party, and no photographer on hand to take pictures. We were two young people very much in love, ready to take on whatever challenges life threw at us.

We made a day of it in Nashville, walking along Broadway Street hand in hand and taking in the sights. We got to Birmingham late—around 10 p.m.—and pulled into the driveway. The lights were on, so we figured his mother was watching TV. So this was our romantic wedding night?

Frank turned off the car engine, and we sat there for the longest time, processing the events of the day. Frank leaned over and kissed me passionately. "I'm sorry I can't afford to get us a hotel room on our wedding night," he said. "I hope you're going to be okay."

"Don't worry, honey. I'll be just fine. We'll take a honeymoon some other time."

We got out of the car and snuck through the front door, tiptoeing through a hallway to the master bedroom. Frank then picked me up and carried me over the threshold—at least we were doing something traditional. We quietly closed the door and couldn't keep our hands off each other. We had no money for a bottle of champagne, but Frank lit a candle in the room, which created a wonderful ambiance. I'll never forget the glow in our bedroom or the flickering light on Frank's happy face.

Our wedding night was not our first time. We had jumped the gun a few nights earlier, but it wasn't because Frank pushed himself on me—I wanted to do it. Frank, who had been intimate with a few girls dating back to high school, was willing to wait because I was a virgin, but I didn't want to. After all we went through, I felt like we were committed to each other and were going to get married any day. Plus it wasn't easy sleeping in the same bed as him and *not* wanting to share all of myself with him, so we went ahead and took our fill of love.

We didn't disclose this in *Shattered*, but I am choosing to do so now out of a sense of transparency. Over the years, when I've spoken in public, I've been asked by curious women when we consummated our relationship. Each time I ducked their question with a roundabout answer and found it amusing that people who didn't know me very well wanted to know such a thing, but that's the world we live in. The main reason I'm volunteering this information now is because I want everyone to understand what Frank and I were like when we got married.

I had been raised a strong Catholic and knew sex was reserved for marriage, so I can't claim that I was naive about this. I simply wanted to give myself completely over to Frank: physically, emotionally, and spiritually. Frank was willing to wait, but I couldn't wait any longer.

They say that when you marry someone, you also marry his family. I married into a dysfunctional family.

Even at the age of sixteen, I understood that Frank's family had its quirks. While my mother and I tangled and didn't see eye to eye on many things, I still grew up in a stable home environment. Sure, there was hot Italian blood as well as boisterous outbursts, but at the end of the day, there was plenty of *amore* to go around the table.

Frank, an only child, outlined his tangled backstory about his parents in *Shattered*: moving from house to house—as well as to different school districts—in his elementary school years because his parents were skipping out on back rent; being raised in a home where his mother called the shots and hurled verbal abuse at Frank Sr. like a brushback pitch; and how his parents had no contact with extended family, didn't make friends, and didn't allow visitors to the home. In other words, his parents had very few interpersonal relationships with the outside world.

My parents were total opposites. Their front door was always open and there was always extra room at the dinner table. That's how I got to know Frank, who hung around our house a lot more than he did at his parents' place.

At the time when Frank and I got married, Frank Sr. and Elma Pastore were happily divorced, as they liked to tell friends. But Elma—who was always on the lookout for an easy mark to take care of her—had chosen wrong when she brought Buddy into her life and allowed him to move in with her. Instead of him supporting her, Buddy was looking for her to support him.

I guess you could say they deserved each other, but when things didn't work out between her and Buddy, she needed a new Sugar Daddy. Mrs. Pastore would have been happy having my Frank pay her bills, but we would barely be scraping by on Frank's minor league salary. So Mrs. Pastore hatched a scheme: get her claws on Frank Sr. again. He had just turned sixty-five and hit retirement age, so he had a pension and Social Security coming in.

But she knew that Frank Sr. would see right through her intentions if she called him back in California and asked him if he wanted to come live with her in Birmingham, Alabama, so she got my Frank to do her bidding.

"You need to call your father," she told Frank. "Tell him that you want him here with you and Gina, that you want us to live together under the same roof. He won't listen to me, but he'll listen to you."

"But Mom, Gina and I are leaving in a few weeks for Instructional ball," Frank protested. After Frank had called the Reds front office in Cincinnati and smoothed things out regarding his marriage to a sixteen-year-old girl, he'd been told to report to the Florida Instructional League, where young major league prospects hone their skills from the end of September through October.

Mrs. Pastore knew exactly what to say. "Frankie, if you don't call your father, you're going to lose your house and all your money. Everything you put into this house will be gone."

She had Frank backed into a corner since she had borrowed $20,000 for the down payment but hadn't repaid him yet. Frank was stuck between the proverbial rock and a hard place, so he made the phone call and sweet-talked his father into leaving his one-bedroom apartment in Upland and living with us in Birmingham.

To show how no good deed goes unpunished, while driving his bronze 1963 Buick Riviera through the California desert—the same car we used to make our getaway to LAX—Frank Sr. got stopped by the California Highway Patrol. The state trooper must have run his license number because that's how he learned there was an all-points bulletin out for a guy named Frank Pastore—a low-lifer wanted in connection with kidnapping an unsuspecting sixteen-year-old for nefarious reasons.

So, imagine the scene on a lonely patch of sagebrush and sand in the middle of the desert under a canopy of triple-digit heat: Frank Sr. sees a red flight in his rearview mirror, pulls over to the highway shoulder, and hears a CHP officer ask for his driver's license. The name says "Frank Pastore," and the cop thinks he has a child molester on his hands. The next thing Frank Sr. knows, he's told to step outside the vehicle—when he's suddenly whipped around and told "Hands up and spread 'em" while he's frisked for weapons.

Backup is called, and the two officers open his trunk, expecting to find a teenage girl scared out of her wits and bound in duct tape. All the while, Frank Sr. is protesting, saying they have the wrong Frank Pastore.

It was hours before the mess got cleaned up and the CHP officers let Frank Sr. get on his way to Alabama. Fortunately for us, my father-in-law had two days of open road to put the encounter behind him.

We weren't one big happy family living together in the same house, and with Mrs. Pastore, there were always unexpected surprises—like finding out there was no washer and dryer in the house.

"You need to get us a new washer and dryer," she said before Frank Sr.'s arrival. "It's your house."

Frank, the dutiful son, went out and bought a new washer and dryer, which meant we were down to no money until we got to Instructional League. We ate a lot of peanut-butter-and-jelly sandwiches until his dad arrived and bought us some groceries.

We couldn't wait to hit the road for Florida, which is why Frank and

I had the biggest grins when we packed up our Ford LTD and headed off on a nine-hour drive to Tampa for the start of Instructional League.

Our grins weren't shared by some of the Cincinnati Reds coaching staff or front office personnel. Not only did the news of our elopement create waves within the Reds organization, but Frank hadn't pitched well when he started with the Triple A club and then broke his finger in Double AA during the 1978 season. The deck was getting stacked against him.

I had no idea what it would be like stepping into the world of baseball, so I was nervous. Would I fit in? Would the other wives and girlfriends like me? Just thinking about my future was overwhelming.

My comfort level was raised when Frank said we'd spend our first night in Tampa with the Arena family, who owned an apartment complex and had a one-bedroom place waiting for us. Andrew and Judy Arena had three children: Richie, Melody, and little Andrew. They lived in a nice ranch-style home at the end of a lovely cul-de-sac. Frank beeped the horn as we drove into their long driveway, which prompted the kids to come running out with squeals of joy.

Andrew, a handsome Italian-looking man and his beautiful wife, Judy, were close behind and gave Frank and me warm welcoming hugs. They were also checking me out, as in: *Okay, here's the girl Frank eloped with.*

They smiled as we stood in the driveway and talked. They had lots of questions:

"How are you doing, honey?"

Fine, just fine. We're so excited that this is over and that we're finally married. Now we have the rest of our lives together.

"Frank said your dad was madder than hell when you two ran off and got married."

Yeah, he wanted to break Frank's legs, but we're much better now. We've talked, and he gave me his blessing.

"What do you think of Florida?"

This is my first time to the South, and my first time in Florida. I love Southern hospitality, and that you've opened your arms to us. So far, so good!

And a final question:

"Are you hungry?"

We're starving!

Andrew spread his arms and pointed us toward the front door. "Let's go inside. We have some pasta cooking on the stove. You like spaghetti?"

Did we ever . . . a big plate of spaghetti with a simmering meat sauce sounded like heaven to a young runaway bride and her hungry husband.

I could easily see why Frank had fallen in love with this family. The next morning, they helped us move into a furnished apartment at a complex they owned with Andrew's brothers, Sammy and Anthony. The apartment was simple and nothing fancy, but we were only going to be staying there for six weeks. The apartment manager was Grace Arena, the family matriarch and typical Italian grandmother who bustled about her day speaking an energetic mixture of Italian and English, so I felt at home, especially when she invited us over for dinner, which was always Italian and always way too much food.

Our time in Tampa was my introduction to something called the Baseball Life. Don't ask me to explain exactly what that means, although I can tell you that it involves a lot of waiting . . . waiting for Frank to emerge from the locker room after practice or games . . . waiting for the team bus or plane to arrive after a road game . . . and waiting for interminably long games to end. Baseball, one of the few sports without a clock, has a lot of dead time between pitches, outs, and innings.

I'll never forget the first time I drove Frank to the ballpark, which happened to be the Red's spring training complex known as Al Lopez Field. (The ball field was named after New York Yankees Hall of Fame pitcher Al Lopez, a Tampa native.)

The Cincinnati Reds had just finished their 1978 season, compiling a glittering 92-69 record—good enough these days to qualify for post-season play, but back then, only four teams qualified for the playoffs, two from each league. That left the Reds on the outside looking in as the Los Angeles Dodgers and Philadelphia Phillies fought it out to become the National League's representative in the World Series.

I pulled into the parking lot at Al Lopez Field when Frank suddenly got quiet. I steered the car into a parking slot right next to a silver Rolls Royce; you don't see cars like that very often.

A couple stepped out of the Rolls and made their way to the clubhouse door. The player stopped, gave his wife or girlfriend a peck on the cheek, and kept moving, not making eye contact with anyone.

Frank was about to have a heart attack. "That's Pete Rose!" he whispered.

Pete Rose was one of the biggest stars in baseball. He had dominated the sports pages during the summer when he stitched together a 44-game hitting streak, tying the National League record and coming within sniffing distance of Joe DiMaggio's immortal 56-game hitting streak. If my dad could only see us now. . . .

The small-framed attractive woman walked back toward the Rolls. She was dressed in white and wearing a casual blouse, tight shorts, and tennis shoes. Her tan neck was dripping with diamonds, and she wore three diamond rings.

"Let's go say hi to Karolyn!" Frank said.

"Who's she?" I wanted to know what I was getting into.

"His wife."

I took Frank's hand as he closed the distance between us. She immediately recognized Frank, which was a good thing—and surprising since her husband was a star and Frank was beating around the minor leagues.

"Karolyn, this is my new bride, Gina," he said.

"Well, hello," Karolyn Rose said, extending her hand. I could feel her eyes appraising me. She was in her mid-thirties, so I had to look so young to her. I certainly felt intimidated. We made small talk, and I felt like I had passed some sort of test.

Karolyn had been around the game of baseball ever since she married Pete Rose during his rookie season in 1963. She was nineteen back then, so I would imagine that she saw a bit of herself in me: young, idealistic, and having no idea what the future held.

After the crazy events of the last month, I was ready for anything. As the umpire says before the first pitch, it was time to "Play ball!"

13

Introductions Are in Order

The Instructional League was an excellent introduction to professional baseball and a low-key opportunity to get acclimated to my role as a baseball wife.

We were excited to set up house in a tiny furnished apartment owned by the Arena family. I remember driving to a nearby supermarket with Frank for our first-ever grocery shopping experience. Frank pushed a cart as we slowly walked through the aisles. I dropped familiar foods into the cart: bananas, apples, and oranges from the produce section; Shredded Wheat and Life cereal from the breakfast aisle; crackers and chocolate chip cookies from the baked goods area; and milk, eggs, and cheese from the dairy section.

We were careful about what we put into the shopping cart. Frank's paycheck was $65 a week, or about $250 in today's dollars, meaning he wasn't close to earning minimum wage. My father had graciously sent us a $400 check to help us get by, but much of his generosity went toward paying the Arena family for our short-term rental.

Frank looked at the half-filled cart. "What are you making for dinner tonight?"

I fought for the right words to say. "Um, well, I don't know," I stammered. "What do you feel like?"

"What do you like to make?" Frank asked.

There was a long pause. Because I had prepared scrambled eggs in Birmingham, Frank thought I knew my way around a kitchen, which wasn't the case at all. Now that Frank and I were on our own, the moment of truth had arrived.

"I really don't know how to cook," I said.

Frank looked shocked.

"Really?"

I would imagine that Frank thought he had married a budding *mama mia* who could whip up rib-sticking comfort foods like the ones he enjoyed at my parents' dining room table. Here I was, from an Italian family that loved to entertain and was known around town for the amazing dinners that came out of our kitchen, but I was confessing that putting a hot meal on the table was beyond me.

Frank cracked a smile. He wasn't mad or even disappointed. Just another bump in a road littered with potholes. "We'll figure something out," he said.

We bought some hamburger meat, a few chicken breasts, tomato sauce, a couple cans of beans, and different packages of pasta. These days, you can watch a YouTube video on how to make Italian meatballs or boil angel hair pasta, but back then, you were on your own. You could study a cookbook or ask someone to show you, but those options weren't available to me.

Frank had an idea. "I heard some of the guys in the locker room saying their wives were making great meals with their Crock-Pots." Slow-cookers, as they were also known, were the rage in the 1970s as more women began to work outside the home. Even though my mom was a stay-at-home mother, she loved making chili in her Crock-Pot, so I had seen this cooking appliance in use.

We decided to visit a Sears department store and purchase a Crock-Pot as well as a set of Corelle dishes, a few pots and pans, a half-dozen plastic cups, and cheap flatware since we had eloped and didn't have any household items. We were careful to buy the very minimum since we were on such a limited budget and wanted to bring everything back with us when Instructional League was over.

The Crock-Pot turned out to be a lifesaver. The slow cooker came with a cookbook, which I showed to Frank. We picked out a chicken dish that seemed easy enough to make: all I had to do was slice up a pair of chicken breasts, add a can of cream of chicken soup, a can of mushroom soup, chopped celery and carrots, a can of mushrooms, a dash of minced garlic, and let everything simmer for eight hours.

We invited Rick O'Keeffe, a pitcher and Frank's old roommate in Nashville, and his girlfriend over for dinner with Crock-Pot Mushroom Chicken as the main course. Frank was thrilled that we were entertaining friends with a home-cooked meal because his mother rarely cooked and *never* invited anyone over when he was a kid. This was the beginning of many years of preparing delicious meals and entertaining friends and family, something we grew to love doing.

It was also fun discovering that Frank and I were social butterflies. We fell into a fun routine on weekends. Friday night was Disco Night, when we went out dancing with other baseball players and their wives and girlfriends. The disco craze was at its peak in 1978, and Frank and I danced up a storm under a mirror disco ball and colorful strobe lights to the sounds of "Saturday Night Fever," "More Than a Woman," and "You Should Be Dancing."

John Travolta didn't have much on Frank Pastore. My husband was a great dancer—and wasn't a stranger to Tampa discos, as I discovered. One time at a nightclub called the Brass Balloon, we sat out a dance and rested around a table. A curvy and sexy girl walked in our direction and stopped by to say hello.

"Hi, Frank! Howya doing, you handsome man?" she gushed.

Frank pulled back. "Uh, hi, Ginger. Have you met my new wife?"

I'll never forget the look on her face. "You got married?"

"Yeah, let me introduce you to Gina."

Within seconds of the awkward introduction, Ginger was gone.

"Who's she?" I watched her disappear into the mass of humanity on the dance floor.

"We dated a few times when I was here for spring training. That's all."

Silence ensued. Frank and I told each other everything, so I figured there was more to the story.

There was. "We spent the night together a few times," he confided. "I told you that I wasn't celibate before we decided to elope. I sewed my wild oats. But that's all in the past, now that I have you. I never liked playing the field anyway because it didn't feel right."

I could tell that Frank felt bad about his promiscuity and was ready to put that in the past. Still, laying eyes on one of Frank's old flames wasn't easy for a sixteen-year-old bride feeling her way in an adult world.

The following night, a Saturday, we were invited to Andrew and Judy Arena's home for dinner. Every weekend, Saturday and Sunday, the Arenas had us over for dinner, which gave us a sense of family and helped stretch our food dollar.

While in the kitchen helping with the clean-up, I poured my heart out to Judy, who had become like a mother-in-law to me. I described coming face-too-face with one of Frank's "old girlfriends" inside the Brass Balloon.

Judy stopped me there. She put her hand on my chin and sternly said, "Gina, what happened in the past is over. You need to focus on your husband and your future right now. You are his wife now and he loves you."

Her dose of wisdom snapped me out of my wallowing, which was a good thing.

My innocent days of childhood were over.

Frank pitched well in Instructional League, which was good news because our elopement certainly raised eyebrows in the locker room and the Reds front office. Since reputations are hard to lose once they become ingrained in people's minds, the last thing Frank needed was to be known as a flake—a baseball term for an eccentric person who can't be relied upon on or off the field. By the end of Instructional ball, Frank's reputation as a flame-throwing prospect was intact.

While we were in Florida, Frank became convinced that there was something fishy going on with the house in Birmingham. During a phone conversation with his mother—we couldn't afford a telephone so we asked the Arenas if we could borrow their phone—Mrs. Pastore didn't react well when Frank asked if the property was really in his name. "Frankie, I told you it's your house, and that's it!" she huffed.

Frank wasn't convinced everything was on the up and up, so he called my father for advice. Dad listened to Frank outline the situation and agreed that things didn't add up. My father suggested that Frank ask his mother to show him the house deed, which would reveal once and for all if he really was the rightful owner. We were planning to stop in Birmingham on our way back to California, where we would spend the off-season, so that would be the perfect time to get to the bottom of everything.

We drove to Birmingham after Instructional ball was over and stayed a couple of days with my in-laws. Frank Sr. was thrilled to see us. Mrs. Pastore? Not so thrilled.

When Frank brought up the touchy subject of the deed again, she got angry and said we were making a mountain out of a molehill. Of course, Frank's name was on the deed, she claimed.

"Okay, let me see it then," Frank said.

My mother-in-law made a show of searching for the legal document but was unsuccessful. "I don't know where I put that piece of paper," she said. "It has to be around here somewhere."

It was evident that she was stalling and hoping we'd get back on the road to California as soon as possible. The following day, she and Frank Sr. were out of the house, so we began a scavenger hunt. Every drawer was opened, every piece of paper scrutinized. And then we found the deed. Everything we needed to know was there in black and white: Elma Pastore was listed as the owner of the house!

Another deception . . . and one of many. When his parents returned, Frank told them that he found the deed, which touched off a heated argument. Frank said he wanted his money back and instructed his mother to get a new loan to reimburse him for borrowing the $20,000. She promised to repay, but even I knew that wasn't likely to happen.

I was glad I witnessed their quarrel because I felt like Frank was fighting for me and our future. If baseball didn't pan out, that money was going to finance Frank's college education so that he could get a good job and provide for me and any children we brought into the world.

As usual, nothing was resolved. Within hours, we hit the interstate and started the thirty-hour journey back to Southern California. My parents said we could move into my old bedroom during the off-season, which would save on renting a place. Dad went a step further and offered Frank a job doing construction clean-up, which meant the world to me because we needed to put some money in the bank. Living off love was taking us only so far.

I had never been on a cross-country drive in my life, so the open road was a revelation to me. Frank had done the long trip several times and was an old pro. He usually stayed in the slower lanes so that faster cars could pass, and then he blinked his lights to indicate that it was clear for a passing car or truck to pull in front of us.

Since we didn't want to spend money on a cheap motel, we drove right on through, switching drivers so that the other one could catch a few winks. One night at 4 a.m., however, Frank was behind the wheel and I dozed in and out. He got so tired that he pulled into a New Mexico truck stop to snatch a couple of hours of shut-eye before getting back on the road.

We parked and did our best to sleep in our seats. Next thing I knew, I opened my eyes—and saw a weird man with his unshaven face pressed against my window!

"Frank!" I grabbed my husband's arm.

Frank freaked out and instinctively started the car as quickly as he could. With his right foot jammed on the accelerator, we peeled out of that truck stop so fast that I'm sure we woke up half the truckers sleeping in their rigs.

Two days on the open road was conducive to long, deep conversations. We discussed everything from the stars and the planets to Frank's baseball goal of becoming part of the Cincinnati Reds starting rotation. Frank and I were more alike than we knew.

Once we crossed the California state line at Blythe, though, my stomach tied up in knots. In just a few hours, I would be arriving in Upland as a . . . married woman. What would that be like? How were Mom and Dad going to treat me? What would our old school friends say? How would they act toward Frank? Those were huge concerns.

We pulled into our old driveway late at night. In just ten weeks, I had gone from being a simple schoolgirl to the wife of a professional ballplayer, from living in a teen world to finding my way among adults. Would my parents treat me like a kid or a grown daughter who had left the nest? I wasn't sure what to expect.

I ran to the front door, which was locked, given the late hour. I rang the doorbell.

"Is that you, Gina?" my mom cried out.

Back in those pre-cell phone days, we couldn't call and let her know where we were on the road. She just knew we were coming sometime.

"We're here, Mom!"

Mom quickly unbolted the door and immediately hugged me. That felt so good. Frank walked up, lugging a pair of suitcases. They hugged as well.

"Where's Dad?" I knew he'd wake up for us, no matter the hour.

"Your father is on the way home from his annual hunting trip. He could arrive later tonight or sometime tomorrow morning. I know he can't wait to see you."

We slugged our stuff inside the front door, and Mom led us to my old bedroom. Talk about an awkward moment—for all of us.

Mom opened the door. "You'll see that things haven't changed much around here," she said.

My bedroom looked untouched—like the morning I left it.

"Thanks, Mom," I said.

Frank and I took much-needed showers and then fell into my old bed, which was king-sized. I had shared my bedroom and the bed with my sister, Marina, before she got married. (Remember, she was nine years older than me.) The king-size bed was handed down from my parents when they purchased a new one.

We were exhausted and bone-tired from not having slept in two days. We climbed into my old bed—another surreal experience—and were asleep within minutes.

The next thing I knew, I awakened. Something stirred in the middle of the night. I focused on my surroundings—and saw Dad!

"Dad, what are you—?"

"Hi," he whispered, careful not wake up Frank. "I just wanted to see you."

My father's eyes glistened in the semi-darkness. He was obviously very moved by the moment. I could only imagine the emotions he was dealing with. I was teary-eyed as well.

Dad leaned over and kissed me on the cheek, which caused Frank to stir. Then my father walked around the bed and kissed Frank on the cheek as well.

I will never forget that moment for as long as I live.

We had my father's complete blessing, and I knew things were going to be okay.

14

Not a Good Deed

A day or so after arriving in Upland, Frank visited his friends at Chino Valley Bank, where he learned his $50,000 bonus check had whittled down to $10,000. Sure, he had spent $15,000 on buying two cars (the 280Z for him and a Riviera for his mom) and lent Mrs. Pastore $20,000 to buy the house in Birmingham, but bank records showed that she had been dipping into the account for small withdrawals that didn't seem like a lot at the time but added up to a significant amount.

At the time Frank opened the account, he was seventeen and a minor who needed one of his parents as a signatory. He didn't know that his mother would be using his savings account like a personal piggy bank, but that's what she had been doing for the last few years.

Frank did what he had to do: he took his mother off of the account and placed the money into a money-market certificate of deposit.

Living at home during the off-season was certainly interesting. When Mom and I were home alone, she'd tell me that she was afraid everyone was laughing at me for eloping. "It's so bad that I can barely say hi to any of my friends," she said. I did my best to stay out of her way.

My father was the peacemaker. Although I had gone ahead and eloped, he still wanted to give me a church wedding and a reception with all the trimmings. Frank and I thought that was a great idea.

The plan was to have a simple repeat-the-vows ceremony at St. Joseph's, our parish church in Upland, followed by a large reception at the Magic Lamp Inn, a classic red-leather steakhouse owned by Pat Vernola, a close family friend. There would be a lovely sit-down dinner followed by toasts, dancing, and white rum cake—a must for any Italian wedding.

But the drama! My mom got riled up when a relative called and asked, "Will Gina be wearing a white dress?"

In those days, white dresses were reserved for virgin brides, although I'm sure many a bride walked down the aisle to "Here Comes the Bride" having jumped the gun. Nonetheless, protocol had to be followed. Since Frank and I had been married for several months, it was evident that I had to wear an off-white dress, which I had no problem with. I understood what people would be thinking if I wore a shimmering white dress while on my father's arm.

Because we were already married, Mom thought it would be prudent to send out invitations that invited people to the reception only, which was explained in a small card that said this:

> *Prior to the reception, there will be a church ceremony held beforehand at St. Joseph's Catholic Church where Frank and Gina Pastore will repeat their wedding vows.*

Leading up to the wedding day, the producers of the reality show *Bridezilla* would have loved filming the behind-the-scene commotion at the Pignotti household. My mother was frustrated, saying things like, "This whole thing is a farce," even on the night before our church wedding.

That evening, I cried myself to sleep and woke up with puffy, red eyes and feeling extremely nervous. After all the family drama, my emotions were on edge. I ran to the bathroom and vomited. Somehow, I got through my Big Day, wearing a beige gown, not a wedding dress. Frank looked smart in a burgundy tuxedo, in keeping with the fashion of the times.

We expected our guests to skip the church ceremony, but we were wrong. Nearly all the invitees—more than 200—came to see us pledge our love to each other "till death do us part," which filled my sails at a time when I needed encouragement.

This time we didn't spend our wedding night at a parent's house. We made our getaway from the reception and checked into the Uplander Motor Hotel, a Route 66 motel in Upland that was next to the Arbor restaurant. Nothing fancy . . . a type of place with Magic Fingers vibrating beds . . . but it was sure nice to be alone with my husband in a private, quiet location.

I will admit that after the scandalous elopement and the big "church wedding," I felt like we were under a microscope. We heard the rumors rumbling around town: "She must be pregnant" or "It won't last!"

I was quickly learning that I didn't like life in the public eye or being the subject of people's dinner conversations.

After our church wedding, we could focus on baseball. In mid-February, we drove coast-to-coast from Southern California to Tampa. The Ford LTD was equipped with a CB radio popularized by the film *Smokey and the Bandit*. Frank loved using all the "10-4" trucker slang and bantering with other truckers, including those who warned him over the radio that he had a "bear at his back door," meaning a highway patrolman was rapidly up coming from behind. Our handles were "Romeo" and "Juliet."

We arrived in Tampa and drove to the International Inn, where the Reds organization had negotiated a discounted rate for players and their families. That helped since $250 a week in meal money was the only income paid to the players during spring training.

Regarding his future in baseball, Frank had taken a wait-and-see attitude. "I know I haven't lived up to the Reds' expectations," he told me. "I'll probably get sent to Double A. If I pitch well in Nashville, then we move up to Triple A in Indianapolis." My husband was clearly managing his hopes.

His pitching coach did tell him that our elopement had been accepted by the Reds management based on what they saw at Instructional League. The scouts liked me and thought I was an asset to Frank and his baseball career, which was good to hear. One scout even noted, "She's a great girl!" in his report.

Frank was placed on the 40-man major league roster during spring training, meaning he was among the players who could be called up at any time to the 25-man roster during the baseball season. That was a positive development.

I remember dropping Frank off at Al Lopez Field on the first day of spring training. As we pulled into the parking lot, I noticed a well-built man exiting his late-model Mercedes.

"There's JB!" Frank exclaimed.

It was Johnny Bench, in the flesh. Frank jumped out of the car and practically ran Johnny down. They had no sooner exchanged a warm handshake when Johnny looked over to me and gave me a knowing nod. I wanted to melt into the car upholstery. He had obviously heard about the elopement.

"Gina, come say hello to Johnny Bench!" Frank bellowed.

Inside, I was dying. I'm extremely shy in these types of situations, especially because Johnny was so famous. For most of my childhood, I had heard my dad and my brother Johnny go on and on about what a great catcher Johnny Bench was. Posters of the Reds catcher lined my brother's bedroom, and now I was shaking his hand.

He gave me another look over, as if to appraise my worthiness as a baseball wife. I passed. "Way to go, Frankie. Good job!"

Johnny Bench would always call Frank "Frankie" or "the kid." I don't know why, but Johnny took a liking to Frank and would watch out for him in coming years. He won our hearts, and we loved him.

Frank was right about spring training—the high energy was sure different than the low-key Instructional League. I felt like the new kid on the block as I saw other players and their wives hugging each other in the players' parking lot or in the stands during spring training games.

While dropping off Frank one morning, he introduced me to another pitcher he had played with in Nashville—Bill Dawley. Bill was also on the 40-man roster, and I soon met his wife, Karen, who I found to be fun and outgoing.

After a few days, they asked us if we wanted to "apartment share" with them as they had rented a two-bedroom place. Hotel living and eating out all the time—usually at fast food places so we could pocket leftover per diem money—was getting old quickly. I thought that Karen, who'd been a baseball wife for a couple of years, could show me a few things, so I was all for moving out of the International Inn.

Karen was an excellent cook who also used the Crock-Pot, so we took turns preparing meals. I learned how to make a great spaghetti sauce from her that I would tweak over the years with ingredients to Frank's liking: big chunks of onion, diced mushrooms, and slices of Italian sausage.

Bill and Karen were from Connecticut, so when they mentioned one night that they had never tried Mexican food, I knew what I was preparing the following night.

After Frank and Bill got back from the ballpark the next day, Karen announced, "Gina made Mexican food with rice and refried beans!"

Her hungry husband had a puzzled look on his face. "Refried beans? What are those?" he asked.

When I served our new friends tacos with Spanish rice and refried beans, Bill liked the tacos but wasn't impressed with the refried beans.

"You don't have to serve those again," he said.

For years after that, Frank loved doing an imitation of Bill and his first encounter with refried beans—like a baby being served a spoonful of cod liver oil.

The pitchers and catchers always report five days before the position players. When the rest of the Cincinnati Reds team descended into camp with their families, the entire complex was abuzz. I saw swarms of reporters and photographers, and sitting behind the Reds dugout with the other players' spouses was a revelation. The wives of Tom Seaver, Tony Perez, Ken Griffey, Tom Hume, George Foster, and Joe Morgan seemed like baseball royalty to me. I was struck by how all the Reds wives seemed to have their husband's number in diamonds around their gorgeous necks. If I was going to wear a necklace featuring Frank's No. 35, it would have to be made out of costume jewelry.

Since I was so young—remember, I would have been in the middle of my junior year at St. Lucy's—I was extremely shy around the players' wives and girlfriends. The other dynamic was that Frank was a minor leaguer and they were part of The Show, as the major leagues were called by the players, so there was a caste system in place. I certainly wasn't going to approach them and introduce myself, so I sat quietly on the sidelines.

Things were different in the clubhouse, where the other players weren't shy about teasing Frank. They had a merry old time at Frank's expense, saying things like, "Hey, Pastore, does your wife have her driver's license yet?" or "Pastore, we didn't know that you were that desperate to rob the cradle!"

Hearing Frank get ribbed like that—which I knew was a time-honored baseball tradition and actually a sign that his teammates liked him—was a reminder to me that I was in over my head with these very famous and mostly wealthy ballplayers. I kept telling myself, *It's only for a few weeks*, and then we could move on to a minor league team and be among our "own" people, as it were.

One of those people was Jackie Oester, whose husband, Ron, was a second baseman and a Cincinnati native like Jackie. He, too, was tabbed as a player of promise but had played in only a handful of major league games the previous season. I liked Jackie, a pretty blonde who was down-to-earth and twenty-one years old, which made her a lot more approachable since there wasn't as much of an age gap.

When the spring training exhibition games started, Frank got a chance to pitch—with Johnny Bench behind the plate! We were both so excited. I felt very nervous as Frank took the mound, but he performed well and didn't give up any hits, which made headlines in the *Cincinnati Enquirer* sports page the following morning.

The next time he pitched, the same thing: Frank gave up no runs and acquitted himself well. And then another excellent outing. By now the beat reporters were abuzz about Frank, calling him a "21-year-old wunderkind." Johnny Bench told Reds manager John McNamara, "The kid's ready."

Meanwhile, pitchers were getting cut every day and being sent to minor league camp, but Frank was still hanging around, still mowing 'em down. As we got to the final week of spring training, Frank still hadn't been sent down, prompting reporters hungry for a story to surround him in the locker room and pepper him with a variation of the same question: "Pastore, do you think you're heading to Cincy with the big team?"

Frank had no idea, but that didn't stop columnists from speculating that Reds management was deciding whether to keep Frank by cutting loose veteran pitcher Pedro Borbón, a right-handed power pitcher from the Dominican Republic who'd been with the club for nine seasons.

Tension was building! We had assumed that since Frank had a good spring training, we were headed to the Triple A affiliate in Indianapolis for more "seasoning," as they say in baseball, but now anything was possible. We kept my family apprised of what was happening, and I think Dad was more excited than we were.

My father offered to fly out to Tampa and drive with me to Indianapolis—or Cincinnati—so I wouldn't be alone in the car. He arrived in Florida on Monday, April 2, 1979, two days before the end of spring training camp. The Reds still hadn't decided who got the last roster spot. The following morning, Dad and I decided to start driving toward Indiana, knowing that *if* Frank made the parent team, we could easily detour to Cincinnati since the Queen City was in the general direction of Indianapolis. Either way, we were looking at a 1,000-mile journey.

Dad and I left Florida on Tuesday, the day before Opening Day, still unsure of Frank's fate. Just think: today, Frank and I would be texting or calling each other on our cell phones—instant communication. But Dad and I could only sit in the car as the miles passed and wonder what was happening back in Florida. The Reds were playing their last game of Grapefruit League season and then flying to Cincinnati afterward for their home opener on Wednesday, April 4, against the San Francisco Giants.

Somewhere in Georgia, we stopped at a restaurant for lunch and called the Reds spring training complex at Al Lopez Field. A locker room attendant found Frank, who told me, "I still don't know if I'm going to Cincinnati after the game, but I'm told that it's looking good. I say you and Dad drive to Cincy and we'll see what happens."

That was exciting. "Where should we go?"

We needed a plan since Frank and I didn't know when we'd be able to talk to each other next.

"The Reds are staying tonight at Stouffer's, a hotel real close to Riverfront Stadium. If I don't get sent down, I'll leave you tickets at Will Call and see you after the game."

Dad and I made it as far as Kentucky before finding a roadside motel. We got up in the morning and drove straight into Cincinnati. We had to stop and ask for directions to Stouffer's Cincinnati Towers (which is the Millennium Hotel today). After a short detour, we managed to find the hotel entrance and drive up to the valet station.

Dad spotted a bellman walking in our direction.

"Hey, do you know if Frank Pastore made the team?" he asked.

I didn't think my husband's name would mean anything to him, but I quickly found out that Cincinnati fans were all about their Reds.

"I believe so, sir!" the bellman replied.

That sounded like a yes to me! I jumped up and down like a junior high cheerleader, and Dad was misty-eyed. We couldn't believe this was happening.

Getting out of the car was like stepping into a walk-in refrigerator; the late-morning temperature was in the high-thirties. After being in tropical Florida for six weeks (and growing up in sunny Southern California all my life), I was freezing.

Dad and I checked into a room, which was an ooh-la-la experience. I had never been in such a nice hotel before. After freshening up, we took the elevator downstairs to the lobby and asked the concierge for the best place to quickly buy a coat since the Opening Day game had already started.

"Good idea about a coat, ma'am, since we could have snow flurries this afternoon," the concierge said. "There's a department store across the street. I'm sure you can find something."

We were pointed to a covered walkway that took us straight into Shillito's Department Store, where Dad offered to buy me an attractive light brown coat with fake fur around the neck. I protested, saying the coat was way too extravagant.

"Honey, this is the big leagues!" he said.

I cried and thanked him.

We quickly drove over to Riverfront Stadium with no idea where we should park.

Dad, who didn't have a shy bone in his body, yelled out to the parking attendant, "Hey, I'm Frank Pastore's father-in-law, and I have Frank's wife in the car. Where do I park Frank's car?"

The attendant snapped to attention. Apparently, Dad had said the right words. He pointed us toward the player's parking lot, where Dad repeated the same spiel. I almost laughed when Dad pulled our ordinary Ford LTD next to all the Mercedes and BMWs in the players' lot, but we were part of the club.

We hustled over to Will Call, got our tickets, and took our seats—where we found Andrew and Judy Arena! They had flown up from Tampa that morning when they heard the dramatic news that Frank was part of the 25-man roster. They were as excited as we were. We hugged like long-lost friends and made quite a scene, which prompted a few raised eyebrows from other players' wives, but we didn't care.

We settled into our seats as the Giants were in the midst of a second-inning eight-run explosion, shelling starter Tom Seaver. The score was 11-5 for the Giants in the sixth inning when my dad looked out to the bullpen and saw Frank warming up.

My heart leaped. When Frank came in to pitch the top of the seventh inning, Dad, Andrew, Judy, and myself jumped to our feet and cheered so loudly that Frank later told us that he heard us loud and clear.

Frank pitched like a ten-year veteran, not a rookie pitcher making his major-league debut. He pitched three scoreless innings, giving up a measly single and showing that he belonged in The Show.

After the game, we didn't know where to go. Dad asked Connie Bair, wife of pitcher Doug Bair, how we could see Frank, and she said, "Follow me."

She led us to an exclusive elevator, only for VIPs, which took us down to the locker room area, where there was a room set aside for wives, girlfriends, and families. The room was crowded because of Opening Day.

I felt out of place and underdressed since the players' wives were wearing *real* fur and their big diamonds. Nobody said hello or offered to introduce themselves.

Just as the four of us were wondering what was going to happen next, a Reds front office employee, dressed in a suit and tie, came in and yelled out, "Is Gina Pastore here?"

I craned my neck and raised a hand. "Over here," I said.

"If you can follow me," he said.

With a shrug to my dad and the Arenas, I left the family waiting area and was led to the press room, where Frank was sitting on a raised platform.

"There she is," he said. "Gina, come on up here."

Frank, still in his uniform, gave me a quick hug as I took a seat next to him. I didn't know what this was about. I felt overwhelmed, underdressed, and painfully shy.

Reporters started shouting out questions—to both of us!

"What's it like to be in the bigs, Gina?" asked one scribe.

"Frank, are you the next Tom Seaver?"

"Did you two really elope?"

We spoke while cameras flashed every few seconds. The experience was so surreal that I wondered if I was in the middle of a dream.

I wasn't, of course, but it sure felt that way.

As I sat there, soaking everything in, I wondered if my life was going to change as much as it did when I hopped into Frank's Riviera on an August morning just six months earlier.

It was.

My parents, John and Ann Pignotti, were married in their hometown of Chicago Heights, Illinois, after my father served in the Korean War.

They moved to Southern California, where my father got into the construction trade and built our home in Upland, a sunny suburb east of Los Angeles. Next to the mirror (right), I was the third of four children.

My father took this photo of us all dressed up for a family wedding in front our family Cadillac. Friends often said my mother struck a resemblance to Jackie Kennedy. My older sister, Marina, is in the back, and I'm flanked by my brothers, John and Nick (in the tie). I was four years old.

One Easter, when was I was twelve years old, I wore an "Anne of Green Gables" long gown.

A few years later, I entered a local beauty pageant, and following the swimsuit competition, I placed third.

My sophomore year of high school is when Frank Pastore and I started dating. Frank, twenty years old at the time, was four-and-a-half years older than me. He was playing professional baseball as a pitcher, but he'd had his eye on me for a long time.

Frank, blessed with a great arm, was a young phenom. The Cincinnati Reds called him up when he was twenty-one years old, making Frank the youngest player in a major league uniform during the 1979 season.

I loved going to baseball games, especially with my father. I enjoyed participating in the Cincinnati Reds wives' annual softball game.

One year, none of the other players' wives wanted to pitch, so I took the mound and hurled all three innings. Frank beamed from the dugout.

After Frank's second year with Cincinnati, I got pregnant during the off-season with Frank Jr. Jackie Oester, whose husband, Ron, was the Reds second baseman, got pregnant at the same time. The players' wives gave us a wonderful baby shower.

Frankie was still in diapers when Frank escorted him to home plate to bat during the Reds' kids game. Frank was actually a good-hitting pitcher and hit two home runs during his pitching career.

After our second child, Christina, celebrated her first birthday, she was pooped, so Daddy kissed her and put her to bed.

While Frank pitched for the Reds, we were asked to do several print and TV commercials for hotels and restaurants in Cincinnati, plus appearances on local TV shows.

His best season was in 1980, when Frank compiled a 13-7 win-loss record with a 3.27 ERA record for the Reds.

Following baseball, Frank got into radio broadcasting with KKLA, a major Los Angeles radio station. As host of the *Frank Pastore Show*, he's pictured at a live remote with evangelist Greg Laurie (center) and Terry Fahy, his boss at KKLA.

Frank was asked to welcome those attending Greg Laurie's Harvest Crusades as well as deliver the opening prayer, which he took seriously.

While at KKLA, my husband became good friends with talk show host Dennis Prager because they shared the same studio at the Glendale headquarters for the Salem Radio Network.

Finally, the *Frank Pastore Show* was named "Best Radio Talk Show of the Year" by the National Religious Broadcasters (NRB). Frank is joined by (from the left) program director Chuck Tyler, "Engineer Ann" Aragon, and KKLA general manager Terry Fahy.

Frank cuddles with our first grandchild, Michael Pastore, when he was one week old. Frank was excited to become a grandpa, and "Poppa" was his name.

In this family photo, taken shortly after Christina and Josh Smallwood (to the right) were married in 2011, Frank and I are joined by Frank Jr. and his wife, Jessica, with grandson Michael perched on Frank's shoulder. (Brady Puryear Photography)

Frank and I really enjoyed our empty nest years, a time when Frank pursued his hobby of riding motorcycles. We loved traveling the open road together, including this trip to the Banff region of British Columbia.

My life today: grandkid time with (from the left) Frank William Pastore (known as Will), Finley Smallwood, and Michael Pastore.

Here the entire clan is pictured at a recent vacation to Newport Beach.

And now I carry the broadcasting torch as co-host of *Real Life with Gina Pastore and David James* at KKLA. I'm pictured with my co-host, "Big Wave Dave" Benzing, along with Boston Red Sox pitcher and close friend Steven Wright, his wife, Shannon, and their daughter, Ella, following a taping.

15

Major League in Every Way

They say the difference between major league baseball and the minor leagues is like the difference between night and day.

You're traveling in style on chartered aircraft instead of surviving long bus rides. Staying in shiny five-star hotels instead of drab motels. Everything is taken care of for you, from schlepping bags to transportation to the ballpark. On road trips, the daily allowance—known as the per diem—was $77 a day for meal money instead of $12 for minor league players. Frank even noted that the chewing gum in the locker room was free. In the minors, he'd have to pay 50 cents for a wad.

Our lives changed in ways we couldn't imagine when Frank made the jump to major league baseball. I had no idea what would unfold, but it was exciting to think about the possibilities. Anything could happen.

One thing was clear: Frank was the new star! At twenty-one years of age, he was the youngest player in the National League as well as handsome, articulate, and most importantly, the possessor of a major-league 94-mile-per-hour fastball. Since Frank latched onto the Reds at the tail end of the "Big Red Machine" era, the local newspapers, always looking for a fresh angle, described Frank as the new face of the future.

Sportswriters also noted his similarities to the legendary Tom Seaver. They had similar wind-ups, which didn't surprise anyone in my family because Frank grew up emulating his pitching hero in our backyard. Frank and Tom actually resembled each other in appearance as well: they had similar builds, similar haircuts, and similar gaits. On a few occasions, after taking my seat at the ball game, I'd look down to the dugout and see Frank and wave to him, only to realize—it wasn't my husband. Whoops! Tom Seaver would meet my gaze and crack up every time.

My face would turn as red as a Cincinnati ball cap, but it was all in good fun. I chalked up my new-every-day experiences as part of my crash-course on becoming a Baseball Wife. Besides figuring out a new city—even getting around Cincinnati's one-way downtown grid was new to me—I was also adapting to a new lifestyle, which meant staying up late since night games often started at 7:35 p.m. and didn't finish until way after 10 o'clock—or later if there were extra innings.

By the time Frank grabbed a snack from The Spread, socialized a bit with his teammates, showered, and changed into street clothes, it was usually 11 p.m. or midnight when we got back to Stouffer's. We decided to stay at the team's downtown hotel since we understood that Frank, as the last pitcher on the roster, could be sent down at any time. All it took was one bad outing, and we were in Indianapolis.

I worried about where I fit in as well. It was tough breaking into the "sorority" of players' wives. I'd get to Riverfront Stadium, take my seat in the family section, and watch these older, more mature women talking and laughing with each other. They had an incredible bond after watching their husbands play together for years and from the success of winning four National League pennants and two World Series championships. They weren't rude or cold to me, but I was simply the new kid on the block—and an incredibly young one at that.

Being shy, I kept to myself and only spoke if spoken to. The exception was Connie Bair, who walked over to where I was sitting and introduced herself. After Frank pitched three scoreless innings on Opening Day, she escorted me to the post-game waiting room. She will never know how comforting that simple gesture was to a young rookie wife.

Over time, other players' wives began smiling and saying hello. Some of them were pregnant—Susan Hume, Terri Knight, and Cindy Norman. I saw lots of little kids running around in the section of seats reserved for the families of players and the Reds front office.

Since I was a young newlywed and childless, I would go on many of the road trips. Back then, however, wives weren't allowed on the team's chartered flights, nor were wives allowed on the bus that ferried the players from the airport to the hotel, from the hotel to the ballpark, or from the ballpark to the airport. I had to buy my own plane ticket, take a separate flight on a commercial carrier, and arrange my ground transportation.

Sometimes I'd arrive in a city before the team got to their hotel. I love the memory of the players stepping off the team bus, smartly dressed in coat-and-tie (the Reds had a strict dress code), and worship-ful fans waiting in the lobby for autographs. Pretty girls seemed to be everywhere, hoping to catch the eye of a ballplayer. I'm positive the players noticed their curvy bodies and suggestive demeanor because I sure did.

One time, the Reds flew commercial instead of a charter, which meant I could join Frank on the flight. We sat together toward the very back—coaches and veterans took the front half of the plane—but I was the only wife onboard. I caught a vibe from a few players that they were uncomfortable with me accompanying my husband. While in flight, Frank leaned over and softly said, "You may see some things on this road trip, but honey, you have to keep what you see to yourself. Does this make sense?"

I nodded. I was learning that what happens on the road stays on the road. But hearing Frank whisper those words was a real-world acknowl-edgment of the temptations that every ballplayer faced in a new city.

Would Frank remain faithful? I pondered that question in my heart.

Second baseman Ron Oester didn't make the final 25-man roster and was sent down to Indianapolis, which was a disappointment since his wife, Jackie, and I had clicked in spring training. Since Ron and Jackie were Cincinnati natives and lived year-round in the Queen City, they kept a small apartment close to downtown. Shortly after Opening Day, Ron offered us their furnished one-bedroom place, which worked perfectly for us. We moved our stuff from Stouffer's into their cozy apartment.

One of the Italian restaurants in the neighborhood was Ciuccio's, owned and operated by Pat and Lillian Ciuccio, so it was authentic. Ciuccio's was one of the few restaurants that stayed open late, so many nights after a home game, we hungrily devoured our favorite Italian foods at Ciuccio's: chicken piccata and homemade pasta slathered with wonderful cream sauces. Pat and Lillian became our family away from home, and we became fast friends with their son, Jim, who managed the restaurant. When Andrew and Judy Arena came into town, we loved hanging out at Ciuccio's.

Frank pitched okay for the first couple of months of the season.

When the Reds made their first West Coast swing, you can imagine the excitement back in our hometown of Upland. I flew out ahead of Frank and felt like a red carpet had been laid down from my old driveway to the front door, where Johnny and his friends were excited to see me and hear what life was like in the big leagues.

We had probably thirty friends and family members who wanted to see Frank pitch, but Frank could only get six comp tickets, so Dad worked with Doug Berman, the Reds travel secretary, to buy up two dozen more tickets to each game. On Friday, May 25, 1979, in the first of a three-game series, Tom Seaver took the mound. Although Tom would pitch well in 1979, compiling a 16-6 record, he didn't have his best stuff again that night and was relieved by Tom Hume in the bottom of the third inning. Down 7-2 in the bottom of the fourth, manager John McNamara turned to Frank for long relief. When my husband jogged in from the bullpen to the mound, our group jumped to our feet and cheered.

Soon, it was the Dodgers fans' turn to raise the roof because Frank got into trouble quickly. With two runners aboard, he served up a hanging curve ball, which was knocked out of the park for a home run. Then he gave up another home run. And then another blast into the blue bleachers. The Dodgers scored five runs to go up 12-2.

A scoreless fifth inning was a mirage for what was to come. In the bottom of the sixth, the first batter up hit a home run. Then Frank got into more trouble: a walk and a couple of infield singles scored another run. Then leadoff man Davey Lopes, who stood just five feet, nine inches, stepped up to the plate with two men on. He took a big cut at Frank's offering and smacked the ball deep into the left field bleachers, making the score 17-2.

Mac, the team manager, made the slow walk to the mound. Frank dropped the ball into Mac's hand and hung his head as Dodgers fans jeered him every step of the way. "Hey, Pastore, when's my turn to bat?" was one of the kinder remarks. That's what allowing five home runs and ten runs in three innings will do for you.

Not long after the shelling in Los Angeles, Frank was sent down to Indianapolis. Instead of letting the Los Angeles home-run barrage eat away at his confidence, Frank worked on his off-speed deliveries and pitched well, compiling a 7-2 record. The Reds called him back up. This time, we were determined to stay in the big leagues. With this second bite of the apple, we had both matured and weren't so "starry-eyed" about the major leagues anymore.

Frank straightened his shoulders and took the mound with a confidence that I shared. This time around, I wasn't bothered if none of the player's wives and girlfriends talked with me. What was more important was how Frank performed, and he pitched awesome on a team that would win the NL West division.

Instead of being relegated to long relief, Frank worked his way into the starting rotation. He pitched two shutouts during the pennant chase, including a nifty four-hit blanking of the Atlanta Braves to clinch the NL West on the next-to-last day of the regular season. He also pitched in the National League playoffs against the Pittsburgh Pirates, starting Game 2, which was a thrill. Frank did his part and pitched well, but the team lost in extra innings. The Pirates, with the catchy "We Are Family" as their theme song, would sweep the Reds in the League Championship Series as well as defeat the Baltimore Orioles in the 1979 World Series.

When the 1979 season was over, I thought about how much our lives had changed in one short year. I was still a couple months shy of my eighteenth birthday and wasn't considered a legal adult, but I had grown up in many ways. I can illustrate this newfound maturity by describing a conversation I had with Frank when we traveled to the Cincinnati airport at the start of a road trip. This would have been after he was called up from Indianapolis.

As Frank drove, I sat with a team roster on my lap and held a red pen in my hand. I went down the 25-man Cincinnati Reds roster, circling the names of those who couldn't be trusted. By this time, more than halfway through the season, I could tell who the "players" were on the team—the womanizers and those being unfaithful to their wives and girlfriends.

He's okay . . . no, not him . . . nope . . . yes, he's good . . . no, he's a wild one . . . .

Frank took his eyes off the road. "Honey, what are you doing?"

"I'm letting you know who you can hang out with on road trips," I said.

"Oh, really?"

I wanted to make a big deal about this, so I laid down a marker. "If I hear you've been hanging out after the game with any of these guys

I've circled, then I won't be in Cincinnati when you get back. I'll be at my parents' house."

Frank blinked. He saw that I meant business—a side of me he had never seen before.

As Frank described in *Shattered*, he had many occasions to be unfaithful to me. The baseball groupies were readily available in every city. While Frank admitted that it wasn't any religious or moral grounds that kept him from sampling the forbidden fruit, the idea that he would lose me if he cheated gave him pause. On this he saw that I wasn't kidding around.

I didn't know it at the time, but I had consigned Frank to hanging out with the Christian players on the team.

So, place yourself in my shoes during the 1979 baseball season: I was seventeen, living in a very adult world, and feeling I had matured ten years in a matter of months. I was comfortable around baseball players because I had been around baseball all my life, having watched Dad coach teams and my brother Johnny become a star catcher.

Feeling very grown up, I made a suggestion to Frank one night as we drove back to Stouffer's following a game. (After getting called up from Indianapolis, we stayed at the downtown hotel for the rest of the season.) "Whaddya say we stop and get a *Playboy* magazine?" I asked.

Frank nonchalantly looked in my direction. If he was surprised, he wasn't letting on. It was all part of being mature and cool at the same time.

"Sure, we can do that, but why?"

"I want to see what the fuss is all about. Plus, I hear everyone reads *Playboy* for the interviews."

Frank cracked up at my little joke. At the first convenience store, we walked in. I grabbed a Dr Pepper—my favorite soft drink—and an A&W Root Beer for Frank, as well as a bag of sunflower seeds. Frank visited the magazine rack and reached for the latest edition of *Playboy* with Miss August on the cover.

Back in our hotel room, I sipped my Dr Pepper and turned the glossy pages, blushing at the air-brushed nudes and trying to act unfazed around Frank. I knew he and the other players had copies of *Playboy* in the clubhouse and thought the girlie magazine was the greatest thing ever, so I wanted to make sure Frank knew I was cool with this. We were a married couple, after all. Even though I was putting my foot down about him hanging out with guys who cheated on their wives, I wanted Frank to know that I wasn't a prude or a "fuddy duddy."

I rationalized that this was our private sexual life, something between us and us only.

When the 1979 season was over, we lived with my parents again, which was convenient and saved us money. It wasn't like we were rolling in dough. Free agency was just starting to happen in the late 1970s, but the big money was stacked at the top. For rookies like Frank, clubs doled out the major league minimum, which was only $21,000. And he didn't make even that much because he spent two months in Indianapolis on a minor-league salary!

Today's star players should kiss the cleats of Frank's generation. The three highest-paid baseball players during the 2017 season were all pitchers: Clayton Kershaw, Zack Greinke, and David Price. They made between $30 million and $34 million each, which works out to nearly $200,000 for every single game in a 162-game season.

What can I say . . . anyway, from the money we did earn as well as playoff bonus money, we decided to trade the tired LTD for a spankin' new brown Cadillac DeVille that we garnished with custom license plates that read REDS 35. When we tooled into Al Lopez Field for spring training in February 1980, you can imagine the teasing Frank got from his teammates.

Hey, Frank. Aren't you getting a little big for your britches?
Frank, what's with the custom plates on your pimpmobile?

The ribbing came from players who had their numbers on their license plates as well as on the diamond necklaces that hung around the necks of their wives or significant others. I guess seeing two California kids arriving in a boat-sized DeVille bearing REDS 35 on the license plates seemed funny to everyone.

When the 1980 season began, we planned to get our own apartment, but Stouffer's made us an offer we couldn't refuse: they asked Frank to be their official spokesperson, which involved cutting a few commercials and making a handful of appearances. In return, we received a free room and food for the entire baseball season. We were beyond thrilled!

My friendship with Jackie Oester deepened. Now that her husband,

Ron, had stuck with the parent club, I stayed with her when the Reds left town—unless I traveled with Frank and the team. Home or away, the major league life was a ball. Frank and I were living the dream.

Frank was pitching unbelievably as part of the starting rotation. He sported a 10-5 win-loss record at the All-Star break, meaning that Frank was on track for a 20-game win season, which meant he was one of the best pitchers in the National League. Everyone was shocked when Pittsburgh Pirates manager Chuck Tanner didn't name Frank to the NL All-Star team. We were deeply disappointed.

The disappointment didn't last long. With Frank pitching so well, he thought about purchasing his dream car. The Cadillac, he decided, was for old people. The cool car for a 22-year-old hotshot pitcher was a Porsche.

When the Reds made a West Coast swing, I joined Frank in Los Angeles but stayed in Upland for a few days when the team traveled on to San Francisco. Frank beat me back to Cincinnati, and on his day off, he cruised over to the Porsche dealership to kick a few tires. He wasn't planning on buying a sports car. He was just browsing and dreaming.

I arrived the following day in Cincinnati. Frank greeted me at the gate as I got off the plane in those pre-9/11 days. I immediately noticed a strange smile on his face.

We hugged and kissed, but something was up.

"Frank—"

"Honey, don't get mad at me . . . ."

"What happened?"

"I got us a new car."

"What did you do?"

"I traded in the Cadillac for a new car. I'll show you."

After retrieving my luggage, I was giddy with excitement as I followed Frank to the main airport parking lot. He led me to a black Porsche 911 Targa, a flashy coupe that took my breath away.

"Oh, my . . . ." My hand covered my mouth. I was in a bit of shock.

"I got it at the dealership yesterday," Frank said. "Check this out. They told me Pete Rose was the previous owner."

Well, if Charlie Hustle owned this car, then it was meant to be.

The trunk wasn't big enough for one piece of decent-sized luggage. We somehow managed to squeeze my suitcase into the back seat, which looked like it had enough room for two preschoolers.

We jumped into the luxurious leather seats, and I admired the German engineering. Frank started up the car, and the turbocharged engine roared to life. Frank reached down to manually shift the car into reverse as he pumped the gas and kept the car in neutral.

"You got a stick shift?" I asked.

"That's all they come in." Frank had trouble finding reverse, but managed to find the right spot.

"I've never driven a stick," I said.

"Don't worry. I'll teach you how."

"But, but . . ."

Frank smiled. "You'll do fine, honey. I promise."

With that, we roared out of the parking lot with the distinctive Porsche engine note heralding our departure.

For the next several days, we visited empty parking lots around town, where Frank gave me lessons on driving a stick shift. He forgot to mention that a Porsche is a difficult stick to drive because the clutch and power combination can be tricky.

I wasn't the smoothest driver and hated climbing hills and then having to stop at a steep intersection. Keeping the car from rolling backwards or stalling the engine was challenging and made me a nervous wreck. Cincinnati is a hilly place, so it took me a while to get used to driving the Porsche through foothill terrain. Fortunately, it was flat driving to the ballpark.

Once news of buying Pete Rose's old Porsche hit the clubhouse, Frank's teammates had more ammunition to tease him. When Frank would look toward the grandstands to see if I arrived safely, one of the guys would say, "Pastore, did your wife wreck Pete's Porsche?"

Sirens in the distance provided another opening. "Hey, Pastore, must be a car accident. Sure hope Pete's Porsche is okay." The guys didn't know how to let up.

His teammates played well behind him, though. Frank would post his best statistical season in 1980, finishing with a 13-7 record and an ERA of 3.27 in 27 appearances for a club that finished 89-73, which was very good but only good enough for a third-place finish in the NL West.

My dad asked us to stay with them again in the off-season. Mom and I were getting along a little better, so I gave in. That fall, Dad asked Frank to go on a week-long elk hunting trip that he went on every year with Pat Vernola and his buddies.

One day, while the men were roughing it in the Colorado Rockies, I realized my period was a little late. I was also feeling tired and lethargic, like I had a bit of the flu.

Could I be pregnant? I had heard that pharmacies sold pregnancy test kits, which was something new. I took the test, saw the red line, and screamed with delight. And then I felt overwhelmed. I hadn't turned nineteen yet, and I was going to be a mother.

Once the elk hunt was over, Frank called from a pay phone in Grand Junction, Colorado, to let me that they were on the way home.

I couldn't restrain myself. "Frank, I'm pregnant!"

I heard the pay phone drop—*clunk, clunk*—and Frank yelling in the background, "Dad! Gina's pregnant!"

I heard cheers and was thrilled to hear how excited Frank was to become a father.

I was also thrilled to get rid of the Porsche since a two-seater sports coupe wasn't going to work for a growing family.

We traded in the Porsche for another Cadillac, which was a very sensible and adult thing to do.

After learning I was pregnant, I received more good news: my best friend Jackie Oester was expecting her first child as well. She was due about six weeks ahead of me.

When Frank and I drove the Cadillac to spring training in February 1981, life couldn't be better. Frank was an entrenched starter, we were in a family way, and the money was getting better. That spring, we lived at Sail Port, a condo complex where many of the Reds players stayed during spring training. We loved eating out at Malio's Prime Steakhouse in downtown Tampa and hanging out with the Arenas and their growing children.

The pressure of wondering if Frank would make it to the major leagues was over. He had arrived and was feeling like a veteran, even though this was only his third season in the big leagues.

In our quiet times together, we both felt a check in our hearts. Something was missing. What was it? We didn't know.

When the season started, we purchased a condominium in Newport, Kentucky, located just over the Ohio River and just ten minutes from downtown Cincinnati. I liked stepping out onto my balcony and taking in the tremendous view of Riverfront Stadium. I remember standing there, rubbing my swelling tummy, and thinking about where this crazy thing called life had taken us.

To the world, Frank and I appeared to have it all at a very young age. But something was missing . . . for the both of us.

16

Striking a Deal

The unease that Frank and I felt stayed with us right into spring training before the 1981 season.

Part of our anxiousness stemmed from talk of the players going on strike because the owners were trying to take back several hard-won victories that related to free agency. Remember, this was a key time in the grand old game's history, and the players had recently secured the right to do away with the "reserve clause," which bound a player to one team for his entire career and didn't allow him to enter into a contract with another team—even after the present contract was completed.

Opening Day in 1981 also marked the start of my seventh month of pregnancy, a time when I had a good-sized baby bump. A nice touch was when the Reds' wives threw a baby shower for me in Cincinnati. Jackie Oester and Carol Rose—Pete's second wife and pregnant with their first child—took the lead. Those attending the shower didn't know whether to present me with blue or pink infant outfits since we didn't know whether we were having a boy or a girl. The ultrasound technology was new and I underwent several sonograms, but neither of us wanted to know the sex of our baby before he or she was born. I guess we were old school in that department.

In the middle of May, around six weeks before my due date in late June, talk of a possible baseball strike dominated the sports pages. I originally planned to have my child in Cincinnati if there wasn't a "work stoppage," as the possible strike was being called in the papers, but if the players *did* go on strike, then I wanted to be in Upland, close to my parents and extended family.

I looked at the schedule. The Reds were making a West Coast swing beginning with a Friday, May 29 game against the Los Angeles Dodgers. I had maybe four weeks before my due date, so if I was going to fly out to Southern California, this was my last opportunity, even though my obstetrician-gynecologist in Cincinnati strongly advised me not to fly so late in my pregnancy. "I really wish you wouldn't do this," he said. "You're at risk of going into premature labor."

Frank and I discussed what we should do. Knowing there was a strong possibility that a strike would happen or that Frank could be on a road trip when I went into labor anyway, we both agreed that it would best for me to be in Upland, where I could count on a lot of family support.

Then we learned a bit of good news: the Reds were not chartering an aircraft but flying commercial, so I could accompany Frank. When he checked with traveling secretary Doug Berman, however, he informed us that every seat was booked.

Frank freaked out when he heard that news. "I can't let you fly alone," he said. "We're going to have to figure something else out."

If I couldn't get a seat on the team flight, that meant the two of us taking a different flight to the West Coast—and breaking team rules. Frank asked the traveling secretary to book us on a Delta nonstop from Cincinnati to Ontario just in case nothing opened up on the team flight.

When John McNamara, the team manager, heard about the arrangement, he wasn't pleased.

"If you're not on the team flight, you're going to get fined," Mac told Frank in the clubhouse before the start of the afternoon day game against the San Francisco Giants on Thursday, May 28.

"Then fine me," Frank said.

Not even a 7-4 victory over the Giants softened Mac's stance. Rules were rules.

Frank showered and met me after the game. We drove straight from Riverfront to the airport with Frank muttering that he was in trouble. "It's never good to make waves in the clubhouse," he said. "But I know this is what we have to do."

I think Frank said the fine was $500, which was enough to sting. Frank had gotten a raise to $32,500, but that was just 4 percent of what Ken Griffey ($700,000) and 8 percent of what Johnny Bench ($400,000) were knocking down. Being around baseball, I understood why the big stars made the big bucks.

During the nonstop flight, I started feeling crampy. I got up to use the lavatory. Uh-oh—I was starting to spot. I mentioned to Frank what had happened. He turned as white as a sheet. "Are you going into labor?" he asked.

I had done some reading about pregnancy. "I don't think so. Maybe this is some sort of pre-labor thing."

We were both sitting on pins and needles, knowing that if we had to tell a flight attendant that I was going into labor, then it would be a major deal—and potentially inconvenience a lot of lives since the pilot would divert the flight and land at the nearest city. We decided to stay calm and see if we could stick it out.

As the minutes passed by slowly, we were grateful when the pilot announced that we were descending and would soon be landing at Ontario airport.

My condition seemed to have stabilized that evening, but I woke up early at 6 a.m., which was partially due to the time change and partially due to feeling crampy again. Once again I determined that I was spotting. Call it a mother's intuition, but I could tell something wasn't right.

Frank and my parents were deeply worried, as well as they should have been. One of Dad's best friends was Dr. Preston Merrell, who had been *my* pediatrician when I was a young girl—which hadn't been that long ago, come to think of it.

When Dad called him and described my symptoms, he became immediately concerned. "I'm calling Dr. Rawle," said Dr. Merrell, referring to an ob-gyn colleague.

Five minutes later, Dr. Merrell called Dad. "Get her down to San Antonio as soon as possible," he said, referring to San Antonio Community Hospital in Upland.

We rushed to the hospital, where Dr. Gerald Rawle and Dr. Merrell were waiting for me. Dr. Rawle examined me and determined that I was already dilated at 3 centimeters.

"You're starting labor," said Dr. Rawle.

Hearing the word *labor* sent everyone into a tizzy. Frank called the team hotel and spoke with one of Reds coaches about the situation.

"You be with Gina," the coach said. Back then, there was no such thing as "paternity leave" in the baseball world. Players were expected to take the least amount of time as possible away from the team, but there was compassion, too. "Do what you need to do, Frank. We'll be just fine," the coach said.

I steeled myself for what was to come as Frank stayed by my side. He coached me to breathe as labor progressed, and I huffed and puffed. Seven hours later, Dr. Rawle, assisted by Dr. Merrell, delivered a boy. Frank and I had decided that if we had a son, we would name him after Frank, just as his father had done.

As soon as Dr. Rawle delivered my son, I saw looks of concern in Dr. Rawle's face as well as the attending nurses. They were using a lot of big medical words between themselves as they snipped the umbilical cord. Instead of having my son placed on my chest so that I could hold him, Dr. Merrell carried him out of the delivery room with a nurse on his heels. I looked at Frank with a look that said: *What's going on?*

Dr. Rawle noticed our non-verbal interaction and leaned forward. "Nothing to worry about," he said. "Dr. Merrell is having him checked out."

Dr. Rawle then turned to stitching me up. I noticed that he was avoiding my eyes as well as small talk, which made me feel very uneasy and told me that something was not right.

When Dr. Rawle finished, I was wheeled to my room, where Frank and I waited. A distinct feeling of unease filled the air. I had given birth a half hour earlier, and I had yet to *hold* my son.

After another half-hour or so, Dr. Merrell stepped in, wearing a solemn face.

I needed answers. "Are they going to bring Frankie to me?" I asked.

"I have to talk with you," Dr. Merrell said, which are words that a mom who just delivered a baby never wants to hear.

Frank and I nodded for him to continue.

"This is very serious. We think Frankie has a breathing disorder called hyaline membrane. Are you familiar with that?"

"No," I said.

"Basically, hyaline membrane disease means his lungs are under-developed, which means he needs extra oxygen to help him breathe. It's very serious."

"How serious?" Frank asked.

"Serious enough that his life is at risk," the doctor replied.

"How much of a risk?" I asked.

"I'd say he has a 50/50 chance of pulling through."

My son might not live?

As if reading my thoughts, Dr. Merrell continued. "The good news is that he weighed seven pounds, three ounces at birth, even though he was at least three, four weeks premature. That's a good sign. But we don't have a neo-natal unit here at San Antonio, so we're going to have to send him to Queen of the Valley."

I was in shock. I lay back in my bed, feeling totally numb. If—and it was a big *if*—my son survived, then I wouldn't be able to hold my son until I visited him at Queen of the Valley Hospital, which was twenty miles west of Upland in West Covina. But I wasn't going anywhere.

Frank had a question. "Can I go with him?"

"Of course," Dr. Merrell said. "Frankie's going to be transported by ambulance to Queen of the Valley, and you're welcome to follow."

My parents and other family members were in the waiting room. When Frank delivered the tough news, the decision was made for Frank and my dad to accompany Frankie to Queen of the Valley while I recuperated. As I was giving birth, some nerves in my legs got cut off, which happens sometimes but was scary nonetheless. I could barely stand on my feet and had to stay in bed.

Frank returned to my room that night and told me everything that happened: Frankie was being well taken care of in the neo-natal unit. He was a fighter. Every hour that passed was a good sign. I would later learn that Patrick Kennedy, son of President John Kennedy and his wife, Jackie, had died of hyaline membrane disease after being born premature. Patrick lived thirty-nine hours before dying on August 7, 1963.

Frank wanted to spend the night with me at San Antonio. Nurses brought in a cot to accommodate him. We talked about what Frank should do the following day because he was scheduled to pitch against the Dodgers at Chavez Ravine.

"Frank, if Frankie is stable, you should pitch," I said.

I knew that when a starting pitcher doesn't take his turn, it kind of screws up the whole rotation. Whether Frank pitched or not wasn't the first thing on our minds, but if Frankie was doing well in the neo-natal unit, then he should take the mound.

"Let's decide in the morning," Frank said.

When Frank woke up, he felt chipper. "I have all this nervous energy," he said. "I think I'm going to pitch."

"Good, you do that," I said. I hadn't slept well at all, but if Frank felt up to it, he should do his job. We called Queen of the Valley and spoke with the nurses, who said Frankie was responding well.

Frank called team manager John McNamara at the team hotel. He'd gotten word the day before about Frankie's birth and was waiting to hear from Frank about whether he was coming in to pitch.

"Frank, it's all over the news, what's happening with your son. You don't have to pitch today. Don't worry about it! We'll find somebody."

The news that Frankie had been born prematurely and could die had been leaked to the press. The local newspapers and TV stations had been all over the story.

"Mac, I spoke with Gina. She's doing fine, and things are looking better for Frankie, so I'll be ready. I'm coming in."

"You sure?"

"I'm sure."

Back in 1981, ESPN and cable sports were still in their infancy. If a baseball game was nationally televised, then it was one of the Big Three networks: ABC, NBC, or CBS.

"The Game of the Week" on NBC featured a Saturday day game of interest around the country. On Saturday, May 30, 1981, NBC sports programmers chose to air a game between the Cincinnati Reds and the Los Angeles Dodgers, the host team. Longtime Dodgers announcer Vin Scully, who had an agreement with the Dodgers to moonlight on Saturdays by doing the play-by-play for NBC, was in the booth that day. Joe Garagiola provided the color commentary.

Vin Scully had read our story in the local newspapers as well. As Frank took the mound in the bottom of the first, Scully—a masterful storyteller—regaled his national audience with a description of Frank and Gina Pastore's lives in the past twenty-four hours.

I had grown up listening to Vin Scully. My father held him in the same high regard that he reserved for the Pope. So when his melodious voice described how "baby Pastore" was "fighting for his life" in a local hospital, he painted a heart-tugging, dramatic picture of a young father—unable to do anything for his son except to pray—deciding to pitch although he had no idea what the outcome would be. Vinnie hailed Frank as a ballplayer with "tremendous courage" and "inner resolve" in the face of a possible tragedy.

Back in San Antonio hospital, I watched the game on a wall-mounted TV and never saw more nurses in my life inside my room—their eyes were glued to the set. Frank had that determined eye-of-the-tiger look going up against pitcher Burt Hooton, who had a perfect 7-0 record. My Frank pitched great, setting the Dodgers down most innings and giving up just one run in seven innings until he was relieved by Tom Hume, leading 5-1. The final score would be 9-1, Reds.

Watching that game was a weird experience for me. I wasn't into the game because my focus was on Frankie, but I had nurses coming in and out of my room sayings things like, "When is Frank coming back? My kid wants his autograph." A couple of nurses left baseballs to be signed.

Frank checked in on Frankie on the way home from the game and then came to see me. He reported what Dr. Merrell was saying: Frankie was responding well in the incubator and things were looking good.

In the morning, Dad arrived with copies of sports pages from several different newspapers. The typical headline read "Reds' Pastore Handles Crisis, Beats Dodgers." Mike Davis, the beat reporter for the *San Bernardino Sun*, wrote this:

As it was, there were enough problems in Frank Pastore's life. He hadn't been pitching in the best of luck, as indicated by his 1-2 record and 3.78 ERA, and Saturday afternoon he was assigned to work a rather important game against the Dodgers and their unbeaten right-hander Burt Hooton.

Add to this the fact that on Friday his wife, Gina, had given birth to a baby boy, who arrived early and with more complications than the Pastores were expecting, and you can begin to imagine the strain Frank was pitching under yesterday.

The 23-year-old right-hander's reaction to all this had a touch of heroism to it. He went out and shackled the Dodgers on six hits for 7 1/3 innings that produced a 9-1 victory before 43,582 at Dodger Stadium.

After recapping Frankie's premature birth and the seriousness of the breathing difficulties, Davis used these locker-room quotes from Frank:

"This was a very emotional day for me," Pastore said after Saturday's game. "It kind of put things in perspective. The game was very secondary. My wife and child were on my mind all Friday and all the time I was out there today. They're on my mind now.

"I had all this emotion in me, and maybe pitching was a good way to vent some of it. It probably helped me to relax. I do feel very blessed to have been in the delivery room when my child was born, and I look on this whole experience as a good one."

After all the local publicity as well as Vin Scully broadcasting our story to the world, we were inundated with baby gifts. I'm talking hundreds of gifts, perhaps more than a thousand. The gifts came to San Antonio Community Hospital, Queen of the Valley, and even my parents' home. (How people found out their address I'll never know.) Just as many gifts were mailed to the Reds' front office in Cincinnati and to Riverfront Stadium.

All this attention helped me cope with Frankie's condition. I had nurses tell me how serious hyaline membrane disease was. They said Frankie's lungs would either get over the disease and adapt well, or he would die quickly. There was no in between.

Not being with Frankie nearly killed me. While Frankie's life hung in the balance twenty miles away, I had to stay in the hospital for three days until feeling came back to my legs. As soon as I was released on Monday, Dad drove me to Queen of the Valley Hospital. Frank had left the day before for the next series against the San Francisco Giants. The report on Frankie was good. It looked like he was out of the woods.

I'll never forget the first time I saw my son—except for the quick glimpse after his birth. When I stepped inside the neo-natal unit, the first thing I saw was a sign above the Frankie's incubator that read, "Go Reds! Daddy Loves You!" My son was like a little celebrity.

I was allowed to step up to the incubator. Frankie lay on his stomach, wearing a diaper and hooked up to all sorts of monitors. My heart nearly burst. I was allowed to don gloves and reach inside and touch my son, which was a weird, conflicting feeling. I consoled myself by repeating what doctors had told me: *Frankie was going to live.*

And for that, I was grateful to God.

Frankie was two weeks old when major league baseball players went on strike on June 12, 1981. Although no one wanted the baseball season to stop and meant that Frank would stop getting paid, there was still a bright side: Frank could join me in Upland and have a little father-son bonding time with Frankie.

The three of us camped out in my old bedroom once again. Mom and Dad enjoyed their new little grandson, and many nights Dad got up with me for one of the middle-of-the-night-feedings.

Frank worked out, keeping himself in shape and his arm loose. It was a good time to reconnect with my family. My brother Johnny had been drafted by the Oakland A's the year we got married, but two seasons of minor league ball and never rising above Single A ball were enough. Johnny and his wife, Staci, moved to Phoenix, where my older brother had taken a position with Transamerica in sales.

My younger brother Nick was looking forward to his senior year at Damien High School, where he was also a standout pitcher. One of Nick's close friends was a tall red-headed and kind-hearted teammate named Mark McGwire.

Mark was a pitcher, too, and he and Frank would go to the mound in my parents' backyard, where Frank would work on Mark's windup. Frank discovered that he liked tutoring young players on the finer points of pitching.

Dad, who loved cooking, loved feeding the Damien High ball-players even more. He'd try to get Mark to eat different things like greens cooked in olive oil and garlic, but when Mark would turn his nose up, Dad would reach over and teasingly smack the back of Mark's head, saying, "You don't know what's good!"

I only heard him say that a thousand times.

On weekends, Dad loved cooking a big breakfast for the baseball kids. He came up with a new dish just for Mark: pancakes stacked with a fried egg on top and slathered in maple syrup, which Mark loved so much that our family referred to this dish as "The Mark McGwire."

In the fall, Mark enrolled at USC as a power-hitting power pitcher. He pitched two seasons for the Trojans and then decided to concentrate on hitting: 583 major league home runs later, I would say he made a great decision.

When Frank wasn't working with pitchers in our backyard, he played some celebrity golf tournaments during the strike. Frank made some interesting connections, including meeting a guy who headed a large advertising agency.

We were invited to attend a private backyard dinner at the Beverly Hills home of Robert Evans, who'd produced films like *Love Story*, *The Godfather*, and *Chinatown*. We received a fancy invitation in the mail and were excited to be included in such a star-studded event. When the night arrived, I wore a beautiful black dress with a fuchsia-colored sash around my waist. Frank wore a dark suit with a fuchsia-colored tie. We looked ready for Hollywood!

When we arrived at Robert Evan's private estate, we entered a long winding road to a circular driveway, where a parking valet took our car. We were nervous since we didn't know anyone at this party.

Standing next to a huge front door was Robert Evans, wearing a dark blue bathrobe (something that the late Hugh Hefner of *Playboy* was famous for doing). Out of the corner of my eye, I saw several celebrities staring at us, trying to figure out who we were.

As Robert extended his hand to Frank, my husband blurted, "Frank Pastore, Cincinnati Reds!"

Robert's face lit up. "A ballplayer! Welcome to my home. And who do we have here?" he asked, looking at me. "Is this Jaclyn Smith's younger sister?"

I blushed. Jaclyn Smith was famous for being one of *Charlie's Angels*, the popular TV show that also starred Farrah Fawcett and Kate Jackson.

"No, I'm Gina Pastore," I said as graciously as I could.

We quickly realized we were way overdressed. This wasn't the Academy Awards; people were dressed casual. We were escorted to the backyard area, which was teeming with A-listers: actor Ron Howard, singer Andy Gibb, *Dallas* actress Victoria Principal, actress Morgan Fairchild, actress Donna Mills, and two of Charlie's Angels—Farrah Fawcett and Kate Jackson.

The experience was rather surreal, but as I quickly learned, everyone loves a major league baseball player. As Frank was introduced around, these Hollywood elites were impressed in meeting him, and I couldn't help but notice that some of the starlets were smiling at Frank a little too friendly—just another reminder of the temptations that baseball players face.

The owners and the players didn't reach an agreement to end the baseball strike until July 31, which resulted in the loss of one-third of the regular season.

I flew with Frankie to Cincinnati when the strike was over, where the Reds' front office had received hundreds of baby outfits for our son. While the outpouring was amazing, there were some weird fans out there. One lady continually wrote and said she couldn't wait to hold Frankie. That freaked me out.

Having a son was a life-changing experience, as it is for all new parents. As we dedicated ourselves to this sweet little new life, our focus shifted from all the glitz of baseball to a more grounded reality: waking up during the night for feedings, putting Frankie in a stroller and taking walks around the neighborhood, and going straight home after games instead of hanging out with our friends at Ciuccio's.

I also noticed some of the baseball wives were treating me differently at the games, as now I had something more in common with them. The first night I brought my baby to Riverfront, many wives came over to see and greet him. I remember Susan Hume asking to hold him, which pleased me. Her husband, Tom, was known as a team leader, a down-to-earth man of faith respected by team members. Tom was one of the people I hoped Frank would hang out with on the road.

While the team was traveling, I was invited to barbecues by a few of the players' wives. It felt great to finally be part of the group.

During this time, I attended church every so often. My friend Jackie Oester was a devout Catholic, so that was something we had in common. When the guys were on the road, I'd drive up to Jackie's house in a nearby suburb, and we'd attend her Catholic parish.

Interestingly, even though Frank was a skeptic, he always attended Sunday morning chapel services at the ballpark, hosted by Athletes in Action, a division of Campus Crusade.

That summer, I remember talking to Frank about how I had this weird empty feeling. "Maybe we need God at the center of our lives," I said, but Frank didn't engage me on that topic. I could tell he was thinking, though.

As our third season in the big leagues came down to an end, we were enjoying our status. Frank was recognized around town from various commercials and public appearances, where he did some speaking. I participated in fashion shows, even doing a few odd jobs modeling.

One night as Frank and I left Riverfront Stadium, we noticed a car tailing us. Frank purposely didn't drive to our condo complex. When the car kept following, we decided to drive to the nearest police station. It took us a while to find one, but when we did, the car tailing us sped off in a hurry.

That experience frightened me quite a bit, and I wondered who else was stalking us. Back in those days, fans would write and mail letters by the hundreds to their favorite players, often asking for an autographed picture. Frank would bring home bags and bags of mail and sign black-and-white glossy photographs or Frank Pastore baseball cards. We found it to be very overwhelming. At times, I felt like we were living in a fish bowl.

When the strike-shortened 1981 season ended, the Reds didn't make the playoffs even though Frank's team had the NL West's best full-season record of 66-42. The owners decided to split the season into two separate halves, which kept us from post-season play.

Frank, as sportswriter Mike Davis wrote, didn't have the best luck out on the mound either. He finished the 1981 season with a 4-9 record, but Mac and the coaches felt he gave the club a lot of good outings.

The 1982 and 1983 seasons were statistically more of the same. Frank compiled 8-13 and 9-12 won-loss records in those two years, but he was pitching for a struggling team that lost over 101 games in 1982 and finished 74-88 in 1983.

It was during this time that Frank began to exhibit his gifts of leadership. Frank was elected as the Reds' union representative for the Major League Players Association. One off-season, we attended the player union's annual meeting held at the exclusive five-star Kapalua resort on the island of Maui. We left Frankie with Mom and Dad and looked forward to some alone time in Hawaii. A romantic interlude would do us well.

All the player reps were there. There was one incident I'll never forget. Frank and I went out for dinner with another player and his wife. After a lovely meal overlooking the Hawaiian twilight, this player had a limo waiting for us in front of the restaurant. "Hey, the night's still young," he said, and we were invited to join him and his wife for a "nightcap." We hit several nightclubs, where we danced and had a few drinks.

As the evening wound down, the limo took us back to our hotel. As we exited the black Lincoln, the ballplayer sidled up to Frank and whispered something. I saw Frank straighten up. "No way," he said, shaking his head. "No way that's going to fly."

We said our goodbyes and walked into the marble-lined lobby. "What was that all about?" I asked.

"He asked me if we wanted to swing," Frank said.

Swing? I didn't know what that meant. Frank saw my quizzical look.

"Gina, he meant swing as in wife swapping. Get it?"

"Oh, no!" I covered my mouth with my right hand. I couldn't believe what I was hearing.

Afterward, we shared a good laugh. I always made sure that Frank was taken care of in that department. I knew I was the only one for him and he was the only one for me. As a testament to our love, I was thrilled to learn that I was pregnant when the 1984 season rolled around.

Little did I know that something even bigger was on the horizon.

17

Shattered

I f you had asked me in 1984—the start of Frank's *sixth* season pitching in the major leagues—if I was happy or not, I wouldn't have
hesitated to say yes.

Remember, I had eloped at age sixteen with no expectations for
what the future would bring. Oh, I probably hoped Frank would have
this great pitching career in the major leagues and we'd live happy ever
after, but that's not why I married him. I married Frank because I was
in love with him. If the pitching thing didn't pan out, then we'd get
serious about Frank earning a college degree while I worked to put him
through school.

That's as far as my thinking went when I was sixteen years old. While
I may have thought I had it all together at the time, the reality is that I
was at the starting gate of life and was mature as any girl who was sweet
sixteen.

My maturation process sped up rapidly when Frank and I jumped
out of the gate and eloped, which was crazy back then and even crazier
today. I mean, who elopes these days? Certainly not young couples
since there is no longer cultural tsk-tsking about living together without
benefit of matrimony. In many precincts, young couples are *expected* to
live together before marrying, to see if they are "compatible."

I've been digressing for a moment, but I want to set the stage for
where Frank and I were at during the summer of 1984, a time when
the world would look at us and say, *Wow, what a great couple. They're
handling fame and fortune so well.* Little did we know that everything
would change that summer when our lives were *shattered*, as Frank's
book was titled.

Like I said, life was good and we were happy. I had gotten used to
Frank being on the road three months a year during the baseball season.

I leaned on friendships with other baseball wives as well as my family for support. I had a three-year-old son who had not only survived a life-threatening disease but was thriving. I had a bun in the oven, which kept me positively focused on the future. We didn't know if we were having a boy or girl, but it didn't matter. We were going to become parents again, and thoughts of raising two children filled my sails.

The Reds were pitiful in the early '80s, and even though Frank pitched well, his record suffered, losing more games than he won. The days of the Big Red Machine were long gone because star players like Pete Rose, Joe Morgan, George Foster, and Ken Griffey bolted to other teams via free agency. Left behind to "rebuild" the Reds were young up-and-coming players like Frank, who could still fire the ball hard and fast over the plate.

There's something else you should know about No. 35 when he took the mound: he didn't take guff from anybody. Frank pitched like he had a chip on his shoulder, like he had something to prove. That was a good thing because his take-no-prisoners attitude gave him tunnel vision. I wouldn't say that Frank was a cocky pitcher, but he gave batters the vibe that he wasn't scared of pitching to them.

Pitchers are used to feeling like they're at the center of the universe. The standing ovations, media attention, recognition in public, and signing autographs are all part of being in The Show. At the same time, he took everything in stride because he felt like he *belonged* in the major leagues.

Of course, there's a fine line between confidence and cockiness. His catcher, the great Johnny Bench, who'd seen many young pitchers start off great but lose their edge, gave Frank some great advice during his rookie season. After pitching three scoreless innings against the San Francisco Giants one afternoon, Johnny thought Frank was acting a bit too big for his britches. Between innings, he sidled up to Frank on the dugout bench and offered this advice: "Never get too cocky or arrogant because you're only one pitch away from humility."

Frank took his words to heart, but after five seasons in the major leagues, after signing a four-year, $1.2 million guaranteed contract, after buying a nice condo in Cincinnati, after purchasing a nice single-family home around the corner from my parents in Upland, and after buying his second Porsche, Frank believed he had arrived at the mountaintop named Success.

So, consider where Frank's head was at when the 1984 season started: despite making $300,000 annually (which was *fourteen* times his rookie salary of $21,000 and the equivalent of $700,000 today), despite having a wonderful marriage and a healthy preschooler bearing his name, Frank was not totally fulfilled.

And neither was I. Like I mentioned earlier, there was a weird, nagging feeling looming deep in the background. I couldn't put my finger on what wasn't right, but I felt like there was a "missing piece" in my life.

I would later learn that Frank had the same uneasy feeling tugging at his heart, but at the time, we didn't share our feelings very often, especially if the topic was related to spirituality or religion. While Frank was a thoughtful person and had a philosophical aptitude, the way he talked about the Christian players on the team wasn't very complimentary. He'd make fun of them at times and let it be known that he thought they were religious fanatics. I heard him say that the born-again Jesus freaks on the Reds believed in fairy tales. Jesus dying on a cross and rising from the dead on the third day never happened.

The irony is that these "Jesus freaks" were the guys he hung out with on road trips—and Frank enjoyed their company. When, during his rookie season, I circled in red the players he couldn't socialize with, I unwittingly left Frank to hang out with the born-again Christians who ate meals together and played cards to pass time on the road, instead of frequenting bars and hotel lobbies, where picking up baseball groupies was like shooting fish in a barrel.

While there were several great guys on the Reds, Frank seemed to bond with five players—Tom Hume, Tom Foley, Duane Walker, Danny Bilardello, and Bruce Berenyi. They weren't holier-than-thou types or Bible thumpers; they were great, dependable, and trustworthy guys. Even though Frank thought they were religious fanatics, we both knew they had his back.

Tom Hume, a relief pitcher, was the Red's chapel leader and had the most in common with Frank. I couldn't help but notice that after Frank signed his long-term, million-dollar contract, my husband went out and bought a fire-engine red Porsche, but Tom—who made $833,333 a year, or three times Frank's annual salary—drove a simple, well-worn SUV. He and his wife, Susan, were salt-of-the-earth people. They loved entertaining in their home and hosted many outdoor barbecues for the players and their families.

Another thing I noticed about Tom was how he never let fame go to his head even though he was one of baseball's top relievers, having won the Fireman of the Year award in 1980. But I also observed how he handled life when the breaks didn't fall his way. He tore cartilage in his right knee midway through the 1982 season and was out the rest of the year recuperating from knee surgery, which wasn't nearly as sophisticated back then as it is today. Tom didn't pitch well in 1983 and was struggling to find his old form as the 1984 season took shape.

Yet Tom hadn't changed. He was still as low-key and humble as when he was one of the National League's top relievers, and he was still the same unassuming, things-are-going-to-be-fine guy when he was demoted from closer to set-up man on the Reds. Frank and I both noticed that Tom had his priorities right, which is why the biggest stars on the team often took Tom into their confidence. That's a true sign of a person of integrity.

All this was the context when Frank took the mound at Dodger Stadium on Monday night, June 4, 1984, for the start of a three-game series against the Dodgers.

This wasn't just another weeknight ballgame. There was extra excitement in the air because Frank was pitching in our hometown before family and friends as well as for those watching the game on local TV with Vin Scully describing the action. Frank was going *mano a mano* against Fernando Valenzuela, the left-handed screwball artist from Mexico who'd set off "Fernandomania" in the City of Angels.

Frank brought his best stuff to the ballpark that night. He mowed down the Dodger batting order . . . once, then twice, allowing just one hit in six innings. In the bottom of the seventh, though, a double by Ken Landreaux scored a Dodgers run that tied the game 1-1. But the Reds came right back in the top of the eighth, working Valenzuela for two runs, including a gusty suicide squeeze play that gave the visiting team a 3-1 lead.

When Frank took the mound in the bottom of the eighth, he was six outs away from besting the great Fernando on his home turf. I sat next to Dad, loving every moment. Mom was back home, watching Frankie and the game on TV from our living room couch.

Second baseman Steve Sax stepped up to the plate. Sax was built like most major-league second basemen—not that tall or big and certainly not a power hitter. With a 2-1 count, Frank threw a fastball on the outside part of the plate to the right-handed hitter. Sax swung and hit the pitch on the screws, rocketing the ball back into the box, as they say in baseball when a batted ball goes straight for the pitcher.

Frank, still in his follow-through, instinctively raised his arm to protect himself from the rocket coming right at him. The line drive smacked him in the pitching arm and ricocheted harmlessly toward first base. The infield had no play on Sax for the out.

When Frank was struck by the line drive, I immediately flinched, throwing my hands over my face. Frank circled the mound in pain, holding his arm. Players ran to his aid, as well as manager Vern Rapp, pitching coach Stan Williams, and trainer Larry Starr. They gathered around Frank with concerned looks on their faces.

I stood up for a better look, which wasn't so easy since I was in my fifth month of pregnancy. I was seated behind the Reds dugout on the third-base side.

Did he break his arm? I wondered.

I wanted to pray, but I didn't feel worthy enough to do that because I didn't feel right with God. Praying happened on Sundays during the not-so-often occasions when I went to Mass. The rest of the week was "my time." This was a Monday night.

Frank was escorted off the field by his manager and coaches as Tom Hume jogged in from the bullpen to relieve Frank. Fear gripped my heart. Something was terribly wrong.

Why was this happening?

I told Dad I would be right back. I left my seat and walked to the area underneath the grandstands—where the locker rooms and the waiting room was for players' families. I showed my pass and then banged on the Reds' locker room door, hoping someone would answer.

When no one came, I returned to my seat to tell Dad what happened. When Tom Hume got out of the inning, I hustled back to the Reds' locker room again. This time when I banged on the door, Larry Starr, the trainer, emerged.

"How's Frank?"

Larry shot me a sympathetic look. "He's injured. The line drive hit him in the elbow, so he's in a lot of pain."

I felt sick inside. "Can you tell him to come see me?"

"I'll do that. Don't you worry. He's going to be all right."

How could I not worry? I paced the concrete hallway outside the Reds' locker room until Frank came out, his right arm in a sling. He looked like he had seen a ghost.

"This is really bad, honey," he said, as I drew close.

"How bad?"

Frank tugged at the sling. "My elbow's swollen like crazy. Could be a game-changer."

I had never seen Frank so upset or rattled. My husband was scared. I put my hands to my face and began to silently cry.

"Now, now." Frank drew me close with his good left arm. "The club wants me to fly back to Cincinnati tomorrow for X-rays and see the team doctor. Then we'll know a lot more."

I took small comfort in those words. Here we were, on top of the baseball world—well, maybe not at the top but we were pretty high in altitude—and we had been caught in a sudden avalanche. Frank was pitching well, making good money, playing with the security of a guaranteed contract, adoring our son, and looking forward to our second child—and then we got buried.

I stayed behind at our home in Upland while Frank flew to Cincinnati for an evaluation of his arm. I was miserable without Frank, and we talked on the phone constantly.

Frank, usually upbeat, was as down as I'd ever heard him. Of his time in Cincinnati, Frank wrote in *Shattered*: "There I was, without my wife and best friend, Gina, without my son, with no friends or teammates, and my career possibly over. I was physically, emotionally, and psychologically wounded."

During one of our daily phone calls, he waxed philosophical. "What'll we do if I can't pitch anymore?" he asked.

That was a great question but one I didn't want to face. It slowly dawned on me that his identity . . . my identity . . . was wrapped up in his baseball career. The fame, the fortune, the lifestyle, our friends on the team, living in Cincinnati, the fun and excitement of being part of major league baseball—that all happened because Frank stepped inside the chalk lines every fourth game. If pitching was taken away, what would we do?

The medical exams on his bruised elbow didn't give us much to go on. Even though the team doctors poked, prodded, and twisted Frank's arm, studied X-rays, and even used a newfangled diagnostic tool known as a CAT scan, they couldn't tell us exactly what happened to his arm. The only medical determination they could make was that no bones had been broken and a few existing bone chips had become dislodged. Nothing could be done about those, however.

Frank was told to keep icing the elbow and wait for the swelling to go down and for the bruises to heal. The team doctors said, *You'll be a lot better in a few days. You'll miss a start or two and then be good to go.*

I wasn't sure if this was good news or bad news, especially after Frank told me that he could feel stuff moving around inside his elbow joint. When Frank told his doctors that something was really wrong with his elbow, they thought he was overreacting. One sports medicine physician actually told Frank, "It's all in your head."

With our lives in turmoil, I decided to fly back to Cincinnati with Frankie to support my husband.

When Frank picked me up at the airport, he told me how four of the Christian players on the Reds found him in the trainer's room after the final out in Los Angeles. Frank's arm was in ice when Tom Hume, Tom Foley, Duane Walker, and Danny Bilardello filed into the training room, sharing looks of concern.

After asking Frank how he was doing, Tom asked, "Can we pray for you?"

Under different circumstances, Frank would've offered a funny retort to maintain his image of being a skeptic of Christianity, but being struck by Steve Sax's line drive was no laughing matter.

"Yeah, you can pray!" Frank said without a hint of sarcasm. "You can do anything you want if you think it'll help."

Frank would have never thought to pray—and didn't know how anyway. He was an agnostic at best and an atheist at worst, depending on his mood that day, so the idea of praying ran counter to his belief system. But in the emotion of the moment—getting smacked in the elbow by a line drive and wondering if he'd ever pitch again—Frank didn't mind being prayed *for*, especially for something as serious as his pitching arm.

"It was weird when they prayed for me," Frank told me on the ride home from the airport. "They didn't open a book or anything. Instead, they took turns praying out loud, like Jesus was right there in the locker room with us. They asked Jesus to give me a peace that surpasses all understanding."

"That was nice of them," I offered.

"Yeah, and then a couple of days ago, our off day, Tom invited me over for a barbecue with some of the guys and their families. They were all nice and really concerned about my arm. There's something different about them."

This from a guy who had a take-it-or-leave-it attitude about faith. Frank didn't mind me going to Mass and never hassled me about the Catholic Church. I could even get him to accompany me for Christmas Eve services. But religion wasn't his thing.

What Frank didn't tell me was that he was in the midst of a spiritual journey—one that he had to figure out first. I would learn later that at Tom Hume's barbecue, the same guys who had prayed for him in the Dodger Stadium locker room were there: Tom Foley, Duane Walker, and Danny Bilardello. But there was another recognizable face in Tommy's backyard—Wendel Deyo, the Reds chaplain for the past decade. Wendel was affiliated with Athletes in Action, a ministry of Campus Crusade.

Picture the scene: a handful of Christian ballplayers and Wendel Deyo are standing around with either beers or soft drinks in their hands, watching Tom flip burgers. They got to talking about the Bible, which flipped a switch in Frank. All his hurt, frustration, confusion, and yes, fear came rushing out in a torrent of words. The Bible, Frank declared with the assurance of someone who knew his stuff, was a contradictory work of fiction created by humans to indoctrinate various mythologies to the gullible and explain the unexplainable to the uneducated. "You can make the Bible say anything you want to, and it's been changed many times over the past 2,000 years."

Frank was just getting warmed up. For the next half hour, he launched into the guys, attacking all the ridiculous claims of Christianity and the existence of God. "They sat there and took it, their hair blowing straight back in the hot wind of my tirade," Frank wrote in *Shattered*. "When I felt I'd successfully enlightened the group, I finally stopped spewing."

What happened next was classic. Instead of arguing with Frank, Wendel spoke for the group. "Wow, Frank. I've never heard anyone articulate views with such passion and reason like you just did. I don't think I even understand most of the issues you raised. The guys told me you were smart, but they didn't tell me you were *this* smart!"

Frank beamed. Finally, someone recognized the bubbling genius that had been hidden all these years by a baseball uniform.

"But Frank, we don't want to believe in myths, stories, or anything that isn't true or real either. We're just like you. We want to believe in what's true. Right, guys?"

Wendel didn't ask for an amen, even though he would have gotten a chorus of them from Tom and the rest of the Christian players. Instead, the guys sensibly said, "Right!"

Wendel set a trap. "So, will you help us figure this out?" he asked.

"Of course," Frank replied magnanimously. "You're my friends. I don't want you guys building your lives on lies."

No, of course not.

Wendel clapped his hands. "Great, Frank. Here's how you can help us. I happen to have bought some books that present Christianity better than we can. Will you take a look at them and maybe write in the margins where the authors are wrong and why? Then maybe you can enlighten us and we can become happy and fulfilled, just like you!"

"Sure," Frank said as Wendel handed him several books. "I'm glad to help. Really, guys, disproving Christianity won't be very hard. I'll start with Genesis, and I'll show you why the creation story is an unscientific myth."

"That'll be great, Frank. You do that," Wendel said.

And Frank walked right into the trap.

When we arrived home from the airport, I saw the three books that Wendel had left with Frank. They were:

- *Mere Christianity* by British academic C.S. Lewis, which explains fundamental teachings of Christianity in an intellectual, deep way.
- *Evidence That Demands a Verdict* by Josh McDowell, which addresses challenges to belief and answers questions posed by non-Christians and doubters of faith.
- *Scientific Creationism* by Henry M. Morris, which outlined the scientific evidence of the origin of the universe and Earth from a creationist perspective.

When I saw the books back at our condo, I thought this was a good thing. Maybe Frank would get some answers to his questions because he had always had issues with religion.

Frank returned to pitching only eleven days after getting hit by the line drive in Los Angeles.

That was way too early. These days, baseball clubs "baby" pitchers' arms with pitch counts (no more than 100 pitches per game) and limit innings (no more than seven). Back then, starting pitchers were expected to throw every fourth game and keep throwing if they had a lead or a shutout going.

Even though Frank said his arm didn't feel right, there was a code of honor in the clubhouse that said if the manager pencils your name into the lineup, then you're starting. So Frank sucked it up and tried to do the best he could.

He got hammered on a road trip against teams in the NL West: Atlanta, San Diego, and San Francisco. Instead of getting sympathy or an acknowledgment that his tender elbow wasn't healed, there were whispers in the locker room:

- *He's blaming his bad outings on his arm.*
- *What a head case.*
- *If he doesn't get his act together soon, he's going to Indianapolis.*

Frank shielded me from the locker room gossip, but I could see the angst in his eyes. He was extremely unsettled as well as frustrated. If his arm didn't respond soon, then he'd probably need some kind of surgery—which was the great unknown.

On Saturday night, August 25, 1984, I was inside our Cincinnati condo while Frank was in Pittsburgh with the team. I watched the game on TV. Frank had been demoted to long relief, so unless Reds starter Jay Tibbs got shelled, I wasn't expecting my husband to pitch that night.

I made dinner—meatloaf and mashed potatoes—for Frankie and me while the game was on in the background. The Pirates won a close game, 5-3.

An hour or so after the final out, Frank called me from his hotel—
something he did nearly every night when on a road trip. He sounded
fine as we made small talk about Frankie, and then Frank's tone turned
serious.

"Honey, I need to tell you something."

Uh-oh. I didn't know what to expect.

"What is it?"

"I gave my life to Jesus Christ tonight, and you need to do the same."

I nearly dropped the phone. Once I caught myself, I thought for
a long moment. I didn't know how to respond. Several long seconds
passed by as many thoughts swirled through my head.

Suddenly, I blurted, "Frank, don't become a Jesus freak!"

"Honey, we've been living for the wrong reasons. We need to be
living for the Truth."

I didn't want to listen. The thought banging around my head like a
bell chime was this: *Your husband is a Jesus freak!*

Frank and I were as close as any married couple could be, but hearing him say that he had given his life to Christ felt like an intruder had
entered our relationship.

We talked a bit more, I looked for an excuse to get off the phone,
saying I needed to check on Frankie.

Four days later, I headed to the airport to pick up Frank at the end of
their road trip. I sat inside the terminal where the wives always congre-
gated, letting the kids run around and play as we waited for the players
to arrive. When the door opened, the players dressed in their dark suits
filed out as usual.

I looked for Frank to emerge and then I saw him and waved. He
walked toward me and the strangest thing happened! I couldn't help
but notice the happy countenance on his face, and his eyes that were
crystal blue and nearly sparkled. There was a look of peace on his face.

On the drive home, he described what happened in Pittsburgh:
while sitting on a commode in the visitor's locker room, thumbing
through *Evidence That Demands a Verdict*, Josh McDowell summed up
C.S. Lewis' three possibilities of who Jesus Christ really was: Jesus was
either a liar, a lunatic, or telling the truth.

"That's when I got it!" Frank exclaimed. "If Jesus wasn't a liar or a
lunatic, then He had to be telling the truth."

At the end of the chapter, there was a prayer for those who wanted to follow Jesus. Frank said he sat on that commode and prayed, "Lord, I want to be on your team. I want to commit my life to You."

I exhaled when Frank was done. "Wow, Frank, that's quite a story."

Quite frankly, I didn't know what to do with this admission, so I decided to watch Frank like a hawk.

Throughout the rest of the season, I noticed that something was different with Frank. His countenance had changed. He had a sense of calm about him, a more peaceful spirit. He stopped cussing too. (Ballplayers regularly use four-letter words as adjectives in every sentence.)

He was never much of a drinker or partier, but that sort of stuff no longer interested him. He seemed to have a newfound peace. While he was always a good husband, I certainly noticed that he was more attentive to me.

One morning, I went to the grocery store while Frank played with Frankie. Upon my return, he informed me he had thrown all the *Playboy* magazines away.

"You did *what*?" At the time, I didn't have a problem with *Playboy* magazine. In fact, I liked exploring my sexuality through the advice columns and articles.

As soon as he left for the ballpark, I dug them out of the trash. (I really did this.) When Frank came home after the game, he saw the stack of *Playboys* on the kitchen counter. His grimaced. He was disappointed with me.

He softly held my face and said, "Gina, I love and desire you. I want to make love to you without these images in our heads."

"There's nothing wrong with these *Playboys*. We're adults, and these magazines are staying!"

No sooner had the words left my mouth when I thought, *This man loves you and says he doesn't want* Playboys *in the house, and you're really saying this?*

I remember feeling convicted. Frank and I burned those *Playboys* in the fireplace to really get rid of them.

Frank was constantly reading his first Bible, the one Wendel had given him. My husband wanted to share what he was learning with me, his partner, but I wasn't interested.

I became very defensive. "I already know that," I'd say. "I've been Catholic all my life!"

"That's great, Gina, but what I'm talking about is having a personal relationship with Christ, of accepting him into your heart. Spirit-filled, if you like."

We agreed to disagree regarding the meaning of our sanctification and nature of our relationship with Christ.

Late in the season, Frank ask me to join him at a Bible study that some of the players and their wives attended, along with several Cincinnati Bengals and their wives. (Wendel was also the NFL team chaplain for the Bengals.) The Bible study was held at the home of Anthony Muñoz, a Bengal offensive tackle who was a year younger than Frank and grew up next-door to Upland in Ontario. He and Frank had a lot in common, having played baseball against each other when they were in school. Frank teased Anthony about playing at Chaffey High in Ontario instead of Damien before going on to play college football at USC.

Whenever Frank invited me to this couple study, I always bowed out gracefully. I figured they were all talking about me and trying to get me "saved." I didn't want to be around these people.

One day, while I was big and pregnant with Baby #2, Frank was on a road trip. The doorbell rang—and standing there was this Wendel Deyo guy along with Anthony Muñoz, who looked like the Incredible Hulk since he stood six-feet, six-inches tall and weighed 280 pounds.

"Hi, Gina," Wendel said. "This is Anthony Muñoz."

"Oh, hi, Anthony," I said, extending my right hand while Frankie held on to my leg. "Frank's been telling me how he enjoys the Bible studies at your house."

"Nice to meet you, Gina," Anthony said.

Wendel spoke next. "Would you mind if we came in for a visit?"

"Well, sure," I said, caught a bit off guard. "If you don't mind the mess."

It wasn't total disorder inside our condo, but I did have a three-year-old running around and toys all over the place.

I offered them a soft drink as we sat down at my dining room table. Wendel didn't waste much time after the small talk.

"Gina, what's holding you back from giving your life to Christ?" he asked.

"I was raised Catholic, so I know Christ," I responded.

Anthony spoke up. "I was raised Catholic too, so I know what you're going through. We can talk about any questions you might have."

Before I could answer, Wendel met my gaze. "It's all about believing this book," he said, tapping his fingers on a Bible he set on the table. "You either believe what this book says or you don't. It's totally your decision, but you've got to make it."

I thought for a moment. I know both of these godly gentlemen had something I didn't have. But I wasn't sure what that something was. I had a feeling that I wouldn't find out until I completely surrendered myself to God as Frank had. I also sensed deep inside that I was going through the motions when it came to church.

The rest of the conversation went downhill. I was defensive, snappy, and probably wasn't very pleasant to these gentlemen. After they left, I grappled with Wendel's pick-it-up-or-lay-it-down statement: Did I really believe everything in the Bible? Did I really take Jesus seriously enough? I had loved the Lord as a child, but had I pulled away from Him?

These questions prompted a lot of soul-searching. Frank, to his credit, gave me space. He gave me time to sort things out. In the meantime, I saw that his transformation wasn't a flash in the pan. Frank *had* changed. This wasn't a fad for him. He was taking his faith seriously.

I wasn't like Frank who surrendered his life to Christ in a moment. I took my time getting there, but I knew I was ready to make a decision to make Jesus No. 1 in my life while I was giving birth on October 31, 1984. The Halloween delivery was no trick or treat, which whipped up memories of nearly losing Frankie. In the midst of super painful contractions, I made a personal pact with Jesus in the delivery room: "You get me through this, and I will completely surrender my life to You. And to show You that I mean it, I will name this baby in Your honor."

And that's how Christina Pastore got her name.

18

Transition Time

The plea I made to the Lord before Christina's birth wasn't a foxhole prayer of convenience. I *knew* God had gotten me through tough times and dramatically changed Frank. The Lord also filled a hole in my heart because something was missing in my life.

Wendel kept in touch while we lived in our Upland home during the off-season. He told us that the way to grow as new believers was to read the Bible daily, pray about our needs, lift others to the Lord, and find a good church.

We were still attending St. Joseph's Catholic Church, more out of expediency than anything else. We both sensed we were ready to be part of a Bible-teaching church with contemporary music. Then I happened to run into Pam Lahr, an old friend who lived across the street from us. We got to talking about what was happening in our lives. When I mentioned the spiritual journey that Frank and I had been on, her face lit up.

"I know a great church right here in Upland," she said. "And Frank will love it because the pastor is a sports guy too. He used to play for the Oakland Raiders."

"What's the name of the church?"

"Life Bible Fellowship. Ray Schmautz, the pastor, preaches right from the Bible. He used to be a linebacker with the Raiders, so he knows what it's like to be a professional athlete."

Frank, who wasn't as tied to the Catholic Church as I was, was all for trying out a non-denominational, evangelical church. The electric guitars, bass, and drum set behind the worship singers resulted in a very different church experience than what we were used to. From our first Sunday, we loved worshipping at Life Bible Fellowship.

Mom and Dad were not excited about the change. They were

perturbed. Actually, they were angry. Once again, drama reigned in the Pignotti household. Voices were raised, and Dad demanded to know if we were "Jesus freaks," which caused Frank and I to shrug our shoulders and say guilty as charged. Mom complained that we were "Bible thumpers" and part of some cult.

What bothered my parents the most was that we were not raising our two children in the Catholic faith. We had Frankie and Christina baptized in the Catholic Church as infants in scenes that could have come right out of the movie *The Godfather*, but when we stopped going to St. Joe's, my parents thought we were leaving the one true apostolic church. Our decision to attend Life Bible Fellowship prompted arguments and ire.

We couldn't wait for spring training to come around so we could leave the latest round of family drama behind us. But once in Tampa, there was a new dramatic episode evolving: Could Frank still cut the mustard in the major leagues?

That question would be answered by Pete Rose, the prodigal son who'd returned to Cincinnati—after five seasons with the Philadelphia Phillies—and became the Reds' *player-manager*. Not only was Pete deciding the lineup and running the team, but he was playing every day and projected to break Ty Cobb's all-time hits record of 4,191 hits before the end of the 1985 season. (By the way, Rose is baseball's last player-manager.)

As for Frank's status, the good news was that my husband was a known commodity to Pete, who decided to bring Frank along slowly. He got his first start in late April against the Giants but didn't get the decision. Pete then had Frank coming out of the bullpen every week or so for a couple of innings. It was clear he was the forgotten member of the pitching staff—even I could see that Frank wasn't impressive. He still got batters out, but they have a saying in baseball: he was getting out of jams with smoke and mirrors. Guile—not overwhelming heat on the ball—was keeping him in the major leagues.

Frank appeared in just 17 games by the All-Star break. Even though he compiled a surprising 2-1 win-loss record, he kept complaining about his sore elbow after every stint on the mound. Each outing ended with a familiar refrain: "My elbow's killing me." Frank was miserable because of the shooting pain in his right arm.

The Reds' medical staff finally listened to him and agreed that something needed to be done. They arranged for Frank to fly out to Los Angeles to see Dr. Frank Jobe, the famed orthopedic surgeon known for pioneering "Tommy John" surgery, which is a repair of a torn elbow ligament. The kids and I accompanied Frank to Southern California and stayed in our Upland home.

A series of X-rays revealed bone chips and lots of calcium deposits, which earned a whistle of concern from Dr. Jobe.

"I recommend we operate," Dr. Jobe said.

"Good," Frank said. "I'm glad I'm going under the knife."

Frank was operated on the next day. Dr. Jobe paid a visit to the recovery room when he came out of anesthesia.

"Young man, that was about the dirtiest elbow I've ever worked on," said the surgeon to the stars, explaining that the line drive off Steve Sax's bat had broken off pieces of bone that had been floating around Frank's elbow area for a year. "It's a wonder you were able to pitch at all," Dr. Jobe said.

Frank took rehab seriously as we stuck around Southern California. When he returned for spring training, he was topping 90 miles per hour on his fastball, but hitters were feasting on his offerings anyway because his pitches had lost their "hop"—that wicked movement that comes just as the ball reaches the batter. The Reds released Frank at the end of spring training with another year to go on his long-term contract.

Then we caught a break: the Minnesota Twins picked up Frank for their bullpen. Frank actually pitched very well and at one point became their stopper. When the season was over, Frank had appeared in 33 games and compiled a strong 3-1 record.

Frank was a free agent after the 1986 season. He could sell his services to the highest bidder. Just one problem: the baseball owners—tired of paying escalating salaries due to free agency—decided to work together by *not* bidding against each other. This was known as "collusion," and years later, the owners would lose big in court.

At the time, though, Frank was just another small cog in a big wheel. By the start of the 1987 season, no team had extended an offer to Frank to play. The only thing Frank's agent could do for him was get him a tryout with the Texas Rangers' Triple A affiliate, the Oklahoma City 89ers.

You get four starts, Pastore. If you don't blow us away with your talent, you're out of here.

Frank started four games, performed so-so, and that was it. He was released and out of baseball.

He was thirty years old.

Frank left baseball with only one record: eating a 72-ounce steak faster than anyone else in the whole world.

Huh?

Here's what happened. Whenever Frank drove cross-country, which happened a lot during his early years of pro ball, he'd stop at the Big Texan, a classic Route 66 steakhouse in Amarillo, Texas. The Big Texan was famous for its Steak Challenge: eat a 72-ounce Texas steak and all the trimmings—shrimp cocktail, dinner salad, roll and butter, and a baked potato—in under an hour, and your meal was free. Otherwise, pony up. (The cost today is $72.)

Frank said, "I'll take that challenge!"

The first time Frank tried to eat four-and-a-half pounds of Texas steak happened when he was driving toward Tampa and spring training in 1976. Inside the Big Texan, he astounded onlookers by finishing the meal in only twenty-one minutes! The following fall, after Instructional League, he made a beeline for Amarillo. This time, Frank took his last bite of steak in nineteen minutes. Over the years, he finished the Steak Challenge in seventeen, fifteen minutes, thirteen, and eleven minutes, each time setting an all-time record at the Big Texan.

The secret? It was all in the wrist, Frank said. The cutting motion was like throwing a nasty slider.

When the Rangers organization let Frank go in May 1987, my husband knew that this was probably his last chance to step up to the plate—a plate with a huge slab of beef hanging over the edges. While driving back to California to be reunited with us, Frank had his mind focused on setting a new record that no one would ever be able to touch—breaking the ten-minute barrier. Like the four-minute mile, they said it could never be done.

Word spread quickly throughout the restaurant: Frank Pastore was in the house. My husband brought his A-game to the table that night; he ate like there was no tomorrow. The shrimp cocktail, dinner salad and roll, and baked potato were dispatched in a mere minute or two. Then Frank narrowed his gaze and set his sights on the 72-ounce steak, cooked medium rare, just how he liked it.

Showing deft dexterity with his fork and knife, Frank sliced his way into the monstrous steak with a vengeance, like a man possessed. As fans cheered him on, Frank kept biting and chewing—practically inhaling—his steak. He would not be denied.

It turned out to be no contest. If this was a prizefight, the bout would have stopped in the first round. Frank knocked off the steak and all the trimmings in nine-and-a-half minutes, setting a new world record.

That esteemed mark stood up for a long time—twenty-one years in fact—until the greatest competitive eater of all time, the great Joey "Jaws" Chestnut, ranked No. 1 by the International Federation of Competitive Eating and perennial winner of Nathan's Famous Hot Dog Eating Contest held every Fourth of July at Coney Island in New York City, took Frank down on March 25, 2008, finishing the Steak Challenge in 8:52. The future Hall of Fame eater broke the nine-minute barrier, once thought to be impossible.

Frank was surpassed by a professional eater who trained and made a living in the niche world of "competitive eating," which didn't exist when he was playing baseball.

"The professional eaters take the fun out of gluttony," Frank quipped. "Then again, records are made to be broken."

Turns out "Jaws" Chestnut's record was eclipsed as well—by a 120-pound woman! Molly Schuyler, a competitive eater from Sacramento, California, shattered—if I can use that word—the old record by eating the Big Texan steak dinner in four minutes, fifty-eight seconds in 2015. And then to show off, she ate *another* 72-ounce steak, baked potato, a side salad, a dinner roll, and a shrimp cocktail in *ten minutes*.

But Frank held the record longer than anyone—and is still remembered today because of two shows airing on the Food Network: *Craziest Restaurants in America* and *Man vs. Food*. Every now and then, one of those shows will re-air a segment about the Big Texan restaurant and show Frank's baseball card and describe how he wolfed down the Big Texan dinner faster than anyone in the 1970s and 1980s.

I still run into people who say they saw Frank on the Food Network, which explains why my husband often joked he was more famous for eating the Big Texan 72-ounce steak in record time than for anything he did in baseball.

When Frank was pitching in Cincinnati, one of the things he liked doing was public speaking or being an MC at sports banquets or fund-raising events. He seemed to have a natural gift for gab, and I don't mean that in a negative sense. Frank was one of those guys who never seemed flustered when facing an audience and having to come up with something to say. I'm glad he enjoyed public speaking because standing before a crowd was the *last* thing I wanted to do.

Frank got asked to speak a lot when he was a major league base-ball player, and those opportunities increased exponentially when he became a Christian in 1984. When Frank was told that he had a "great testimony," he didn't know what that meant, but he soon discovered that he liked sharing how he came to faith—preceded by the crazy story of how we eloped. As word got around, speaking requests poured in.

This was our introduction to the so-called "evangelical" world inhab-ited by people like evangelist Billy Graham, the Christian Broadcast Network's Pat Robertson, actor and singer Pat Boone, and contem-porary Christian artists like Sandi Patty and Amy Grant. As Frank received pats on the back, I heard him say, "I feel called to ministry!"

Hearing that freaked me out. I wasn't moving our family to Africa and becoming a missionary. Couldn't God figure out something else for Frank to do? I knew my husband was an extremely gifted man: intel-ligent, well read, a born leader, and an articulate speaker. Many people noticed these attributes as well and suggested he go into broadcasting baseball, but Frank wasn't having it. "I don't want to do that," he said. "I want to teach people about Truth—the things that really matter!"

"Yeah, but how do you get paid to do that?" I asked.

"I don't know," Frank said, "but I have the rest of my life to figure it out."

That was his attitude when his baseball career was over. Frank wasn't bummed that he could no longer pitch, even though the baseball life was all he had known since he was seventeen years old, when he was drafted and signed out of high school.

In fact, Frank rubbed his hands in glee when we returned to our home in Upland. I was caught up in the excitement of a new beginning as well, although I didn't know how we were going to pay for it. At least we would get a chance to experience what "real life" was all about, and we could stay in one place and not live half the year in one part of the country and half the year in our hometown.

Plus, we could become a "regular" family—with Frank working during the day and all of us having dinner together in the evening. Frankie was turning six years old and finishing kindergarten, and Christina was an active preschooler.

The first thing Frank did was enroll at National University, taking night classes at the Irvine campus in Orange County. We lived off our savings and a few key investments. Instead of our money working for us, however, our "investment opportunities" went south, which placed more financial pressure on us. While he worked on earning an accelerated two-year degree in business, Frank got a job selling computers with Digital Equipment Corporation, a major player in the computer industry since the 1960s.

At first, the job with Digital was cushy: playing golf and wining and dining clients. But as the company's fortunes changed in the fast-moving computer industry in the late 1980s, Frank had to hit the pavement and actually *sell* computer systems, which wasn't his natural gift.

Still, a job was a job. While making a cold call to the Campus Crusade for Christ headquarters in San Bernardino one morning, Frank was routed to their sports director.

"Wendel Deyo," said the man on the other end of the line.

Frank nearly dropped the phone. He was shocked to be put back in touch with the person who led him to a personal relationship with Jesus Christ. They hit it off and reconnected. When Frank told me what happened, he thought it was more than a coincidence that put him back in touch with Wendel—it was divine intervention.

Frank wasn't very happy or fulfilled selling business computers. He and Wendel got to talking, and over the next few months, his old mentor suggested that Frank come on staff at Athletes in Action. Although Frank would have to raise his own support, we felt this was where God was leading us.

The following year, we moved to Cincinnati because—coincidence again—Athletes in Action moved their headquarters from Southern California to Ohio. The fact that we were comfortable with Cincinnati and knew many people there raised our comfort level with the move.

Frank began leading Bible studies in greater Cincinnati, and Wendel and others encouraged him to think about going to seminary because it was obvious that Frank was born to teach. Wendel figured Frank would attend a seminary somewhere in Ohio, but after researching his options, Frank chose Talbot Seminary on the campus of Biola University in La Mirada, thirty miles from our home in Upland. Frank could commute to school.

I was naturally thrilled to return to our old house in Upland. Frank enrolled in Talbot's School of Theology to work on a master's degree in Philosophy and Ethics. To bring in some money while he studied, Frank gave private pitching lessons in our backyard, which paid handsomely on a per-hour basis. Frank didn't have time to give more than a dozen or so lessons per week, but his young students loved learning from a former major leaguer and saw great improvement. Frank was a born teacher.

Frank then had another idea to save money: commute to Talbot on a motorcycle. He'd been trying for years to get me to say yes to a motorcycle. Each time, I put my foot down. "Too dangerous," I declared. Frank eventually won me over with his childhood story of never receiving the purple Sting-Ray bike he had asked his parents to get him.

When my father heard that Frank was studying philosophy at a seminary, he thought we'd finally gone off the deep end. "Howya goin' to make money with a philosophy degree?" Dad asked over a family dinner one evening.

"God will take care of us, Dad," Frank replied, which elicited another rolling of the eyes. Then my father muttered something about "those Jesus freaks" while taking another bite of Mom's chicken cacciatore.

Frank had one thing going for him at Talbot: he wasn't the typical seminary student. Let me outline the ways Frank was different:

- He was in his early thirties, so he was older than most students.
- He didn't wear a suit or even a dress shirt.
- He rode a motorcycle to class.
- He still dipped tobacco!

I know I haven't mentioned this before, but Frank had started chewing "smokeless" tobacco after he turned pro in high school. Back then, "dipping," as it was called, meant inserting a pinch of snuff between the cheek and gum inside the mouth. That gave Frank a strong nicotine hit, so he tempered things by wrapping a piece of watermelon chewing gum around a wad of Skoal smokeless tobacco and inserting *that* into his mouth.

I actually didn't mind Frank chewing or dipping tobacco because I had been around baseball so long. I was used to watching Frank spew a stream of tobacco juice while he looked toward the catcher for a sign. Frank had become addicted to the stuff during his first season in the minor leagues, taking on the dipping habit because everyone else seemed to chew tobacco in professional baseball. This was a way he could fit in with the other players.

I'm sure the Talbot professors had never seen a student with a chaw of tobacco plugged in the side of his mouth nor a student sitting in the back of the classroom, holding an empty aluminum soft-drink can to spit into. But that was Frank, who was also loud, eager, outspoken, and super friendly.

(When Frank was playing, both of us were unaware of the dangers of chewing tobacco, which greatly increases the risk of cancer of the mouth, irritates gums, and makes your teeth more vulnerable to cavities. Frank quit chewing in the late 1990s and kept only one vice: smoking the occasional cigar.)

Like Frank, I felt like I didn't fit into the Talbot scene either. I got an indication of that whenever I attended a "meet and greet" reception at Talbot, where I would chat with people on staff. As part of small talk, I would invariably hear this question: "So, Gina, how did you and Frank meet?"

Well, you can imagine the look on their faces when I related our eloping story, warts and all. I got good at picking up on the "Christian wince," which was a non-verbal way of saying, *Oh, you're not as pure as we thought you were.*

But Frank's time at Talbot wasn't all for naught. After a couple of years, Dr. Dennis Dirks, the dean of Talbot Seminary, asked Frank to head up a program that gave seminary students a chance to teach lay people in local churches. Frank respected Dr. Dirks, a man of genuine character, and that's how the Talbot Institute of Biblical Studies (TIBS) was born in 1995.

There was just one glitch: since TIBS was a lay program, there was nothing in the university budget to pay Frank a salary. He would have to raise his own support.

We'd been down that road before with Athletes in Action. We rolled up our sleeves and formed Team Pastore. I helped with many of the day-to-day administrative details and fundraising duties while Frank and other Talbot professors taught in local churches as part of the TIBS program. I also collected the $40 fee for classes, which helped keep us afloat and pay other professors.

The TIBS program was a huge success. Over a four-year time, more than 6,000 paying adults took one of our TIBS classes held at one of the twenty-six churches hosting the program. Frank was teaching at least twice a week and was receiving speaking requests, so he was getting his name out there.

Warren Duffy, the host of the *Duffy & Company, Live from L.A.* show broadcast daily on KKLA 99.5 FM, heard about some of the great things Frank was doing. Duffy, as everyone called him, interviewed Frank several times on the air and got to know my husband even better when KKLA did a "live remote" from Biola on occasion. Duane Patterson, Duffy's producer, thought Frank was a natural at radio and saw how easily Frank talked over the airwaves.

"Have you ever thought about guest-hosting before?" Duane asked one time.

"Uh, no," Frank said.

"Wanna give it a try?"

"Sure, why not?" Frank replied. "You'll have to coach me."

Frank was always up for something new, and he also liked the opportunity. Instead of "teaching" dozens at a time, as in a classroom setting, Frank could reach tens of thousands of people within the sound of his voice.

And that's how Frank got his start in radio. Duane took Frank under his wing and showed him how to open shows, segue into segments, introduce guests, go into commercials, and do wrap-ups.

Over the next seven years, Frank drove to Duffy's studio at a Huntington Beach strip mall and sat behind the microphone more than one hundred times as the guest host of *Live from L.A.*, which is where Frank cut his teeth in radio broadcasting and learned the craft. Not only did Frank get good at being on the air, but this led to other broadcasting opportunities, like the time he was asked to guest-host a political talk show that was catching fire: the *Hugh Hewitt Show*.

With all this on-the-ground experience in radio and the ongoing success of TIBS, Frank thought he had a winning idea: go national with a radio talk show broadcast from Biola under the college's auspices. Frank even lined up a donor willing to give $1 million in seed money to make it happen. Dr. Dirks, the Talbot dean, and Biola president Dr. Clyde Cook were in Frank's corner, telling him to go for it.

That's all the encouragement Frank needed. While Frank worked on launching a national radio show under the Talbot banner, my husband juggled other balls. Besides leading classes for TIBS twice a week and guest-hosting for Warren Duffy and Hugh Hewitt, Frank taught an undergraduate apologetics class at Biola and spoke at church conferences and men's retreats on weekends.

And then we were thrown a curveball.

In baseball terms, we got screwed.

While Frank was doing all this great work and finding his way in radio, we didn't know there was a "political situation" brewing in the background at the university. A group of people wanted to overthrow Dr. Cook, the Biola president.

Frank was asked to join in and heard all kinds of petty complaints about Dr. Cook. It was implied, if he didn't join in, that he'd be cut off from certain avenues of ministry. Frank didn't like playing power games; that wasn't his style. He felt a loyalty to Dr. Cook. When Frank said "no" to joining in with the anti-Cook group, they began to undermine him by saying Frank was a "loose cannon" and "not a team player."

All our eggs were in the Biola basket—TIBS, the undergrad teaching, the radio show, the speaking engagements, even our son Frankie's college education. After graduating from Damien High with a 4.5 GPA, Frankie was attending Biola—an expensive private college—at a reduced rate because of Frank's position at the university. The good deal would end if Frank didn't get on board.

During the midst of the upheaval, Frank was invited to appear on *Politically Incorrect*, a late-night, half-hour political talk show hosted by Bill Maher on the ABC network.

The format was simple: Bill Maher, a passionate liberal, and another guest—always a liberal—would gang up to debate the topic of the day with an inept and inarticulate conservative guest. The "debates" were about as one-sided as the lions versus the Christians in the Colosseum.

Frank knew the odds were stacked against him and relished the opportunity to marshal his worldview and passionately debate the other side in the public square. Within the supercharged atmosphere on the set that day, Frank more than held his own. Even Bill Maher was impressed and said so when the cameras stopped taping.

Frank's appearance on *Politically Incorrect* was just the opening that the anti-Dr. Cook forces needed. They thought Frank mixing it up with an in-your-face, anti-God apologist like Bill Maher was unseemly. They felt Frank's appearance on a secular show did not reflect well on Biola University and Christendom and voiced their complaints to Dr. Cook, either in person or in writing.

Dr. Cook, who was fighting to keep his job, had no choice: he had to throw Frank overboard. On October 15, 1999, he asked another high-level administrator to deliver the bad news to my husband: Frank and Biola University were parting ways. No more radio show, no more TIBS classes, no more undergraduate teaching, and no more tuition discount for Frankie. He was being blackballed.

I was beyond crushed when Frank phoned me with the news.

We were shattered once again.

Frank was finished with all this crap. "Screw ministry!" he spat.

There wasn't much I could say. I was in a state of grief, crying throughout the day for weeks. Frank had lost his ministry career as well as his Biola family, his salary, and our son's scholarship. We felt slimed. But even worse, I couldn't get it out of my mind—the idea that my once-vibrant, evangelical husband now wanted nothing to do with ministry. That was such a shame!

At the beginning, I didn't want Frank to "go into ministry" because I didn't know what that meant, but after seeing how thousands and thousands of people reacted to being taught by Frank, I knew this was God's calling on his life. Even the Talbot professors loved him, but now Frank was *persona non grata*.

Frank was right: teaching people Truth was what mattered, but the rug had been pulled out from underneath him.

Why was this happening?

What would we do now?

And who could we trust?

At the time, we were in a small group with several couples from Talbot that included Walt and Marty Russell, who had become very good friends. Walt was a Biblical Studies professor at Talbot, while Marty was Frank's assistant with the TIBS program.

The Russells and our friends in the small group were people we could trust. One of those in our small group had a great suggestion. "Frank, why don't you go to counseling?" she said. "I know the perfect person to help you through this. You have been wronged, and we don't want to see you get bitter."

I wondered what good a counselor would do. Growing up, when my parents would have their terrible fights, I remembered going to my father and saying "Dad, maybe you and Mom should go to a counselor. Maybe a priest or something?"

My dad snapped back at me, "Counselors are for crazy people, and we're not crazy!"

Then, after Frank and I became Christians, there were church leaders who dismissed counseling as "worldly nonsense," even claiming it wasn't a Christian practice. Our friend in our small group suggested that Frank see a female counselor who taught at Talbot and was a former missionary. She seemed safe enough.

Frank began meeting with Dr. Betsy Barber at the Biola Counseling Center once a week. What Frank learned through this process was life-changing . . . and would help connect the dots of his life. Every week, after he returned from his session with Dr. Barber, he'd share with me the interesting things that came out that day: how being a latchkey child at age four affected him; how his mother's deception caused him to seek Truth; and how he was tolerant of "colorful people" with personality disorders because of his mom. He came to realize he was loyal to Biola because he was seeking to be a part of their "family," just as he had been loyal to his mother all those years. But just as he had gotten duped by his mom, he was being duped by this place.

Rather than projecting his anger on the university, Frank made the wise decision to focus on himself. He trusted Dr. Barber, and she ministered to my husband for a little over a year in a small, quiet room in a building at the epicenter of where Frank suffered rejection.

With all that Frank had learned about himself, I wanted to experience this process too, so I began seeing Dr. Barber after Frank's last session. Our sessions helped connect the dots of *my* life, and through this process I became a more integrated, mature woman.

Meanwhile, life went on. Frank ramped up his pitching lessons in our backyard and took on more students, including a young pitcher of promise named Steven Wright. Coaching was how he supported our family, and I was proud of him. He also continued to fill in for Duffy on *Live from L.A.*, which brought in a few bucks.

Frank then decided to do something he had always wanted to do: earn his Ph.D. in political philosophy so that he could go on and teach. During this time, we used the term "Let go and let God," which meant that Frank had to let go of trying to have a "ministry."

This period was one of the most profound times of Frank's life. Along with working on his doctorate, he sat for *hours* and listened to tapes of Christian philosopher Dallas Willard in our garage while he polished our cars and his motorcycle, all the while puffing on a cigar. The great Dallas Willard ministered to my husband in the most profound way on various topics: waiting on God, searching your soul, the art of forgiveness, and living in the Kingdom. Meanwhile, I started attending our local community college, thinking that would do me some good.

This was a fertile time when we focused on what God was doing in us, our children, and our circle of trusted friends. There were no more illusions, no more "setting ourselves up for failure" by trying to fit in with people who had hidden agendas.

When we let go and let God, we didn't know that God had something huge planned for Frank's life.

19

Pick-Off Move

Being counseled by Dr. Barber changed my life in many ways, all for the better. Our sessions initiated a process that helped me "find my voice," which may sound like a cliché but was an important step toward the person I am today.

Think about it: getting married at sixteen propelled a young girl who should have been starting her junior year of high school into the adult world. While eloping certainly matured me, it also robbed me of a certain amount of confidence that comes from working your way through various stages of life: finishing high school, going on to college, getting that first job, locating a place to live, finding your mate, planning a wedding, and starting a new family.

Dr. Barber helped me work through my feelings of disappointment following Frank's abrupt departure from Biola. When I said I wanted to write a letter to Dr. Clyde Cook, the Biola president, to describe how the turn of events made me feel, she was all for it.

I sat at my desk in our home office and poured out my heart, explaining the hurt and betrayal that Frank and I felt. "It's not the fact that you didn't want to go forward with the Biola radio show or didn't want Frank there any longer, but it's *how* you went about it," I wrote.

I was surprised when, just two days later, I received a very kind note from Dr. Cook that basically said, "You're right. An apology is in order for the way things were handled."

His expression of regret paved the way for me to forgive Dr. Cook, which I did in my heart. Over the next couple of years, Frank and I would develop a bond—not a strong one but a bond nonetheless—with him and his wife, Anna Belle. On one occasion, we ran into them at a fundraising event in Orange County and ended up chatting for a couple of hours afterwards. Our interaction helped me connect several more dots. It was all very healing.

We maintained a cordial relationship until Dr. Cook retired from Biola in 2007 and was succeeded by Dr. Barry Corey, who came to Biola from Gordon-Conwell Theological Seminary. We were stunned when, less than a year later, Dr. Cook suddenly died of a massive heart attack. Even though Dr. Cook knew a few people who didn't highly regard his leadership at Biola, he maintained 100 percent support from the Board of Trustees and went on to become the longest-sitting president in Biola's history. Frank and I were glad we had healed and mended our association with this man of great integrity.

Meanwhile, life went on after our chapter at Biola ended. We started attending Calvary Chapel Chino Valley and loved the teaching of Pastor David Rosales. Frank was pursuing his Ph.D. in Political Philosophy and American Government from Claremont Graduate School, just a few miles from our Upland home.

Frank absolutely loved the classes at Claremont Grad School. He would come home in the most exuberant mood, having soaked up everything he could. He delighted in the mentoring he received from Dr. Harry Jaffa, the foremost scholar on Abraham Lincoln in the world. Dr. Charles Kessler also knocked his socks off. They were academics dripping in knowledge and wisdom, and they inspired Frank to love our American heritage even more.

One of the more interesting relationships that formed during Frank's time at Claremont was his connection with Dr. Jean Schroedel, a feminist and author of *Is the Fetus a Person? A Comparison of Policies Across the Fifty States.* She was quite liberal, but her knowledge of American Government was impressive. Frank relished learning from her as well. For one year, he devoured many books, wrote just as many papers, and was immersed in learning political philosophy.

At this time in the early 2000s, Duane Patterson started producing the *Hugh Hewitt Show,* which was really finding its sweet spot. Whenever Hugh Hewitt was on vacation or needed to take the day off, Duane asked Frank to fill in as the guest host. Expounding on political topics on the air was really in Frank's wheelhouse. From picking up a few dollars as a guest host to tutoring kids on pitching to doing a few speaking gigs, we were paying the bills.

The long-range goal was for Frank to finish his Ph.D. and search for a teaching position at a university. Whether that teaching position would materialize after Frank was blackballed by Biola University was something we didn't know—and couldn't control.

While Frank was at Claremont Grad School in 2003, we heard that Warren Duffy was going to "hang up his cleats" and retire from radio. Duffy had lost his precious wife, Terry, to cancer, so he was ready to step back from the grind of hosting a daily talk show on KKLA.

Duffy gave the Salem Radio Network, which owned KKLA, a year's notice to find a replacement host, which touched off a scramble since the 4-7 p.m. afternoon drive-time slot in car-centric Los Angeles was prime real estate for any radio program. This was a plum job in the country's No. 2 media market.

Well-meaning friends would say to us, "So Frankie, you gonna throw your hat in the ring?"

"I don't think so," Frank would say.

Privately, to me, Frank said there was no way he would be hired to sit in Duffy's chair behind the KKLA microphone. "Who starts in L.A.?" Frank asked. He understood that many radio personalities pay their dues in the backwater cities and work their way up into larger "markets." We also knew the competition would be stiff. Frank heard that a lot of radio veterans and popular names in Southern California were applying for the job.

At the same time, I believed Frank was born for this job. He was the perfect person to host a five-day-a-week radio talk show with a Christian worldview and was capable of articulating and applying that worldview to a changing world.

Tempering our excitement was our reluctance to dive back into the so-called "evangelical world," which was known for its politics and intrigue. *Once bitten, twice shy* was our attitude. Frank was leery because of the fakery he'd seen. We didn't seem to fit in with that world, but that didn't mean we weren't willing to give it another shot if Frank were to become the new talk show host.

One day while Frank was thinking about what to do next, he received a call from Duane. The two talked shop for a few minutes, but Duffy's looming departure was a big deal in the radio world, so the conversation quickly came around to whom the replacement would be. When

Duane unexpectedly asked Frank if he wanted the job, my husband responded that he didn't think he was the right guy.

"Ah, Frank, go ahead and audition," Duane said. "It can't hurt."

So Frank tossed his baseball cap into the ring, never thinking he'd get Duffy's old job. The real reason he applied was because he thought auditioning would open up opportunities to fill in whenever the new host couldn't do the show.

Frank was invited to guest host the *Live from L.A.* several times . . . as a "tryout." Frank knew he was being watched closely, just like back at Damien High when scouts in the grandstands took notes of every pitch Frank made. As usual, Frank was himself on the air—animated, engaging, energetic, and knowledgeable about the issues. He asked insightful questions of his guests that sparked lively discussions, and he interacted well with listeners who called in to the show.

Just after Labor Day in 2003, Frank was cramming to finish up his final semester at Claremont and writing his most important papers. He received a courtesy call from Terry Fahy, the vice president and general manager at KKLA, who informed Frank that Salem was narrowing down the "candidates" for the position and that Frank was still in the running. In fact, they asked Frank if he was available to audition again, but this time for a full week—starting on Monday.

When Frank relayed the conversation to me, my first thought was, *Wow, there's a chance Frank could really get this job.* I tried to keep my cool and my expectations lowered. The following week, Frank did his thing at KKLA and thought his time behind the microphone went very well, but he couldn't tell what the honchos at KKLA were thinking.

A month later, on a Monday evening, Terry Fahy called our home asking for Frank. My husband was in the garage, puttering away.

"Let me go get him," I said.

I put the phone down—then dashed into the garage flushed with excitement. This could be the phone call we've been waiting for.

"Honey, it's Terry Fahy on the line!" I was smiling from ear to ear, but my ever-practical and humble husband said, "Gina, he's probably going to thank me for sitting in and tell me they're going with someone else."

Frank walked into the kitchen and placed the phone to his ear.

"Hi, Frank. Good to be in touch again. Hey, we were wondering if you could come in for a little meeting," Terry said.

"Sure," Frank replied. "When would you like to see me?"

I could tell from Frank's body language that something good was happening. When I heard several dates being bantered about, it could only mean good news—he was still in the running.

When Frank hung up, he said, "They want to see me."

"Yes!" I jumped.

"Don't get too excited. They might be bringing me in to let me know that I'm not their guy but thank me all the same."

On the day of the meeting, scheduled for the late afternoon, Frank and I were planning to attend a Claremont Institute dinner that evening with our friends Mike and Joanie Morrell. I arranged for the Morrells to pick me up and drive me to the dinner, where we would wait for Frank's arrival after his "little" meeting with Terry Fahy and KKLA program director Chuck Tyler.

At 6 o'clock, I was sitting in the back of the Morrell's SUV when Frank called my cell. My body shivered with excitement. Could this be it?

"Honey, I got the job!"

"Frank, this is unbelievable!"

I cried—and when Joanie turned toward me in the back seat and I nodded, she cried as well. She and Mike were good friends, politically minded, and wanted Frank on the airwaves.

"We have to keep this quiet until the station makes an official statement," Frank said.

"Got it," I said.

I thanked Frank for the call and said we'd see him soon.

When we arrived at the Claremont Institute, we visited with a lot of dear friends. I didn't say anything about Frank becoming the new talk show host at KKLA—for the first five minutes.

Sorry, Frank!

The *Frank Pastore Show* debuted on January 5, 2004, on KKLA 99.5 FM.

Frank took to radio like a rainbow trout takes to a cold-water stream—naturally and beautifully. The bosses, who didn't really know him very well, watched him like a hawk.

How would he handle this new platform, knowing that millions of listeners were in range of the sound of his voice? Would he let the visibility go to his head or mar his judgment?

On Frank's end, he was feeling out the new landscape. I mean, this was the biggest microphone, the largest Christian talk show in the United States. Within the first couple of months, Frank, Terry, and Chuck felt like the show was settling into a good rhythm, and the three men began enjoying a wonderful run. They became colleagues and good buddies.

In the meantime, our son, Frankie, was in dental school at UCLA, and our daughter, Christina, was taking classes at a local community college, still living at home. Frankie, who came home many weekends, popped in one Friday night and said, "Mom, Dad, I have someone I'd like you guys to meet."

Frank and I looked at each other, each thinking the same thing: *Hmmm, this sounds interesting. It must be a girl!*

The following week, we planned to meet Frankie and his new "friend" at the studio, and then after the show we'd go out to dinner. I drove in with Frank and sat with "Producer Pat" and "Engineer Annie" as Frank did the show. During a break, Frankie walked in with a stunning blonde named Jessica Dangerfield. No, she wasn't related to the famous comedian, but we could tell that Frankie was giving her a lot of respect.

After the show, we drove to Pasadena and sat down at a family favorite restaurant—El Cholo Café on Colorado Boulevard. We sat in a booth, and all I can say is that Frank and I fell in love with Jessica that night. Our son seemed smitten too. The bluebirds were singing.

It didn't surprise me when Frankie and Jessica got engaged a few months later. Life was good. Frank was gaining respect in the radio industry, and listeners loved him. The increased visibility meant a lot of people wanted to reach Frank for one reason or another, or to ask him to preach on a Saturday night or Sunday morning in local churches. It wasn't long before he was preaching all over Southern California several weekends a month.

To help Frank manage his schedule, I took on the role of his personal assistant: answering his e-mails (about three hundred a day, sometimes more); booking his speaking engagements; and accompanying him to live remotes during the week and churches on weekends.

We developed good relationships with executives and management from companies that advertised on the show: Applied Financial Planning, American Vision Windows, Galpin Ford, Berglund & Johnson Law Firm, and Phil Liberatore IRS Problem Solvers—the list was a long one.

Frank and I often reflected on how all the things in his past had shaped him for this job: playing professional baseball in the major leagues, which meant he was used to being in the public eye and hearing cheers as well as criticism; learning to deal with adversity, which happens in baseball and in life; going through counseling after the Biola debacle, which gave him a broader perspective of the big picture; and earning two advanced degrees, which gave him the confidence to debate in the public square. God was using it all!

Frank, a good listener, also turned out to be an excellent interviewer, kick-starting conversations with the likes of Dr. James Dobson, Chuck Colson, Joni Eareckson Tada, and Jim Daly, and many popular pastors like Greg Laurie, John MacArthur, and Francis Chan. I think Frank enjoyed his interviews with his old mentor, Dallas Willard, the most though. Dallas's smooth, soft teaching made for instructive radio. Frank was also very good at discerning who'd make a good guest.

Lastly, Frank loved taking calls from his listeners. Since Frank made no attempt to disguise his conservative theological and political views, he was a lightning rod, especially in election years. Many Los Angeles residents are liberally bent, so when Frank would espouse or explain the conservative point of view, the call lines would light up with callers wanting to take Frank to task.

After a verbal tussle or two, Frank had a way of calming down his callers. By the end of many of these phone calls, they either agreed to disagree or were carrying on like the best of friends. Frank was good with people because he loved people.

The year 2006 was a big one for the *Frank Pastore Show*: Frank won the National Religious Broadcaster's "Radio Talk Show of the Year" award, just two years after the first broadcast.

Even bigger, though, was the joy we experienced when Frankie married Jessica in Temecula, sixty miles southeast of Upland, on June

24, 2006. Temecula, blessed with a favorable climate for growing grapes, was home to forty wineries. Frankie and Jessica pledged their love to each other in a gorgeous setting with acres of vineyards as a backdrop. We were surrounded by family and close friends who joined us for the weekend to celebrate this joyous occasion. Two years later, we received more wonderful news: Jessica was pregnant! Michael John Pastore was born June 11, 2009, healthy and happy as can be.

The year 2006 was tempered, however, by the loss of my precious father. Dad had been in failing health in recent years, dealing with a common form of memory loss known as vascular dementia, caused by an impaired supply of blood to the brain. When he died at the age of seventy-seven, more than seven hundred people showed up at St. Joe's for his funeral. He was a great man who impacted countless others, and while we had our differences, I loved him deeply. Mom continued to live in our old family house around the corner from our home.

Following my father's passing, Frank interviewed his friend Greg Laurie, the famed pastor and evangelist behind the Harvest Crusades, on the show one afternoon. When they were finished, Greg said to my husband, "Hey, Frank, have you ever thought about writing your story?"

"No, man, I don't have the time for that!" Frank replied.

"That's why you need a writer. I have a good one for you—Ellen Vaughn. She does a lot of my books."

After Greg left, Frank did a Google search of Ellen. Besides being a prolific author in her own right, he noticed that she'd collaborated with Chuck Colson, who converted to Christianity following his role in the Watergate scandal as President Nixon's special counsel.

Frank found Ellen's website, hit her Contact button, typed out an email, and sent it off, thinking he probably wouldn't hear back from her for days, if at all. Greg had said she was very busy and picked her projects carefully.

By the time he drove his motorcycle on the 210 and came roaring up the driveway, Ellen had replied: *Sure, I'm interested. Tell me more,* she wrote.

This was the start of a great association between Frank and Ellen on the collaboration of *Shattered*. Focus on the Family/Tyndale House published the book in 2010, and when my husband's autobiography hit the streets, Frank became busier than he'd ever been. The success of

Shattered and news of his NRB award resulted in a lot of out-of-state speaking requests too.

The hits kept right on coming . . . and 2011 was another big year. Frank won the NRB's "Radio Talk Show of the Year" for a second time, and then our daughter Christina came home one day and said, "I want you guys to meet Josh, my boyfriend."

We met them at Outback Steakhouse in Upland for dinner. Christina had a few serious boyfriends dating back to her sophomore year of high school—boys who Frank and I liked—but this one seemed different. Josh Smallwood was mature, serious about life, and seriously smitten with our daughter.

When Frank and I left the restaurant, he said, "I like this guy, I like him a lot." Protective Papa gave his approval. Several months later, Christina and Josh were married in a sunset ceremony at Laguna Beach. When the barefoot wedding party walked onto the beach, the tide was rolling in and even hit our feet. Our close friend Bruce Erickson, a pastor from Life Bible Fellowship, performed the ceremony. We held the reception at Las Brisas, a Mexican restaurant overlooking the Pacific Ocean.

When we waved goodbye as Josh and Christina drove off to their honeymoon, the realization hit me that Frank and I were officially "empty nesters" since Christina had been living with us before she got married.

Frank was thrilled to enter into this new season of marriage. I had a bit of a hard time as I grieved the empty house, although the kids would come over often and spend the night. Life was good. Life was so good.

Frank loved getting on his Honda motorbike every mid-morning and going to work and seeing the people he worked with. Every day, as he came out of the elevator inside the high-rise building in Glendale that was home to the KKLA offices and studios, Frank would march over to Terry Fahy's office, passing Terry's assistant and saying, "Hi Boss!" He *loved* working for Salem Radio.

After checking in with Terry, he'd head over to his cubicle, stopping to talk with the sales team and the Salem L.A. staff, giving giant hugs to Balvina, Victoria, Big Wave Dave, Richard, Bob, Katherine, Donna, Chuck, Big Sean, JJ, Dann, Bill, Erica, Lara, and so many others.

Frank shared his radio studio with the great Dennis Prager, host of the *Dennis Prager Show*. Dennis would stay in the studio afterwards, taping commercials and talking to his producer Allen. It wasn't unusual for Frank to peek his head in, and the guys would summon him in for a conversation or political discussion. Frank and Dennis loved to talk to each other. The two became friends and respected each other beyond words. I would have loved being a fly on the wall, listening to Frank, a Christian, and Dennis, a Jew, bat around their perspectives of what was happening in the world.

When 2012 rolled in, we received more good news: Jessica was pregnant again. We would learn that she was expecting another boy. I can still see the huge grin on my husband's face when he heard that news. We couldn't be more excited.

Frank loved me deeply, and our marriage was never better. We loved spending time together: talking, taking long walks, babysitting, hanging out with our friends, eating long, unhurried dinners, making love, going on little road trips: visiting our friends Mark and Cindy Stapleton in Gardnerville, Nevada, or my brother Johnny and Staci in Arizona, or just going to the beach.

In 2012, we even drove out to Arizona to visit our dear friends Steven and Shannon Wright during spring training. Frank had tutored Steven in pitching when he was just ten years old, and the two formed a close bond over the years. Although Steven had yet to reach the major leagues, Frank encouraged him to hang in there because he was so close to making it to The Show.

Steven and Shannon had a surprise for us too—Shannon was pregnant! We went out after a spring training game and celebrated with a lovely dinner. Frank, who hadn't been to spring training since his baseball days, was thrilled to be around major league baseball again.

Yes, life was so good.

Too bad it didn't last much longer.

20

The Foreshadowing

Shortly after we got home from spring training, I was combing through Frank's Facebook page when I noticed that a listener named James Grainger suggested an interview guest: Frank Sontag, who was a producer on the *Mark & Brian Show*, a hugely popular morning drive-time show on KLOS 95.5 FM, a classic rock station that garnered huge ratings in L.A.

"I hear that Frank Sontag has a great testimony of where he came from and how he came to Christ," James wrote. "I think it would be interesting to hear how he handles being a Christian and working in the environment that he does—a rock station on a typical morning show." James included links to the pair of YouTube videos in which Frank Sontag shared his conversion story.

Frank loved fish-out-of-water stories like Frank Sontag, so he checked him out and was satisfied that his story was legit. On April 25, 2012, a Wednesday, Frank Sontag was an in-studio guest and shared his testimony of how he was a New Ager for most of his adult life—twenty-five years—until he had an incredible coming-to-Christ moment after a round of golf with buddies who shared the Gospel with him.

This is how their conversation unfolded on that April day. I share it because this will give you a sense of how engaging and how much fun Frank was when he was in his element—behind the KKLA microphone with tens of thousands listening in:

> **Frank Pastore:** *(talking over the lead-in music) 99.5 FM, KKLA Los Angeles. The intersection of faith and reason right here on the* Frank Pastore Show. *Hee-ha and welcome aboard.*
>
> *Get this now. You guys, I've shared my testimony several times*

on the air. Briefly, I'm a major league baseball player with the Cincinnati Reds. Forced to hang out with the Christians on the Reds because if my wife found out that I was going out and clubbing with the non-Christians, she was going to go home. Leave me. A long story.

A pitch is thrown in Dodger Stadium. The batter swings, and the ball crashes off my elbow. My world is rocked. These Christians I'm hanging out with invite me to a Bible study. Of course, I don't want to go, but I go. I'm challenged to simply disprove Christianity. I was asked to read two Christian books—I didn't even know Christians wrote books. I thought they were all stupid. But I read C.S. Lewis' Mere Christianity *and* Evidence that Demands a Verdict *by Josh McDowell.*

I got to that 50.1 percent place where you go, "You know, I don't have all the answers yet, but I've got enough answered." I'm at that tipping point, right? I chose to become a Christian.

I don't want to offend people, but there is something about Christians who come to Christ in adulthood. There's a flame that burns hotter, brighter, and more distinctly than those who always grew up in the church.

The way it should work is this way: Everyone should grow up in a Christian family. *That's the ideal, right? Let's not sensationalize and make heroes of the heroin drug dealer who comes to Christ. No, the goal for our children is for them to say,* You know, I never knew a time when I wasn't a Christian. *That's the goal.*

Nevertheless, there's something about hearing from people who come to Christ late in life and their perspective on things. For me, I never signed up for "Churchianity." When I came to Christ and self-identified as a Christian, I didn't have a fish on the car or a leather Bible or know who Petra was or Sandy Patti or Stryper or Amy Grant. I didn't have the lingo down. My guest, Frank Sontag, is not a new name in radio. In fact, he has been in radio for more than thirty years now. If you listen to 95.5 KLOS, then you know of the Mark & Brian Show *and Frank Sontag. Maybe you've seen his testimony on YouTube.*

Frank grew up in Cleveland, playing the accordion in an Italian-Catholic family. He moved with family to L.A. in the mid-1960s when he was ten years old. He went to Catholic schools and probably had the nuns beating him over the knuckles with a ruler, just like me.

But get this. In 1984, he got into a motorcycle accident that rocked his world and sent him on a search for God and significance and meaning that ultimately culminated in him coming to Christ just a few years ago in 2009.

I've invited him on the show to share his testimony because I often say, "Listen, if you know of a neat ministry or someone I ought to have on the show, let me know." Jim Grainger sent me an email that said, "Dude, you have to have this guy from that heathen pagan station over at KLOS because he's a believer and he's solid. I heard him speak."

We vetted Frank through the team and Frank Sontag got the green light, and now you're here, bro. Welcome aboard. How are you, man?

Frank Sontag: *I can't tell you what an honor it is to be on your show and thank you for your radio ministry, Frank. I'm thrilled to be here.*

Frank Pastore: *I can't believe we look somewhat alike. You've got no hair like me but a scratchy, fuzzy thing on your chin. Very cool. You're very hip, by the way.*

Frank Sontag: *Well, you are a little younger and a little better looking than me.*

Frank Pastore: *(laughs out loud): Good answer! He sucks up* *right from the beginning. So you're from Cleveland, the accordion thing. You still into music?*

Frank Sontag: *I wanted a guitar growing up. I grew up with the Beatles, and my parents stuck me with an accordion. I had a permanent black and blue bruise on my chest from eight to nine years of age. I hated the accordion. Finally, I said no more. I don't play music anymore, even though I love listening to music.*

Yeah, we came out here from Cleveland in '65, as you said. I remember the first thing I wanted to do was go to the beach. I had never seen a beach before. Lake Erie was our body of water, and as you all know the joke, Lake Erie caught on fire because it was so polluted and disgusting back then.

So we went to the beach, and I felt, Wow, California. I'm here. *Went to Notre Dame High School. All-boy Catholic school. Raised in Catholicism.*

Frank Pastore: *Me, too.*

Frank Sontag: *I remember that summer, when I graduated in 1972, my thought was I was never going to go to church again. I just didn't feel it. I didn't like church. So from that time on, through my twenties, I wandered. I was lost. Did a lot of different things. Lot of different jobs. You know what it was like in your twenties—which happened yesterday. Life was so right there, and you felt like you had life by the tail.*

You mentioned my crash. That's where I want to start this. It was June 17, 1984. I'm in the San Fernando Valley on my motorcycle. No helmet laws back then, so I wasn't wearing a helmet. I did have hair—long hair—to fly in the breeze.

Frank Pastore: *What kind of bike?*

Frank Sontag: *It was a little dinky Honda FT 350. Single* *stroke. I'm driving on the 101, coming up Balboa, and there's a long straightaway there . . .*

Frank Sontag described how a brand-new Corvette, doing 110 mph, came out of nowhere and mowed him down, sending him sprawling on the paved freeway:

Frank Pastore: *You were on a little 350 without a helmet. Dude, are you kidding? You're lucky to be alive!*

Frank Sontag: *Well, yeah, that was my proverbial wake-up call. Frank, I had no broken bones. I had nothing but road rash. But I had no relationship with God whatever. I had walked away from the church some twelve years earlier.*

Frank Pastore: *Did you believe in God?*

Frank Sontag: *Remember, I was raised a Catholic, so I believed in God, whatever that meant.*

Frank Pastore: *That would have gotten you a B on the Christianity 101 multiple-choice exam.*

Frank Sontag: *Probably a C-minus.*

Frank Pastore: *So you believed in God but had no personal relationship. You weren't into organized religion. Would you consider yourself, at that point, a spiritual person?*

Frank Sontag: *I began to perceive myself as a spiritual person. Like I said, I locked myself inside a cabin in Sunnyside in Lake Tahoe, in the middle of winter, and I started to read books. It was weird, Frank. I graduated from high school when I was sixteen, and I learned to dumb down because I had skipped the fourth grade. I became a jock. Learned to play basketball and got stupid. So after this crash, I decided to start reading everything I could get my hands on. I found Gandhi and Dr. Martin Luther King. New Age authors. After a handful of*

*months up there, freezing with no heat, I decided to come back
to L.A.*

Frank Pastore: *Dude, stop—we have to take a break. When
we come back, we're going to continue with Frank Sontag. If
you're a fan of KLOS, then you know a bit about him. Frank
Sontag is sharing his story today. You're the on-air technical
engineer for* Mark & Brian—*is that right?*

Frank Sontag: *Yeah.*

Frank Pastore: *When we come back, we'll continue with
Frank's story with how he came to Christ in December 2009,
when his life got really interesting. We'll find out why when we
come back.*

That was a nice teaser. My husband was a real pro. Coming out of
the break, my Frank said this:

Frank Pastore: *I love genuine testimonies. They aren't
churched up. Frank Sontag . . . I'm just hearing this story for
the first time like you guys are. What's neat about this is that it's
not like you're a "professional Christian" yet. It's only been less
than two-and-a-half years.*

*So I'm trying to do the math in my head. What age were you
when you became a Christian? Fifty-five?*

Frank Sontag: *Let's see. In 2009, I was fifty-four.*

Frank Pastore: *That's my age now. So for fifty-four years, you
lived without Him, and now His grace has overwhelmed you.
So let's open up the phone lines. It's Jenna in Anaheim . . . .*

That gives you an idea of how Frank rolled while he was on the air.
He looked for ways to connect with his guests and his audience, and his
listeners sensed that and appreciated that about him.

Frank also liked talking to me about the guests he had on the show.

That night, over dinner, he told me, "I really liked this guy. He's a big dude, bald head, wears jeans and boots, and looks like me!"

Frank Sontag shaved his head, a practice that my follicly challenged husband had started doing in the past year. But the way Frank carried on about Frank Sontag that night was funny because my husband didn't normally dwell on guests. Frank and his program director were picky about having guests back for a second time because they often repeated themselves or didn't have anything new to say.

They sensed Frank Sontag was different because of his unique testimony and radio background, so Frank invited him to come back on the *Frank Pastore Show* two months later on Friday, June 29. Ironically, that happened to be the day Frank Sontag learned he was losing his job on the *Mark & Brian Show* because one of the hosts, Mark Thompson, announced that he wanted a change of scenery and was leaving the show after twenty-five years.

Frank began the second show with Frank Sontag this way:

> **Frank Pastore:** *A few weeks ago, I had the great Frank Sontag on the show. I didn't know who he was or how important he was. Frank gave his life to Christ on December 17, 2009, so it was just a few years ago. He's with his wife, Erin, in the studio.*
>
> *Now the big news today is that the* Mark & Brian Show *may be ending because Mark Thompson wants to move back to North Carolina. What's happening with the show?*
>
> **Frank Sontag:** *Listen, you're as surprised as I am. We've been hearing rumors, and honestly, I didn't know anything this morning until Mark addressed the staff and said that as of August 17, that was going to be it.*
>
> **Frank Pastore:** *So what are you going to do?*
>
> **Frank Sontag:** *I know I would love to do a Christian talk program. Maybe I'll end up here. I don't know.*
>
> **Frank Pastore** (grinning): *Now that's immediately threatening to me. Dude, we're done. Next!*

I was listening from the radio in our kitchen as they shared a long laugh. It was all in good fun, and they were trying to bust each other's chops. After a commercial break, Frank said this:

Frank Pastore: *I wish you could have heard what we talked about the last two minutes or so. Frank and Erin are so transparent and so real in their relationship and their walk with Christ. You rarely hear that these days. I don't want to talk out of school here, but typically on KKLA, it's sermon shows all day long—and then me. Those of you who are struggling and don't want the academic, apologetic answer, you're asking,* How do I deal with what I'm going through? *Where were you spiritually, Erin, before Frank became a Christian? Be brutally honest.*

Erin Sontag: *Part of his appeal to me back then was that he was a broad, spiritual man, very accepting of all faiths. I was with him and felt the same way. When he gave his life to Christ, though, I thought he was nuts. I thought he was going through a mid-life crisis. I didn't know what to do with it. I was angry because I felt that he didn't take my needs into account. I felt he was moving away from me. That set off a hard time for us, almost to the point where we divorced. Things were bad.*

Frank Pastore: *Did he have to sleep on the couch? I'm prying, but I want people to understand what really happened.*

Erin Sontag: *It was really bad. I probably hit my bottom. At that point, he had found Reality Church in Carpinteria. He said, "Erin, come with me." I was so desperate for anything that I went with him. I fell in love with his church.*

Frank Pastore: *Wait. You're into all the Eastern stuff—mysticism, Taoism, etc. But dudette, he's going to Reality Church in Carpinteria. He asks you to go. So why did you go?*

Erin Sontag: *At that point, we were into counseling because we had decided that we wanted to make our marriage work. Counseling helped. But there was this desperation for some-*

thing bigger than myself. The other things in my life were not working.

When I went to Reality Church, I started to be fed. Then Frank bought me a Bible, and I couldn't put it down. Since I was raised Catholic, part of me felt that I was coming home when I read the Bible. When Religious Science was my thing, I never felt like it was enough.

Frank Pastore: *In Religious Science, God is not a Supreme Being but a Force. Would you pray?*

Erin Sontag: *Sure, all the time.*

Frank Pastore: *Who was listening?*

Erin Sontag: *The one God, the Creator of everything.*

Frank Pastore: *In the Eastern religions, God is not a personal being. It's a Force. There is no God. There is no heaven. There's no life after death. You just pop out of existence and nothing becomes nothing.*

The reason why I asked you the prayer thing and the reason it caught you is because you were praying largely because of your Catholic roots. The thing with Religious Science and "mind" cults is that you have to get back in sync with the "energy field" and "energy force." Hence all the New Age and Harmonic Convergence and the crystals and pyramid stuff.

But you never felt fulfilled by that.

Erin Sontag: *That's right. I was told that if you think positively, positive things will happen. But how often can you do that? It doesn't happen like that.*

Frank Pastore: *Please don't exaggerate this. Did you ever have that sense of fulfillment or warmth or glow at any time when* *you were into the Religious Science stuff?*

Erin Sontag: *You know, I felt connected on some level, but it never lasted beyond those brief moments. Since I've become a Christian, I don't feel that "aahh" moment all the time. It's not an easy walk at all times. But I keep going because I see the miracles happening.*

Frank Pastore: *That's great to hear. Name one.*

Erin Sontag: *Our marriage for one. We have had a lot of obstacles. We have a big age difference. With that comes a hard dynamic. But our marriage is better now.*

Frank Pastore: *Did Frank become a better man and husband?*

Erin Sontag: *Oh, yes. Before he gave his life to Christ, he was very stubborn and full of his own opinions. That was one of the things that caused us to drift apart. After he gave his life to Christ, he became much more open and even exuberant, like many do. He wouldn't stop talking about what Christ was doing in his life, and that caused a rift between us. After we went through everything, he had to back off to keep me interested.*

When I was able to find Christ on my own, that's when everything started to change. But yes, he has become a much more humble man. He's much more loving.

Frank Pastore: *So, Frank, there's not going to be a* Frank & Brian Show. *Dude, what are you going to be doing?*

Frank Sontag: *Only the Lord knows. I have no clue. I have no idea. My sense is they like me at the station and they'll keep me there. But ever since my walk started a few years ago, I'm like, "Lord, use me for Your glory. Whatever it is and in everything I do."*

I really feel called to be a pastor. I don't have a penny saved to my name. The Enemy is very active: What are you doing? You're an awful provider.

Spiritual warfare goes on in our house a lot. I don't know what's going to happen, but I pray that I get out of my own way, whatever the plan is.

Frank Pastore: *Let me jump in here since you guys are being so vulnerable. Let me ask some probing questions here. When you said, "I don't have a penny to my name," I know you don't own a yacht down at Malibu or have a ton of money. So here's my encouragement to you: Don't go into the pastorate to make money.*

Frank Sontag: *I know that.*

Frank Pastore: *Look, there are some people who say, "I've failed at everything else. God must be calling me into the ministry." Dude, it's not that way at all. Being a pastor is more than delivering three messages on Sunday. Unless you have a counselor's heart, then my encouragement is no, go in a different route.*

Look, it doesn't mean you have to be the "pastor" of a church. There are all sorts of pastoral roles that you can fulfill. Dude, just sharing your story like we're doing now is something you could do. Erin, you're nodding your head. He's good at this, right?

Erin Sontag: *He's in his element. I cried when I listened to his interview with you on KKLA six weeks ago. It was a beautiful thing. He's just great behind a microphone. I could see him doing some sort of pastoral thing on the radio.*

I share this exchange to show how Frank could explain what different religions believe or why they were false religions. You can also see that when he liked someone, he called him "dude" and her "dudette."

When the trio was done at the top of the six o'clock hour, there was one more hour of air time left. My Frank invited Frank and Erin to hang around and kibitz with him during commercials breaks. When the show was finished, Frank accompanied them to the parking garage next to the KKLA offices. They came upon my husband's mode of transportation—a Honda VTX 1800. Frank Sontag whistled in appreciation.

My Frank was proud of his Honda VTX 1800 and talked of his love for motorcycle trips. "Yeah, there's nothing like it, riding the open road," Frank said. "Gina gives me grief, though, about riding the freeways here," he said. "When I bought my bike, she got pretty upset, but I told her, 'Look, life is life, and you're gonna go when you're gonna go.' I'm not a reckless rider. I ride very safe."

When Frank arrived home that night and gave me a hug, the first thing he said was, "Hey, did you hear the Frank Sontag interview today?"

"Yeah, I listened to a lot of it. Did Erin *want* to come on the air?"

"Well, not really, but I kinda talked her into it. She did great, though. I'd like you to meet them someday."

I smiled to myself. *Hmmm, how are we going to fit them in?* Our life was busy and full. Frank and I had a tight circle of trusted friends, and I tried to make sure we did dinners with them on a regular basis. With Frank's career, we were always meeting interesting people that we wanted to get to know better. One couple was Dave and Mary Berg. Dave was a producer on *The Tonight Show with Jay Leno*, and we found we loved Dave and Mary.

"Tell you what, honey. I'll work on getting together with the Sontags."

I was standing at the kitchen sink, washing romaine lettuce for our dinner. Frank came up behind me and kissed me on the neck. Then he wrapped his arms around my waist and lingered a moment. After breaking off the embrace, he started to walk toward the hallway leading to our bedroom to change his clothes and clean up.

"This guy is going to take my show some day," he said, like an afterthought.

He almost said it as a proclamation. I stopped washing the lettuce and turned toward him.

"Are you retiring?" I asked.

"No! Frank's older than me," he said, laughing.

"Well then, why are you saying that?"

He didn't answer. Instead, he turned and continued on to our bedroom without uttering a word.

To this day, I wonder what Frank really knew.

21

Aftermath

B*ecause Mrs. Pastore, your husband is famous.*
        I let the simple declaration from Rosa Saca, the public relations director for the USC Medical Center, settle into my consciousness. The reality of Frank being seriously injured in a motorcycle accident was slowly sinking in, but there was too much to take in. I alternated between feeling numb and feeling out of it. I steadied myself with a reminder that this accident really happened and it was *my husband* and Frankie and Christina's *father* who was in a coma.

Rosa's desire to shield me from intrusive people was born out of Frank's connection with the outside world, something that went far deeper than Frank and I were aware of.

You see, Frank got all that "I wanna be famous" part out of his life when he decided to follow Christ. Once that happened, he wanted to be a normal guy. That's why we lived in a normal tract home, drove a normal car, wore normal clothes, and did normal things. Other than Frank's purple motorcycle, we weren't flashy people. Frank's favorite hobbies were simple: he liked to read, break a sweat doing some yard work, play an occasional round of golf (Frank had a wicked swing and could outdrive anyone), and ride his bike.

Many times, when he wanted to lower the stress in his life, he'd jump on his bike and take a daylong drive on some two-lane road away from the city. He'd call me at lunchtime and say, "Hi, honey! I'll be home by five. Let's barbeque some steaks tonight!" To Frank, a day away from rat race didn't get better than that.

Rosa wanted me to know that the USC Medical Center was being extremely careful with our delicate situation. She explained that several media reporters were asking to speak with me, but it was entirely up to me if I wanted to grant any interviews or decide what information the hospital released to the public.

I didn't know it at the time, but news of Frank's location leaked out when a well-meaning friend went on to her Facebook page while sitting in the waiting room. In a new post, she asked people to pray for Frank and then used the "Check In" tab, where she typed in **USC Medical Center** as her location.

That's all the information people needed to figure out where Frank had been airlifted to following the accident. My friend's Facebook was "shared"—to how many people, I didn't know. But what I did know is that within hours, friends, acquaintances, and fans arrived at the hospital, hoping to visit Frank.

"We're giving Frank an alias," Rosa said. "It's 'Adam 32.' Only give out that name to those who you want to let in to see Frank."

"Got it," I said.

I left the meeting with Rosa and was escorted to Frank's room. He hadn't moved since the night before. His condition had not changed.

This was our new normal. The kids and I would sit in Frank's room, but when the doctors or nurses came in to do certain tests or procedures, they would ask us to leave. We'd head back to the waiting room, where many of our friends and Frank's colleagues were congregating. All of our family and close friends were coming to the hospital, and Frank's bosses at KKLA showed up every day. We had tons of spiritual support: our pastor David Rosales and his wife, Marie; pastor Dudley Rutherford; pastor Steve Wilburn; pastor Raul Ries; and pastor Greg Laurie. They all took turns praying over Frank.

I'll admit that I was in shock for the first three days. I felt shaky and unable to eat. My head was spinning most of the time. Despite my anxiety and unease, I was militant about protecting my husband. Like a mama bear, I snapped at anyone trying to invade my space. I realized early on that other people wouldn't understand what I was doing.

Nonetheless, I wanted to talk to the doctors and find out anything I could about Frank's condition and the outlook for recovery.

On day two of the coma, Dr. John Gruen stepped into the waiting room to meet me. He explained he was one of the neurosurgeons on staff, and I could talk with him.

When I said I did have some questions, Dr. Gruen asked if he could call me a bit later since he was doing his rounds. He took my cell phone number.

When we spoke later that morning, I was blunt. "Doctor, I want you to be honest with me. I don't want you to shield me from the truth."

"Very well," Dr. Gruen replied. "Frank has suffered a traumatic brain injury, and right now, it's hard to know the extent of the damage. But I can tell you that every day he remains in a coma is a very bad sign. The brain scans are showing bleeding all around Frank's brain, leaving little hope for the brain to compensate. The next week will be crucial."

When doctors examined him, Frank reacted to pain but he was not responsive to commands at all. We were told to talk to him constantly, sing to him—do anything we could to get him to show a response. After speaking with Dr. Gruen, I made the decision to let friends into the ICU unit to see Frank. The nurses advised me not to do this, but I wanted people who loved Frank praying over him. We allowed two at a time into Frank's room inside the ICU unit, one group after another: family, friends, colleagues, and pastors, who prayed mighty prayers over my husband.

On the second day, a detective with the Los Angeles County Sheriff's Department stopped by to ask me a few questions for their investigation. I couldn't really provide much information, but after he left, my sister, Marina, pulled me aside.

"Gina, you need to get legal counsel," she said.

I didn't want to hear this; my focus was on Frank getting better. But as I thought about her suggestion the rest of the afternoon, I realized that she was talking sense. When Frank's boss Terry Fahy showed up later that day, I asked him for the contact number for Berglund & Johnson, longtime sponsors of the *Frank Pastore Show*. Frank had always spoken highly of them.

When I called Dan Johnson, he dropped everything and drove to downtown L.A. to meet me. I was struck by his emotion for Frank and shocked at the level of information he had gathered already. He had done his homework and knew far more about the night of the accident than I did.

Frankly, it was too painful for me to hear the details of Frank's accident. It was also painful as a mother to see my children experiencing the aftermath of a collision that left their father in critical condition. I needed to be strong for them, and they wanted to be strong for me.

I was also struck by how our daughter-in-law Jessica and son-in-law Josh cried continually. They loved their father-in-law so much. To be honest, I was shocked by how many people were crying and told me they loved my husband. Frank had impacted so many lives. Even though I was in a "blur" of shock, all of this love and support was sinking deep into my soul.

On the second night of the coma, the kids and I left the hospital late and headed to our house. As we drove up the driveway, neighbors came over to hug us. The message light on our landline phone was blinking and literally alerting me that the "Message Center is full." I had received calls from so many: Dr. Dobson, Warren Duffy, Jim Daly, Dr. Barry Corey, Wendel Deyo, and others.

My cell phone received so many messages that my battery rapidly lost its charge. I immediately plugged my flip phone into the charger because I needed reception. That's how the nurses from USC would be calling me.

Because of the outpouring of love and support, the kids and I realized we had to come up with some form of communication strategy. We decided Christina would be in charge of everything that got posted on the Facebook page for the Frank Pastore Show as well as her personal Facebook page. She informed people to check either page for updates. We all realized we had a difficult, roller-coaster ride ahead of us and girded ourselves for the long haul. Frankie and Jessica, along with Christina and Josh, all stayed with me at the Upland house.

What was especially meaningful was when Christina slipped into her dad's side of our big king-sized bed and slept next to me. We hugged and cried as we fell to sleep, each of us unsure what the morning would bring.

The first thing I did when I woke up was to call the hospital for an update. A nurse told me that Frank's condition was unchanged, but she would call me on my cell if anything changed.

The kids and I hurriedly showered, grabbed a light breakfast and coffee, and then sped off to the USC Medical Center. "Sped off," that is, until we got on Interstate 10, where the major freeway into downtown Los Angeles was snarled with morning commuters.

"Oh, my goodness!"

It was Christina, clicking through Facebook on her iPhone. "Mom, you won't believe how many people are commenting," she said, as her index finger swiped upward. "So many are praying for Dad!"

Truthfully, I couldn't have cared less about Facebook at this time; it was simply a tool to inform those who were inquiring about Frank. I got that. At the same time, I was shocked by how much public interest there was in Frank, which seemed to be growing like a wildfire.

When we finally reached the parking garage, I was shocked at the number of people who recognized me as we made the half-mile walk to the USC Medical Center. "Mrs. Pastore, I just want you to know that I'm praying for Frank," said one nurse on her way to work. Another woman stopped me to say, "Mrs. Pastore, I've listened to your husband for years. Please know we're praying!"

Rosa was waiting for me on the third floor. "Mrs. Pastore, can I talk to you?"

"Yes, but please call me Gina," I replied.

"Sure . . . Gina. I have several reporters who would like to speak with you," she said. "If you're feeling up to that, we can set you up in an office here so that you can talk to these reporters over the phone."

Something stirred deep in my heart. I knew I had to speak on behalf of my husband because of the intense public interest in Frank. I remembered back to our baseball days and how Frank hated it when he was misrepresented or misquoted in an article. I didn't want reporters guessing what happened to Frank or his condition. I had an unbelievable desire to protect and represent my husband, and I was determined that I would follow through as his advocate.

"Okay, but first I want to spend time with Frank," I said to Rosa.

I walked into the ICU Unit and entered Frank's room with my family. He looked the same: a breathing tube was inserted into his mouth, a drainage tube was relieving pressure from his brain, a brace was wrapped around his neck, and there were splints on his broken bones.

I stood next to his bed, thinking, *Frank, wake up. Wake up, Frank.* He never moved. Then I heard a familiar *thomp-thomp-thomp* sound coming from outside. It was an air ambulance helicopter, maneuvering for a rooftop landing. The windows vibrated and the building shook as the massive bird angled for a three-point landing.

I felt sick to my stomach. The arrival of a medical helicopter meant there was someone onboard going through a severe, life-or-death situation. *Dear God, please be with this person's family . . .*

So much pain . . . and so much loss. *God, why is this happening?*

We couldn't stay in Frank's room all day long. After an appropriate amount of time with him, we returned to the waiting room. The hospital asked me to draft a list of people who would be allowed to come up to the waiting room. The biggest group seemed to come from the KKLA office: secretaries, engineers, producers, etc. They loved Frank and Frank loved them, so I kept expanding the list.

Later that day, a couple of the engineers sat and cried with me in the waiting room. One of them said, "It's so hard to believe Frank actually seemed to know what was going to happen. He predicted it. We all heard him say it."

I thought back to Monday afternoon, just three days earlier. It seemed like an eternity had passed. His words from his last broadcast echoed in my mind: *Look, you guys know I ride a motorcycle, right? So, at any moment, especially with the idiot people who cross the diamond lane into my lane . . . .*

"Yeah, unbelievable," I said. There was no other word to describe what he said on the air that day.

"The station has taken the podcast down," the engineer said.

"What? Why is the podcast down?" I couldn't understand that. Frank's broadcasts were always available as podcasts for later listening. KKLA had always been generous in sharing its hosts and its content with the public. Usually within a few hours of the *Frank Pastore Show* ending, the podcast was posted on the kkla.com website.

"They want to respect you and the kids, so they took it down," the engineer said.

Hearing that upset me. "No! Frank would want that up! He would want people to know that God is in control of his life!" I knew that would be Frank's *exact* response.

Within the next hour, the bosses from KKLA showed up at the USC Medical Center. I asked Terry Fahy and Bob Hastings if they could do me a favor: put the podcast back up. "I know you're trying to protect Frank, me, and our kids, but I also know Frank would want people to hear what God placed on his heart and in his mind that day," I said.

Terry and Bob looked at each other.

"We'll do as you wish," Terry said. Later that day, the podcast of the November 19, 2012 show was posted. It didn't take long for Frank's prophetic words to make headlines around the country.

Terry and Bob's attitude was indicative of how the entire Salem L.A. office reacted to Frank's motorcycle accident. They were careful not to intrude and to give me room, but they were available when I needed them. I remember saying, "I know you guys need to think about the station. Maybe you should start finding a replacement."

Terry put his head down and softly said, "We'll trust God in this."

"Who's doing the show?" I asked. We both knew the three-hour program had to go on.

"We asked Kevin McCullough to sit in this week, and he immediately said yes," Terry said.

Hearing that provided some measure of comfort since Kevin was a friend and would have just the right words to say.

Then Terry told me, "We're also going to ask Frank Sontag to sit in. I hope that's okay with you."

 I was momentarily stunned. *That's the guy Frank liked . . . the guy Frank said would take his show someday.* I felt like crying, but I was also piecing together how God had given my Frank a foreshadowing of the future.

"That's fine," I said. Everything was happening so fast.

As the days passed, Frank was showing no signs of improvement. I constantly worried that Frank was in pain, so I stayed on top of the nurses to make sure that he was receiving his morphine.

After about a week, the drainage tube in his brain was removed. The swelling had gone down, but Frank was still in a coma, still fighting for his life.

I hadn't forgotten what Dr. Gruen had said: "Every day he remains in the coma is a bad sign."

In the beginning, I had some hope that maybe Frank would awaken, but that hope was dimming. It was a strange place to be because I didn't want to give up and was still praying for a miracle. However, I knew exactly what my theologically astute husband would be saying: "When it's our time to go, it's time to go. God has our days numbered, and God is in control."

After Frank had been at the USC Medical Center for a week, one of the nurses as the nurses' station called me over.

"Mrs. Pastore, we were wondering if you could stop giving out Frank's alias so much. Way too many people are coming to the hospital and asking to come up to the waiting room," she said, adding that a couple of LAPD officers were called in to monitor the semi-chaotic situation at the hospital entrance.

So that explained why flowers, books, blankets, cakes, doughnuts, pies, and statues were filling up our waiting room. Every day Terry Fahy and Bob Hastings arrived carrying boxes filled with letters from listeners. I couldn't read them all, but nearly everyone expressed his or her love for Frank.

"What do we need to do?" I asked the nurse.

"I need you to make a list of only those people you want to have in the waiting room with you," she said. "Those will be the only people that we will allow to come up to the third floor. I'm sorry that we have to tighten security, but because your husband is so loved, we have to take these measures."

"I understand," I replied.

"I'm glad you do, Mrs. Pastore. We've never seen anything like this, and we've had many high-profile patients before."

Early on, a hospital administrator asked me to bring Frank's "directives" to the hospital. He didn't need to explain as I understood why the hospital needed this information: an advance directive provides instructions about end-of-life decisions, from the determination of what happens to your estate to the use of equipment such as ventilators or "do not resuscitate" orders.

Frank was militant about having his life in order, which started with a family trust. I remembered the day Frank and I updated our family trust a few years earlier. We were in the Irvine office of our attorney, Tim Blied. When we discussed our wishes for the area of medical directives, Tim asked a series of questions—questions addressing our wishes about life support, resuscitation, etc.

Those were questions that we all hate to think about but need to have in writing. Frank was somewhat jovial that day, in keeping with his fun personality. "No life support or extraordinary measures for me," he quipped. "When it's my time to go Home, I'll be with the Lord."

Frank always referred to heaven as "Home"—a place that was real to him, which is why I've capitalized it. Frank and my directives were identical: neither of us wanting to be kept alive, long term, on life support.

The following day, as Frank and I took a long walk before he went to work, we had one of those talks married couples have—the "what-if-something-happens-to-you" conversation.

As we strolled up a beautiful street near our home, I asked Frank, "Yesterday got me thinking . . . do you ever think about where you'd want to be buried?"

"I'd love to be at a veteran's cemetery, but I wasn't in the military," he said. "How 'bout in our back yard!"

I laughed. "Frank, seriously, we need to talk about this."

"Oh, honey, it doesn't matter. It's just my body parts. I'll be Home. I'll be with God."

I got emotional and stopped walking. Turning to him, I said, "I want you to know something, okay? If anything happens to me, I want you to remarry. I mean it."

He quickly stopped me. "Gina, the thought of being on this planet without you is the most horrible thing I can imagine!"

That was sweet to hear, but it still didn't address the reality of being a widower. "I know it's a horrible thought, but will you promise me you'll remarry? I don't want you to be alone."

When Frank frowned, I said lightheartedly, "Just make sure she's a good person and loves our children!"

Frank knit his brow. "I don't think I could ever love anyone else but you, Gina."

And that's how we left things.

Not long after this conversation, Frank came home from a busy day at work and said he wanted to watch a movie with me after dinner. "Remember when we saw *The Notebook*, that Nicolas Sparks movie?" he asked.

I did remember seeing *The Notebook* at the local theater, a chick flick if there ever was one. Frank scored some points with me that night.

"You want to see it again?"

"Yeah," Frank said. "It was a great movie."

By the time we finished dinner and cleaned up the kitchen, however, it was around 9:30 p.m. I was super tired after a long day.

"Sorry," I said, "but I have to go to bed. Can you watch it alone?"

"Sure. I'll stay up a little longer."

"You do that," I said, giving him a goodnight kiss.

I went off to bed, read a while, and dozed off while Frank watched the film in the living room. Suddenly, Frank slipped into our bed and stirred me awake. He was uncharacteristically crying . . . sobbing.

I sat up out of a dead sleep. "Frank, what's wrong?" I exclaimed.

He hugged me tight. "I just finished watching *The Notebook*, and I don't know what I'd do if anything ever happened to you!"

"That's nice, Frank. Now go to sleep."

For the next few months, I teased him to no end. "Don't ever watch that movie ever again," I joked. "It's too sad!"

And now I had a real-life sad situation. After Frank's accident, I knew I had to dig through our files for our advance directives as it became clear that my precious husband's life was being held in what felt like suspended animation.

During week two of the coma, I heard that thousands and thousands of people were praying for Frank. People around the country were reporting of the "prayer networks" and "prayer chains" at their churches and in their communities. Letters poured into KKLA, our church, and our home, far too many for me to even read.

Every day I heard well-meaning people say, "Frank's going to awaken" or "Frank's going to be healed."

Everyone around me was saying this, but in my heart, I was thinking and praying, *God, You know I want Frank to be healed, but I'll trust You, Lord. I know You're in control.*

That thought would sustain me for what was to come.

22

The Passing

I was at Frank's side every day but rarely alone with him. Nurses, techs, and visitors always seemed to be in the room, which was understandable.

Midway throughout the second week, I decided I wanted some "alone time" with my husband and asked everyone to leave the room for a little while.

When everyone was gone, I drew the drape so we could have more privacy. I hopped into the hospital bed and cuddled up to Frank. I stroked his beautiful face and outlined his ears with my index finger. My husband was the most handsome man I had ever seen. I gazed at his wonderful nose, his chiseled jaw line, his high cheeks . . . and tears flooded down my face.

I softly told him, "Frank, I promise to take care of our kids. I will make sure Michael always knows how much you love him, and I'll tell Will all about you. I love you more than my life. No matter what happens, I will carry on your legacy."

I knew there was something else I needed to say. "Frank, I'm not mad about the motorcycle . . . I'm not mad about the motorcycle at all." I wanted him to know that. Then, suddenly, the drapes moved. Standing there was Dr. Gruen.

"Oh, excuse me," he said, realizing that he had just walked in on a private moment.

I set the neurosurgeon at ease. "Dr. Gruen, please come in," I said, motioning with my arm.

Dr. Gruen found a chair and sat down quietly. I appreciated his friendly, caring bedside manner.

"Is there an update?" I asked.

"I would categorize Frank's condition as dim," he began. "He's running a high fever, which is to be expected since infection is common to his condition. We hope for the best, but . . . ."

Dr. Gruen didn't finish the sentence. He didn't need to.

Frank's condition remained unchanged nearly three weeks after the accident, which meant he remained in a coma. A hospital administrator found me in the waiting room and said Frank would be released soon since no signs of improvement were evident.

"What? Released? What does that mean?"

"Mrs. Pastore, I'm afraid there's nothing more that ICU care can do for Frank. He needs to be placed in an acute-care facility for insurance reasons," explained the administrator.

I immediately phoned our primary care physician, Dr. Harvey Cohen. Frank would often have Dr. Cohen on the show to discuss medical topics, and we had become close friends. Dr. Cohen had kept in close contact with me since hearing of the accident. When I phoned him regarding my conversation with the hospital administrator, he explained to me why Frank needed to be transferred. He recommended that Frank be moved to a care facility near our home.

Shortly after my conversation with Dr. Cohen, Frank Sontag called and asked if he could visit Frank. For the last week, I had been following the suggestion of Dr. Gruen and Frank's nurses, who felt that I should no longer allow visitors to see my husband, only family and clergy.

I had never met Frank Sontag in person, but I had a sense that I should allow him to see Frank. Christina and I were at Frank's bedside when a nurse told us that Frank Sontag was in the waiting room.

I walked down a long hall, glancing into the rooms and seeing many wounded people. When I stepped into the waiting room, I noticed a bald man sitting by himself with his head down, as if he was praying.

"Are you Frank?" I asked.

He quickly jumped up, putting his hand out and offering a warm handshake. I thanked him for coming to the hospital and escorted him to Frank's room, explaining my husband's condition.

When we arrived, Christina was standing by Frank's side. Introductions were made. Then Frank Sontag asked if he could approach Frank. I nodded and was struck that Frank began crying as he talked to my husband . . . telling him how much he meant to him and that he was a man of God who touched many lives.

After some time passed, a nurse called me into the hall for a moment. "Is that your husband's brother?" she asked. "They look so much alike."

I smiled. "No, he's a friend."

When Frank Sontag left that day, I knew why Frank spoke so well of him and liked him so much.

At the same time of Frank Sontag's visit, our old neighborhood friend Pam Lahr, who'd moved to Arizona, flew in to stay with me for five days. She provided tremendous emotional support.

Frankie and Jessica were constantly driving an hour to see us, but Frankie had just opened his dental office. "You need to be attending to your practice," I said.

Jessica, who was pregnant with Will, was leaving our grandson Michael with her parents quite a bit since Michael wasn't allowed on the ICU floor. Christina and Josh lived closer, so they popped in and out easier. My immediate family—sister, brothers, nieces, and nephews—took turns being at the hospital and also at our home. My neighbors looked after the house and faithfully visited when I'd get home. From KKLA, the bosses came to the hospital nearly every day. The support we received was unbelievable.

Toward the end of week three, Frank developed pneumonia, which commonly happens when a person is on a ventilator and unable to move. We were told that Frank would still be moved to a care facility in a day or two. Dr. Cohen had found the perfect place for Frank: an acute-care hospital in nearby Rancho Cucamonga that had wonderful security.

Frank was transported by ambulance on Sunday evening, December 9, but we kept this as quiet as possible and asked family and close friends not to breathe a word. Frank was now under the care of Dr. Cohen. I met with him the following day to understand where we were.

Speaking softly, he said, "Gina, this is not good. I'm having Frank evaluated by colleagues, but I have to tell you that he's showing no signs of brain activity."

I began to sob. The last thing I wanted to do was make a decision to take him off the ventilator.

"What do you think will happen to Frank? I'm sure you've seen patients in this condition before."

"Usually in cases like this, the infection and pneumonia take their life," he said.

That week, a hospital administrator contacted me and said they'd like to schedule a meeting the following week on Wednesday, December 19. He didn't mention this, but I was pretty sure he wanted to speak to me about Frank's directives. I immediately started dreading that meeting.

On the morning of December 17, 2012, a Monday, I woke up, quickly dressed, and headed to see Frank. While on my way, one of Frank's colleagues, Dave Benzing, known as "Big Wave Dave" on sister station The Fish, 95.9 FM, called and asked if he could drive out and see Frank. "I want to pray over him," he said.

I didn't know Dave very well and had met him only a few times at the station, but I had a sense that I should let him see Frank. Dave lived eighty miles away, so I was struck by his kindness. I gave him the address of the care facility and said I'd see him there.

When Dave arrived, I ushered him into Frank's room. I noticed a Bible verse on a sticky note above Frank's head. Many of the staff at this acute-care hospital were Christians and consistently prayed over Frank. For the next couple of hours, Dave and I prayed and carried on one-way conversations with my unresponsive husband.

Dave and Frank had always shared a cute relationship, teasing each other constantly, and they had respect for one another. Around noon-time, Dave left and headed into work at KKLA, where he would sit in The Fish's studio for his 3-6 p.m. show.

I left Frank around 1 o'clock to go home, grab some lunch, and fill out disability papers for Frank. Then I'd be back to see Frank in the afternoon.

As I sat at my kitchen table, filling out paperwork, the phone rang. Caller ID signaled that the acute-care facility was calling. I picked up, thinking someone was calling to confirm our Wednesday meeting.

Instead I heard a panicked voice. "Mrs. Pastore, we need you to get back here right now, ASAP!"

"Why?" I shouted. "What's happened?"

"We can't say over the phone," she replied. "Just get here!"

I quickly called my sister, Marina, to meet me at the acute-care hospital. I dashed out my door, endured the fifteen-minute drive, hurriedly parked my car, and ran inside the facility.

A security guard stopped me. "Ma'am—"

"Let me in, now!"

Good thing the guard recognized me and buzzed open the door. I raced down a long corridor to Frank's room, feeling like I was having an "out of body" experience. I saw the CEO of the care facility standing near Frank's room, waiting for me with her head down.

It's hard to explain how I felt seeing her standing there. My legs were moving, but I instinctively dreaded the reality I was about to face.

When I reached her, she didn't say a word. She grabbed and hugged me. Then she whispered, "Frank had a cardiac arrest."

She confirmed what was in my heart: *He was gone.*

I immediately started crying. "I wasn't here, I wasn't here!" I cried out, holding on tight.

My warm tears streamed over her shoulder. She pulled back, teary-eyed, and said, "Gina, your pastor was with Frank, and he's in the room now."

Just at that moment, I looked toward Frank's room. Standing in the doorway were my pastor David Rosales and our church administrator David Bustamante.

More hugs and tears were exchanged.

"We were praying," Pastor David said, "when I said to Frank, 'Frank you need to go home to Gina . . . or go Home with our Lord.' Shortly after that, he went into cardiac arrest. He passed at 1:55 p.m. I'm so sorry."

I mumbled a word of thanks and took comfort in knowing Frank was hearing the voice of our pastor, a man who Frank loved so much, as he exited this world.

Marina arrived, and I heard my sister crying, but everything was a blur. *This doesn't seem real. This feels like a dream. How can I be without Frank?*

Quite frankly, Frank was my world and my true love. We were inseparable. I literally felt like my heart was being ripped out of my chest. A nurse gently held my arm and walked me into Frank's room. The breathing tube was gone, as well as all the other tubes and monitoring machines. Frank was draped with a white sheet over his body, except for his face, which was etched by a faint half-smile. He looked so peaceful. I bent over and kissed his lips, a lingering kiss, knowing this would be our last one.

I leaned over and whispered, "You will always be my husband, and

I'll love you until I join you in heaven."

I stroked every part of his beautiful face as well as his arms and chest, telling myself, *I need to remember every part of his body.* When I finished, I glanced into the hallway and saw Marina and Pastor David crying.

I turned around and sat down next to Frank, stunned and spent. "God, get me through this," I prayed.

Marina came in and sat next to me, putting her arm around me. "Let's call the kids," she suggested.

I stood up and called Frankie, then Christina, who were both at work. Both were shocked by the suddenness of the news. They each had hour-long drives ahead of them, but they assured me they were on their way.

A nurse informed me we could be with Frank for three more hours, and then he would be released by the county coroner to the mortuary.

"What mortuary will you be using?" she asked.

"Oh, my God, I don't know!" I replied.

During Frank's entire coma, even though I knew he probably wouldn't survive, I didn't think about making arrangements with a mortuary.

I looked at the clock in Frank's room. It was now almost 3 p.m. I called Terry Fahy, Frank's boss, who loved and respected Frank so much.

"Terry, Frank passed away."

"Oh, no . . . ."

And that's all he said. He couldn't speak, and I just cried for a few minutes on the phone. When I gathered myself, I said, "Please have this announced on the show today."

"Of course," he said.

One of the hardest things I've ever witnessed was watching my kids entering Frank's room to see their father one last time and say goodbye to the father they loved and adored. The experience was heartbreaking. We all cried like we had never cried before.

I remember standing there, soaking in this private moment, and thinking, *My life will never be the same.*

Around 6 o'clock, after the coroner signed the necessary paperwork, two men from a local mortuary (I picked one in our hometown) came for Frank. I noticed red blotches appearing on Frank's face. My son, the dentist, explained that was from blood coagulating.

In a strange way, I was glad to see that. This meant Frank Pastore was no longer in his body. As he would always teach, "We are living souls who happen to live in these bodies." I knew my husband was experiencing the most unbelievable existence and taking his residence in heaven. Through my pain and tears, I knew that.

The kids and I decided to go into the waiting room while Frank's body was prepared for transfer to the mortuary. Marina and some friends joined us. My cell phone rang, and it was one of Frank's nurses asking me to return to the nurses' desk. "Just some routine paperwork," she said.

When I arrived, I learned that the hospital needed proper identification in order to release the body because Frank had been there under an alias. It all seemed very confusing to me.

I had Frank's wallet inside my purse. I took out his driver's license and signed some papers. When I finished, I noticed the door to Frank's room was open. I took a longer look—and that's when I saw my husband inside a clear plastic body bag on a gurney—a searing image I still can't get out of my head.

After leaving the hospital, my family—Frankie and Jessica (Michael was with Jessica's parents) and Christina and Josh—followed me to my house. They were coming over to spend the night. I just wanted to be alone, just our family.

As we turned in the driveway, my headlights shined on to the front porch. I was stunned to see several floral arrangements had arrived. Actually, it was more than "several" floral arrangements. There were enough flower arrangements to fill the entire porch, and the excess lined the walkway to the front of the house.

This made me a little frantic. My first thought was, *Oh my gosh, I don't want people to spend money on flowers!* In my initial state of grief, I knew this was a waste, and we needed to turn people's expressions of condolence to something eternal.

The kids and I walked into the house, and Frankie said "Mom, we've got to pick a charity or a cause for people to give to. What was Dad's favorite charity?"

Frank had been the MC at many worthwhile events over the years for wonderful ministries like Joni and Friends and Food for the Poor, and for the annual Frank Pastore Show/Cross International fundraiser. Frank loved raising money for Cross International, a Christian relief organization that provided food, shelter, water, and emergency aid to the poor in more than thirty-six developing countries.

Frank always said, "Cross International is the best bang for the buck!" For less than a hundred dollars, a sponsored child would be placed in a Christian school and given a meal every day for one year. When I mentioned Cross International to the kids, they were all on board. I phoned Terry Fahy to have this announced as soon as possible on KKLA. Then we all sat in the living room, still crying, still trying to absorb the emotions we were feeling.

We were exhausted when we went to bed. I slept better than I expected. In the morning, Frankie made breakfast while I checked our answering machine.

I played the messages: Warren Duffy cried throughout his communication, and Dr. Barry Corey, president of Biola, said, "I just heard the news and had to sit down . . . I'm grieving." Dr. Dobson and his successor at Focus on the Family, Jim Daly, also left heartfelt messages.

The outpouring was enormous . . . there had to be three dozen messages left on our landline. I said to the kids, "I think we need to have a public memorial for Dad. I want his memorial to reflect his life in every way."

Both of my children agreed; we were all on the same page. I would hear from a couple of people who said, "I can't believe you're not doing a private ceremony!", but it didn't matter to me what anyone else thought. It wasn't their business.

In fact, this was one of the first things I would learn about losing a husband was how insensitive some people can be, offering their advice when it's not wanted. The kids and I were a team, and *we* would reflect the man, the husband, the father, the grandfather, and the generous person that Frank was.

We began planning the memorial service, deciding to wait until after Christmas, which was only five days away. Reporters were calling the house, the station, and even my cell phone, asking for any information. Rick Warren e-mailed, offering Saddleback Church as a place for the memorial service since he knew a lot of people would attend. The Saddleback sanctuary held 3,500 people.

I felt so honored, but I knew Frank would want his memorial service to be at our church, Calvary Chapel Chino Valley, where Frank loved attending on Sunday morning's when he wasn't preaching somewhere else. Besides, our church was large as well and could seat 3,000 people.

I told the kids I wanted to pray about who would speak. I wanted people who truly loved my husband and knew him well and reflected his life. Over the next several days, we met with Pastor David and were in constant contact with the station.

Meanwhile, I was feeling enormous grief and grappling with the reality of how much my life was going to change. I missed Frank and just wanted to run into his arms—but those open arms were no longer there. I remember wishing this were all just a horrible dream that I would awaken from. But it wasn't a dream.

I remember being aware that all of this hoopla and frenzy over Frank and our family would die down over time. I knew that it would be family and close friends who would be there for me over the long haul. I was also aware that the "sting" was going to last a long time. I felt like my future was uncertain, but with so much planning of the memorial service, I had to focus on that.

My once well-managed household had turned into a bit of a zoo. People, flowers, and food were streaming in and out. Christina was constantly at my side, cleaning up the dishes, making the beds, and making sure I was okay. I remained in a blur of grief. The kids and close friends took turns staying with me at night so that I would never be alone. I didn't listen to the *Frank Pastore Show* during this time, but I heard from others that the guest hosts opened up the lines so that listeners could call in and talk about their favorite memories of Frank or how he impacted them.

What an overwhelming time. I knew I had one more emotional mountain to hurdle, and that was Frank's memorial.

23

Saying Goodbye

I woke up on December 29, 2012, to a rainy sky.

My brother Johnny and his wife, Staci, had flown in the day before and were staying with me at my house. Johnny, always my "big brother," was comforting to me. He was looking more and more like Dad as he aged, which felt good. I needed a familiar reminder of unconditional love.

I went out to the kitchen, where Johnny had made coffee and set out cereal boxes and a plate of muffins. I was quiet, solemn, and not looking forward to this day. It's hard to explain, but I really didn't want to be at my husband's funeral, yet at the same time, I didn't want to be anywhere else.

Such conflicting emotions. I felt like I was tossed to and fro on the high seas of grief.

Johnny, who loved Frank deeply, was very emotional and tried not to cry when he first saw me that morning. I know he hated seeing his sister in such pain. After discussing the day ahead with him and Staci over our morning coffee, I left to shower and get ready. I remember looking in the bathroom mirror and saying to myself, *Why should I put eye makeup on? I'm going to cry all day long.*

We arrived at Calvary Chapel Chino Valley over an hour early, but the parking lot was already quite full. A parking attendant recognized me and directed Johnny, who was driving my car, to a reserved spot near our pastor's office. As soon as I stepped out of the passenger seat, someone from our church escorted me into Pastor David Rosales' office. I was taken by how organized and prepared everything was and felt totally bathed in protection and love.

Pastor David and his wife, Marie, were waiting to greet me. We wiped away a fresh set of tears and settled in on a couple of couches.

In a private VIP room nearby, other family members, KKLA staff, and close friends stood and spoke in muted tones next to tables teeming with breakfast goodies and coffee.

Back in Pastor David's office, I felt numb. I worried that I would have a meltdown during the service, knowing this would be the most difficult public event I would ever attend. I chose *not* to take a tranquilizer, as a few people suggested, because I wanted to experience the raw emotions I knew I'd feel at my husband's memorial. Two church staff members were assigned to me for the entire day, but basically they were my bodyguards. That was something new to me, but I figured they knew what was best.

I remember walking into the VIP room and seeing my family: my mom, Ann; my sister, Marina, and her family; my brother Nick and his family; and Johnny and Staci. I saw Joni Eareckson Tada in her wheelchair and her husband, Ken. They, too, were crying. I was in a blur of grief.

Someone mentioned that Dr. James Dobson had flown in from Colorado Springs, Colorado, and was there at the church.

"What?" I exclaimed. "Dr. Dobson is *here*?"

"Got here a few minutes ago," the acquaintance said.

I panicked. I was sure Dr. Dobson wanted to say something about Frank, but he wasn't part of the program because we didn't know he was coming. I spotted Greg Laurie, pastor of Harvest church, and walked up to him.

"Greg, Dr. Dobson flew in. Do you think we should have him say something?"

Greg showed his true humility. "Do you want him to take my time?" he asked. "I know Frank loved Dr. Dobson."

"Oh, no, don't do that. Greg, I want you to speak too. But maybe we can fit him in?"

"Let me see what we can do," he said.

As he walked away, I was struck by Greg's heart.

I looked at the clock on the wall: it was almost time for the memorial service to begin. As the seconds clicked away, I became very distraught. My stomach ached and my head swirled, but I knew I had to be strong.

I was escorted from the back of the sanctuary and seated right under the podium. I sat with Frankie and Christina, who flanked me on either side. My daughter held my hand during the entire service.

Symbolically, our church blocked off the two seats that Frank and I always sat in for Sunday service. They were in a row toward the middle of the church, in an area where church staff always sat. Frank, having long legs, liked to sit in the end seat so he could stretch his legs.

Over the many years we attended church at Calvary Chapel Chino Valley, members knew where to find Frank. Whenever the service ended, well-meaning congregants would make their way over to say hello to Frank or just say, "Hey, Frank! We love the show!"

As part of the memorial service, the church staff placed Frank's Bible, biking gloves, and his motorcycle helmet on the chair he always sat in. I didn't know this happened until *after* the service, but I was touched when I found out.

I was methodical about who would speak at Frank's memorial service because I wanted people to say something about different aspects of his life. We had decided to webcast the service, which meant that many thousands would be watching online, from every corner of the globe. I choose the following lineup:

- Dennis Prager, the host of the *Dennis Prager Show* and a man who Frank loved for his wide influence in the Judeo-Christian world.
- Terry Fahy, who was Frank's boss at KKLA.
- Walt Russell, a close friend and representative of Frank's Biola years.
- Greg Laurie, another close friend and colleague who displayed Frank's evangelical connection.
- Joe Roggemann, a close personal friend.
- Dr. James Dobson, who we squeezed in, representing Frank's "Focus on the Family" connection.

The first speaker of the day was Dennis Prager, who focused on Frank's intelligence and demeanor. I was struck by his emotion as he explained, "Frank was like a brother to me." He said that he and Frank had a neat connection and great respect for each other. Dennis tried not to get emotional, but he broke down several times as he recalled Frank's "unbelievable intellect" and how he was one of the most joy-filled people he'd ever met.

"It is impossible for me to adequately convey how immense I

consider the loss of Frank to be," he said. "On a personal level, I lost a man I respected and loved. My studio feels empty; I still sometimes have those moments when I think that Frank will walk in, as if nothing happened. And the loss to society is incalculable."

While listening to Dennis's tribute, I held Christina's hand, fighting back the tears. I didn't want to start crying hysterically and become a jumble of tears. I wanted to soak in everything as best I could, but I worried for my children. What emotions were they experiencing? What was this like for them?

I heard sobbing all around me. While Dennis was reminiscing, I remember looking to my right and seeing Marie, my pastor's wife, hunched over and crying. I listened to family members sobbing out loud. The moment was surreal. And then, almost out of the blue, I had a little encounter with God. I was staring up at the back wall of our church and suddenly, quietly, I heard the Lord speak to my heart: *Gina, do you remember what you prayed when you were thirteen years old?*

Is that you, Lord?

Do you remember what you prayed?

I sat there and thought for a moment . . . and recalled a memory deep within my consciousness. I was transported to a time when I was sunbathing in my parents' backyard. I was just thirteen years old and hadn't fully matured yet. While laying on my back with my eyes closed, I prayed to God about a seventeen-year-old boy named Frank Pastore. I was head over heels for him and asked the Lord, "If he loves me as well, could I marry him someday? And could he be loved by a lot of people, even thousands of people?"

And the Lord heard my prayer and gave me an answer that was as clear as the warm, sunshiny day I was enjoying: *Gina, you can be with Frank, but he is going to die young.*

Tears streamed down my face as I felt God's presence in a powerful way in the sanctuary that day. I realized that He had granted me all three things! Frank had loved and adored me completely, we had a wonderful marriage, and thousands loved him.

The circle of life had been completed.

I also realized that by today's life expectancy standards, Frank had died young at the age of fifty-five. But the Lord was gracious . . . Frank had not left me and "died young" at the age of twenty-five, thirty-five, or even forty-five. God had blessed me with thirty-four awesome years together, and for each year, each month, each day, and each hour, I was grateful.

When Dennis was finished, Terry Fahy captured Frank's "radio host" side by describing how he "set the bar so high" as a Christian broadcaster. Then, with a smile, Terry told the story of how Frank didn't like to conform to the standard dress code at KKLA, which was dress pants and button-down shirts. Frank went with the program for a while, but it wasn't long before Frank began showing up in his standard denim shirt and Levi's 501 jeans.

Walt Russell remembered Frank as "undomesticated" and eulogized how Frank didn't play the "evangelical game" but was so real. Walt cried as he marveled how Frank was able to forgive Biola University for the way the school treated him.

Greg Laurie remembered Frank's listening ear and spoke of Frank's heart for the Gospel. Joe Roggemann, a family friend, described how Frank liked to entertain others in our home and live a normal life.

I was especially moved by Dr. Dobson, who softly said, "I loved Frank." He talked about Frank's heart for the Lord, Frank's graciousness toward him and his wife, Shirley, and how much he would miss him.

There was a lighter moment when Dr. Dobson finished. He stepped away from the podium and took several steps, looking for his seat in the packed-out church. It quickly became apparent that his eyes hadn't found where he was supposed to go . . . "Where's my seat?" he asked out loud with a smile, which prompted everyone in the sanctuary to break out in laughter. That was a sweet moment.

The kids and I knew it would be too difficult to get up and say a few words, so we prepared a video. Hearing my children say their goodbyes to their dad was heartbreaking. As for me, I recalled all the times Frank and I had attended memorial services over the years. Each time, without fail, we'd walk back to the car and Frank would say, "Please, I don't want my funeral to be sad! I want it to be an upbeat occasion!"

As I sat in the front row, I thought, *Sorry, Frank, but this is sad!*

And it was . . . a very sad time.

We had a full house that day—3,000 showed up to pay their respects to Frank. When the service was over, I had been prepped for what would happen next: I would be escorted out and taken to a private reception on the church campus.

After Pastor David closed us with touching comments and a final prayer, I stood up to walk toward the pulpit to thank him. I was immediately swarmed by many people who wanted a word with me: relatives, friends, neighbors, and work colleagues. I could tell that one of the gentlemen assigned to me was getting frustrated, but I wanted to hug everyone. But as more and more people pushed and shoved their way to me, I realized that I needed to allow security to escort me to the private reception.

I was turning to leave when a lady I didn't know grabbed me by the shoulders. "Don't worry," she said. "You're young and you're pretty."

That was the *last* thing on my mind at that time—thinking about myself. This was another reminder that though people are well-meaning, they can say weird things at the most inappropriate time—things one shouldn't say to someone in the throes of grief.

As I was being ushered out of the sanctuary, Uncle Reno, my dad's brother, caught my eye. I once again ditched the men assigned to buffer me from the crowd and quickly hugged my uncle. Then Uncle Dante, who looks exactly like my father, motioned that he needed a hug as well. Aunts and cousins saw their chance to express their condolences.

I felt one of my bodyguards gently grab my arm as people swarmed over to me. I had to keep going, but I had to stop for Dr. Betsy Barber, who had counseled Frank during his ministry burnout and had counseled me for a long time after that. With knowing tears in both our eyes, I whispered in her ear, "I think I'll be calling you. This is going to be a hard road for me."

She looked me in the eyes. "I can help you through this," she said.

The church and KKLA worked together to put together a private reception after the service. One of Frank's sponsors, Colombo's Italian Steakhouse, had graciously offered to cater the event. Women from our church supplied dishes also.

After sitting through my husband's nearly three-hour memorial service, I was finally free to move around and greet many familiar faces. Since this gathering symbolized that Frank meant so much to so many of these people, I didn't mind that I was being mobbed and appreciated every moment.

Many cousins, long-time old friends, new friends, church friends,

Frank's colleagues, Frank's buddies from Damien High, neighbors, and many of the *Frank Pastore Show* sponsors were there . . . it was almost too much to take in.

I have to admit that it did feel good to have so much support around the kids and me. I don't remember ever really sitting down to grab a bite to eat because a constant stream of people made their way to hug me. Frank Sontag and his wife, Erin, came over to hug me.

"Thank you for sitting in for Frank," I said. Frank Sontag had been guest-hosting frequently. Dave Benzing, aka Big Wave Dave, brought his entire family over to meet me—his wife, Claire, and their four children.

"Gina, Claire and I would like to support you through this difficult journey," Dave said. "Is it okay if we stay in touch?"

Hearing him say that caught me a bit off guard because he was someone who I didn't know very well.

When I had a moment to catch my breath, I looked around the reception hall. During Frank's career at KKLA, Frank's producer and engineers handled all the on-air duties, and I pretty much functioned as Frank's assistant with anything to do off the air.

I was never employed by the station, but simply attending to Frank's speaking schedule and answering his e-mail seemed like a full-time job and I loved doing it. Through my blur of grief, I realized that all of this was coming to an end.

What will I do with myself? Will I be okay financially?

In many ways, Frank's memorial service marked the first day of the rest of my life. I sensed and understood that I would have to let KKLA and the *Frank Pastore Show* go because that season was coming to an end.

And then the Lord would surprise me all over again.

When the huge memorial was over and Johnny and Staci flew back to Arizona, I never felt so alone in all my life.

To keep me company, my kids and close friends rotated spending the night for the first few weeks, everyone wanting to support me through the rough waters of grief. I was barraged by paperwork; I didn't know there were so many things that needed to be filled out or filed after losing a spouse. Frankie drove an hour twice a week in the evenings to help me get my affairs in order.

I was fortunate that Frank had always been meticulous with keeping life in order: not only did he keep all our records in a safe place, he kept the trust up to date and was on top of his life insurance policy.

I made appointments with my trust attorney and representatives of medical and life insurance companies. It seemed like I was running around all day to get my signature notarized on important documents that needed to get into the mail.

My heart ached for Frank, every minute. I cried several times a day. Often out of nowhere, grief would overwhelm me. It wasn't a conscious thing at all but almost like the depths of my soul knew a part of me was gone.

One day, around three weeks after Frank's death, I returned home from an appointment. I pulled into the garage and walked into the house—still and silent. I was alone.

An unbelievable wall of grief hit. I took a walk through the house, seeing traces of Frank every place I looked. There in the family room was his leather recliner that he loved to relax in while taking in a ball-game. Opening a cupboard in the kitchen, I spotted a large white coffee mug that was his favorite. Inside his home office, where he loved to sit and read, was his desk and favorite chair.

My once-comforting home now seemed vacant without Frank's presence.

I had to go . . . I literally ran out of the house and dropped in on my neighbors. They immediately invited me in, but I couldn't look them in the eye. I was distraught and cried for several minutes.

I don't think I can live in our house any longer without Frank, I thought.

My neighbors were patient and understanding, and they gave me heartfelt hugs and said I would be all right one day. I dried my tears and apologized for barging in, but they didn't want to hear any sort of expression of regret.

For the rest of the evening, I asked myself if it was normal to feel the way I did, paralyzed by grief. I decided I needed to talk to someone about it and knew just the person to call—Dr. Betsy Barber. The following morning, I set up an appointment to begin my grief counseling.

I drove to the Biola campus, where Betsy sat across from me in the same little room where she and I had counseled before. The familiar setting was comforting to me as well as being with her again. She knew me and my husband well, so I felt like I was in good hands. Frank would joke, "Betsy's the only woman who knows me as well as my wife does!"

I couldn't stop crying during my first session of grief counseling. I wasn't sobbing but just quietly crying. Betsy teared up as we talked about Frank's memorial. She softly said, "Gina, I haven't experienced what you are going through, but I have walked people through grief before. There are characteristics of grief. Do you want me to explain the process?"

I nodded yes.

She explained the science of grieving: between the fourth and sixth month, there was usually a psychological dip, but after six months, life starts to look better. She helped me understand that grief was a process that took emotional, physical, and spiritual energy. "Let me caution you not to make any big decisions until a year has passed," she said.

We discussed the disturbing feeling I had in the house and how I fled to familiar surroundings. "Totally normal," she said. "Just be sure to surround yourself with loved ones and don't isolate yourself from people. You did the right thing running over to your neighbors."

Then Betsy said something that stuck with me, "Just grieve, Gina! Don't worry about what you will do in the future. Just grieve!"

And that's what I determined to do.

Pastor David called to check on me. "It may be difficult for you to come to church for a while, but Marie and I want you to know that you can sit in my office if you'd like and watch from there. Marie will be there too."

He was correct: the first time I went back to church, this time by myself, was one of the hardest things I've ever done. About six weeks after the funeral, I drove into the parking lot, tears streaming down my face, feeling so alone and lost without Frank. We had attended our church together for twenty-three years.

I took Pastor David up on his offer and sat with him and Marie in his office while the worship band played, sobbing and holding a tissue up to my face. My pastor didn't say anything: he just let me cry. After about thirty minutes, he walked out to preach and I remained in the office with Marie, silently crying as we watched David preach on the monitor.

Terry Fahy's assistant Balvina—whom Frank had nicknamed "Bal"—kept me posted on what was happening at KKLA. "Gina, you're part of the KKLA family," she said. It was comforting to hear her say that each time we interacted. When I said that I had to clean out Frank's cubicle at the KKLA offices some time, she added, "There's no rush on this."

The Frank Pastore Show continued with Kevin McCullough and Frank Sontag sitting in as guest hosts. Terry Fahy called one day to check up on me and give me some good news: Salem Broadcasting had decided to name Frank's old broadcast studio "Frank Pastore Studio B."

I was so honored to hear this and was invited to the dedication ceremony.

Shortly afterward, Kevin McCullough called and said, "Lady G, would you be up to coming on the air and doing an interview on the day of Frank's dedication?"

I liked his idea. I knew that thousands and thousands of Frank's listeners were grieving with our family. "Sure, we can do that," I said, "but can we tape it in case I break down?"

"No problem, Gina."

On Thursday, January 10, 2013, just twelve days after the memorial service, I arrived at the Salem LA office to dedicate Frank's old studio in his name, which would formally happen live, on the air, sometime after 4 p.m. on the *Frank Pastore Show*. Christina and I arrived an hour early so that Kevin and I could tape our interview, which would air during the special program.

This would be the first time I would talk about Frank on KKLA following Frank's accident. My comfort level was high because Kevin had sat in for Frank over the years when Frank took time off for vacations. After inquiring how I was doing, Kevin asked me to bring listeners up to date on the events of the last few weeks. Then Kevin asked me this: "Gina, what has God taught you through all of this?"

"Well, I've always been a planner, planning ahead on everything, but I couldn't plan this. What I've learned is that we can plan our future, but God is in control and only He knows our future," I said.

My short interview was aired during the show to dedicate Frank's studio, which was filled with tributes from longtime sponsors as well as re-airing some of Frank's "best of" clips. Hearing my husband's cheerful voice so clearly brought back strong memories—and warm tears. The highlight for me was when Frank's old studio was rechristened "Frank Pastore Studio B" on the air.

During a commercial break, Ed Atsinger, the owner of Salem Broadcasting, stepped into the studio where many of us were gathered. I had only met Ed once at a Salem event several years prior. As he approached me to offer his condolences, I reached out and hugged him, tears strolling down my face.

"Thank you for employing my husband, and thank you for your confidence in him," I said.

He responded warmly. "We'll never replace him," Ed said. "Frank was one of a kind. Such a gifted man . . . a rare commodity."

Before I left the Salem LA offices that evening, Christina and I knew there was a chore waiting for us—a chore we weren't looking forward to. But it had to be done.

We stepped into Frank's cubicle. I saw his Bible, Bible commentaries, and various study books that were kept on a shelf. His desk was lined with personal pictures of the two us as well as our children and their spouses, plus the requisite photo of our grandson Michael.

We couldn't clean out his desk. This area seemed "untouchable" to my daughter and me—like sacred territory. Instead, we sat at Frank's desk and cried and told each other that we'd come back in a couple of weeks to clean things out.

I needed time—time to grieve.

24

There Is a Season

I quickly learned that there was no escaping grief.
    I stayed with my kids and grandson as much as possible and was rarely alone in my home. After three months, I started staying home alone at night. I found that I wanted time to be by myself and reflect on Frank and grieve a little by myself. I'm more of an introvert, so constantly being with family for several months was comforting, but now I sensed that I needed alone time.

I wanted to pray about Frank's legacy too. I felt strongly about putting together a format where Frank's past interviews—the ones that were not time-sensitive—could be re-broadcast. As I remained in touch with people at KKLA, I decided to make this suggestion but I never got much of a response.

Christina and I decided it was time to head over to the studio and clean out Frank's desk. After we arrived, we met with Terry Fahy to discuss the Frank Pastore Show Facebook site and what do with all the emails that came into frank@kkla.com. We decided I would maintain Frank's Facebook site as thousands of people still checked in.

When our meeting was over, Balvina gave us some boxes to pack up Frank's books and stuff. My heart sank as I looked at the boxes. As much as I knew this needed to be done, I also knew I *didn't* want to do this.

Christina and I both sobbed as we pulled books from Frank's book-shelf. A large poster of Frank graced the back wall. That had to come down. The entire process was drawn out, but we finished.

About a week later, I received a call from Bob Hastings, one of the sales managers at Salem LA. He left a message, saying, "Hi Gina, it's Bob! Hey, can we schedule a meeting to discuss some ideas regarding Frank's legacy?"

That was exciting to hear. Maybe Salem was open to the idea of replaying Frank's audio clips.

I called Bob back and planned a meeting the following week. I arrived at the studio at 10 a.m. and went into Bob's office. We were talking about what was happening at KKLA when Bob introduced a new topic.

"What do think about you doing a show, a Saturday show?"

I was stunned. "What? Me? Are you serious?"

Bob smiled. "Yes, I'm very serious. People loved hearing from you when we did the dedication show. You really connect with listeners."

I had never thought of myself in that way.

"Well, I've never seen myself doing something like that," I said. "I'll have to think and pray about this."

I'll admit that as I left that day, I was thinking to myself, *No way, I'm not a radio host.*

At the same time, I felt the Lord saying, *I'll be with you.*

During the drive home, I stopped at a traffic light. I glanced up, where I saw puffy white clouds dotting a bright blue sky. Then I noticed a hawk flying over me, gliding through the air with its wings extended as an air current sustained the giant bird.

I'll sustain you, Gina, the Lord said in my heart.

That made me feel a lot better, but I decided to follow my counselor's advice and hold off because I didn't want to make a major decision so soon after Frank's death.

"Wait a year until you make any major decisions," Dr. Betsy Barber had counseled me.

As the weeks rolled on, I still cried every day. My heart continually ached for Frank. I wanted to collapse into his warm embraces, talk to him about many things, stroll with him, see his huge smile, feel his large, soft hands, and hear his cheerful voice say, "Hi, Honey, I'm home!" each weeknight around 8 p.m.

I missed everything about him. Just as Dr. Barber had mentioned, I felt a dip in my emotions around the fourth month. "When you think about not seeing someone you love dearly, at first you miss him," she said, "but after a few months, you *really* miss him."

This was a very difficult time. I remember asking God, "What do I do with this pain?" The pain I was dealing with was the worst emotional tidal wave I had ever experienced. I wanted to talk with other widows, people who could understand my pain. My family and close friends were supportive, but I needed to connect with women around my age who were walking in my shoes.

Just one problem: I was a young widow. Being fifty-one years of age, I didn't know many widows my age. Most of the widows I knew were my mom's age—in their eighties.

I hadn't really voiced this need to anyone, but one day, out of the blue, my close friend Donna called and said "Hey, Gene . . . I have an idea. I have a friend Debi Rooney who went through an awful tragedy. She lost both her husband and eldest son in a plane crash. Would you like to get together with Debi?"

Without hesitation, I said, "Yes!"

Donna set up a lunch for Debi and me at the Cheesecake Factory in Brea. I arrived right on time to find out that Donna and Debi were already seated. As the hostess walked me to their booth. I spotted Donna sitting across from an attractive brunette who was laughing with Donna.

Before Donna even introduced me to Debi Rooney, I thought, *Wow, I'm going to laugh again someday.* She had me before we even said hello.

When Donna introduced us, Debi got up from her seat and we hugged and hugged. We didn't need words. She was a few years out from her deepest pain, but she just looked at me as if to say, "I know exactly how you feel."

I cried a lot that day as we talked and fell in love with Debi along with her vulnerability, her strength, her emotional honesty, and her amazing laugh.

This lunch began a friendship that I would grow to cherish over the next several months, and now years. And yes, she helped me to laugh again.

Another friend, Russ Shubin, introduced me to another woman around this time. Claudia Souser had lost her husband suddenly in a Metrolink accident. I would regularly meet with these women and glean from them as they walked a journey I was now on.

Meanwhile, life went on. On May 9, 2013, Frank William Pastore was born. William was originally going to be his first name, but after

Frank's death, Frankie and Jessica decided to name him Frank in honor of my Frank, but from the first day, everyone has called him Will.

I must admit that Will's birth felt bittersweet. I felt sad that Frank wasn't there for this event. I remembered the day Michael was born. Frank and I both were in the room as Jessica gave birth. Frank was so emotional. I remember him crying and smiling the biggest smile ever as he held his new baby grandson, an image I hold in my heart dearly.

Within days of Will's birth, I received more good news: my daughter Christina and son-in-law Josh learned that they would be adopting a beautiful baby girl after her birth in late September. Again, I was so excited, but the news was bittersweet. In late July, however, I was asleep at 12:30 a.m. when my cell phone rang. Christina was on the line. "Mom, the baby was born tonight, she's here! You're a grandmother again!"

My new little granddaughter was born nine weeks early and ended up in the neonatal ICU for several weeks until we could take her home.

Around this time, a close friend alerted me of a tragedy where her daughter worked at a Christian school in Orange County. One of the boys at the school, along with his father, were killed in a car accident, and his younger brother was seriously injured. My heart sank hearing this, even though I didn't know these people. I immediately thought of my new friend Debi Rooney. She would be perfect to meet the woman who just lost her husband and eldest son. But how could I orchestrate that since I didn't know this woman at all?

That thought remained in my mind for a long time. A few months later, I was viewing my Facebook page one evening when I noticed that Debi was in Canada at a retreat called Camp Widow, a secular-based organization geared toward educating widows and widowers on their journey.

Suddenly, I noticed Debi was tagged in a picture with a woman named Debbie Siciliani.

Wait a minute. Wasn't that the woman in Orange County who lost her husband and son in a car accident? Sure enough, I checked her name with a close friend, and it was indeed she. The two Deb's had met in Canada, so God had worked it out.

The following week, upon their return from Canada, the three of us met for dinner and formed a strong bond. As we talked, the three of us each expressed a desire to help those going through loss and grief.

It was like we sensed a mission for our lives.

Something else happened in May. I received a phone call from Terry Fahy.

"Gina, I want to let you know I've come to a decision. Frank Sontag had been chosen to succeed Frank."

I immediately remembered Frank's words regarding Frank Sontag: "This guy is gonna take my job someday."

A chill went up my spine. I thanked Terry for letting me know and immediately called Frank to congratulate him. I remember Frank crying with me on the phone that day.

After it was announced that Frank Sontag would be Frank's successor, I happened to be visiting the KKLA studios one day because I was invited for lunch with some of the staff. Bob Hastings, the sales manager, walked me over to Frank's old cubicle, which had been taken over by Frank Sontag.

Frank's old cubicle was tucked away in a corner. As I approached his workspace, I saw a pair of jeans and boots, which looked identical to what Frank would have worn.

Frank Sontag, who heard me speaking with Bob, jumped up and spotted me.

"Gina!" Frank nearly bowled me over as he grabbed and hugged me. I sobbed . . . Frank sobbed. We felt a kinship. Then I looked up saw a promotional poster of my Frank, perched on his purple motorcycle, tacked up to the wall behind Frank's desk.

"Oh, that," Frank Sontag said. "That's staying. I want Frank looking down at me every day."

I thought that was a very sweet gesture.

During my time at the studios, I was asked what I thought about doing a radio show. That avenue was still open to me, Terry Fahy said, adding that I could take my time.

I mentioned that I was going to take a year before I made a major decision like that, and that's what I did. As I was grappling with starting my own radio show, I sought advice from Bob Tyler of Tyler & Bursch. He and his legal partner, Jennifer Bursch, had been the attorneys who represented high school student Chad Farnan in a much-publicized religious freedom case. Frank always loved Bob and Jen's hearts, and they formed a special relationship, having them on the show often. I was struck by how saddened they were by Frank's death, and they offered me their unwavering support as I grieved.

After speaking with Bob following the first anniversary of Frank's death—a year of the deepest grief—I felt God's nudging to do a radio show, but if that were to happen, then I knew I needed a co-host with a gregarious personality since I can be the more serious type.

Then the Lord gave me a thought: *What about Dave Benzing—"Big Wave Dave" on the Fish, 95.9 FM?*

Hmmm. He was a busy guy, but I could see doing a show with him. We seemed to have the right temperaments for each other. When I called Dave and dropped the idea on him, he was speechless for a long time, and it's rare for Dave to be speechless at *any* time.

"Wow, Gina, really?" he said. "I'm so honored! I have goose bumps, but let me check with Claire and get back to you."

The next day, Dave called and said his wife gave him the thumbs up. "Let's do it!" he exclaimed.

I scheduled a series of meetings at Salem LA with Bob Hastings, Richard Kennedy, and Dave Benzing to discuss what we'd talk about on the show. When Dave and I got in the studio and made several pilot shows, I wondered, "Do I have what it takes to do radio? Do I like doing this?" But those questions were quickly put aside because I *liked* what we were doing. Dave put me totally at ease and let me be me on the radio.

We had discussions about what to call the show. The phrase "Real Life" kept coming to my mind because I wanted to talk about and grapple with real issues that we all face. I wanted to encourage people through hard times of loss. And that's how *Real Life with Gina Pastore and David James* got off the ground on Saturday, April 12, 2014. We were placed in a half-hour time slot every Saturday from 7:30 to 8 p.m., Dave and I did the program from my co-host's studio, affectionately known as the "Dave Cave" right next door to Frank Pastore Studio B, which was cool. We also played Frank's "evergreen audio," pulling "best-of" clips from the *Frank Pastore Show*.

As I got my feet wet, I thought it would be a great idea to invite Debi Rooney and Debbie Siciliani on the show. We hit it off so well on the air that I made them regulars. As special contributors for *Real Life*,

I affectionately called them "The Debbi's." (I blended their names.) It's neat to see God unfolding a plan for our lives—an unexpected purpose—that the three of us could have never imagined.

Right from the beginning, we had many interesting guests. We invited Pete Rose's first wife, Karolyn, to talk about divorce; clinical psychologist Dr. Mark Baker to speak on forgiveness; Boston Red Sox pitcher Steven Wright and his wife, Shannon, to describe the baseball life; actress Karen Abercrombie, "Miss Clara" from the film *War Room*, to share her thoughts on this moving film; and Biola University president Dr. Barry Corey to discuss his book, *Love Kindness*. I was grateful that Frank and I had struck up a great relationship with Dr. Corey, who was a regular guest on the *Frank Pastore Show*. We were blessed to be invited to his inauguration at Biola.

I was indebted to many of the sponsors of the *Frank Pastore Show* who showed their confidence in me by sponsoring my program and helping me to carry on my late husband's legacy. I will always be grateful to American Vision Windows, Applied Financial Planning, Econo Air, and Phil Liberatore of IRS Problem Solvers.

25

Reflections

Over the thirty-four years of my marriage to Frank, people have asked me, "Did you ever regret getting married so young?"

I guess that's a fair question, and the answer is a resounding "No!" Never once, not for one moment, did I ever regret tying the knot with Frank when I was sixteen years old. Sure, I didn't get to date other guys, experience my last two years of high school, go off to college, or get my first apartment on my own, but I wouldn't have wanted to miss the exciting life journey I experienced with Frank.

Two things can happen when people marry very young: either they grow up together, or they grow apart. In today's world, there's so much emphasis on *not* getting married until your late twenties or even early thirties, and that's reflected in the marriage statistics. The average age for first marriage, according to the U.S. Census Bureau, is twenty-seven years for women and twenty-nine for men, which is up considerably from when Frank and I got married in 1976, when the average age was twenty-one for women and twenty-three for men.

I understand that we live in a culture where you're supposed to "find yourself" before you take a major step like getting married. But in my case as well as Frank's, we "found ourselves" through finding each other.

That's why I can say that so much of Frank lives on in me. Frank was a strong individual, and he helped me become a strong individual. Together we formed quite a union, and anyone who knew us would agree that we were "very married." When Frank and I came to Christ, we allowed the Holy Spirit to be first and foremost in our marriage, and that was our secret weapon. Quite frankly, the Holy Spirit has sustained me through this journey of my life and has been my lifeline through the darkest valleys.

Something I've learned on this journey is that grief is misunderstood. You don't get *over* it, you get *through* it. I didn't fully understand this concept until I experienced it. You have to *live* through grief, not think that you can put it aside in a box.

I remember meeting with a male acquaintance a couple months after Frank's death. This man asked me, "Are you at the point where you're not thinking about Frank every day?"

The question stunned me. This was a very intelligent, well-meaning person, but I realized he simply had no clue about grief.

Another thing that caught me off guard is how people love to help you find another mate. The fact of the matter is this: when you've lost the love of your life, you can't replace that person. Of course, finding another mate is entirely possible and can be a positive thing, but I was stunned about the lack of understanding regarding this. Talk to someone who's lost a child or a beloved spouse, and they'll tell you what I've learned, which is that the heart carries those we've woven into our souls. Traces of Frank Pastore are woven into the deepest parts of my soul, so it's going to take some time before I think I'm ready to remarry, and that may never happen.

Another thing that I've learned is that we humans try to avoid pain. There's no avoiding the pain of losing someone you have loved, however. Through counseling, I've learned to *lean* into the pain. That's the only way to get through it. If you try to avoid grieving properly, that will eventually bite you in the butt and manifest itself as anger, bitterness, illness, addictions, and so on.

It's also vitally important to have a support system, meaning having family, friends, pastors, and counselors around you—any and all. I'm thankful that many people allowed me to cry with them, and they cried with me too. This was healing for me.

I've found that men, especially, become uncomfortable if I start to cry, and they'd say, "Oh, Gina, I'm sorry. I didn't mean to make you cry."

When that happens, I'll quickly say, "No, I want to cry. It's okay."

Since then, close male friends have learned that it's okay to see me cry.

I do have a funny story to share. About a year-and-a-half after Frank's death, I was in my local Ford dealership, waiting for the oil to be changed on my car. I was sitting in the service manager's office, chatting him up, when one of the car salesmen that Frank and I would always talk to spotted me.

He was a big, gregarious African-American man nicknamed "Hutch." He quickly poked his head into the office and said, "Hey there, lady! How's that big, crazy, fun-loving husband of yours?"

I looked like a deer in headlights. I immediately broke down crying, having been blindsided by grief.

Hutch, who obviously didn't know Frank had died, looked stunned. Within seconds, both men were comforting me with hugs. I kept telling them, "It's all right. I'm fine."

When I drove my car off the lot, I could hear my husband teasing me, "Way to go, Gene. Way to make a scene."

After Frank passed away, I heard from people asking me a variation of the following question: "Why was someone who was such a force for the Gospel, someone being used by God in such a powerful way, taken away so young?"

I must admit, I wondered the same thing myself. I leaned on what my husband always said when he preached and taught over the air waves: "God is in control. Even when things in life don't make sense to us, God always has a plan."

I was hearing that some "name it and claim it," positive-confession Gospel teachers were saying things like this on their blogs: "When Frank Pastore talked about getting hit while riding his motorcycle home, that gave Satan an invitation to wreak havoc."

Thankfully, my husband held a good and strong theological perspective that rested on this foundational thought: "God's will is first . . . it's not my will, it's Thy will."

It was perfectly fine for us to pray for God to intercede and ask Him for a miracle, and to beg God to spare Frank's life. However, God chose to take Frank Home. His will be done.

I had an interesting dream one night, about two months after Frank died. In the dream, it was night time and I was walking down a set of stairs to walk on a beautiful beach, lit by moonlight. The air was breezy and balmy, and the sound of waves crashing on the shore filled the air. As I approached the ocean, the tide rolled up and hit my feet. Suddenly a beautiful, majestic lion came walking out of the water!

I cried out, "What are you doing here? You're a lion. You're not supposed to be in the ocean!"

Suddenly, a voice gently said, "This is my domain, and I take whom I choose to be with me."

Then I woke up, a little startled, wondering what that dream meant. Within moments, I knew it was God explaining to me that Frank belonged to Him. This dream brought comfort to my aching heart. As hard as it is to do, we need to realize God is in full control of our lives and this entire universe.

We're all going to go through transition times. I remember the day Frank and I brought Frankie to Biola University and helped him organize his new dorm room. We were all excited that our son was starting college, but after Frank and I left the campus, a sad feeling came over me. I remember thinking, *Our lives will never be the same.*

I began to tear up on the hour-long drive back to our home. When Frank saw that I was crying, he tried to cheer me up. "Awww, honey, he's only an hour away. He'll be home a lot on weekends."

When we got back to our house, Frank drove up the driveway and parked in our garage. I went to walk into the house and turned to ask Frank something when I noticed my husband had tears rolling down his cheeks. He had spotted Frankie's golf clubs in the garage. Frank loved golfing with Frankie, and our son frequently practiced his chipping on the front lawn.

We hugged each other in the garage that day and sobbed. Life was changing for us. We were moving into the next phase of life, which was terrifying, especially because we were so content with the way things were.

One of my favorite portions of Scripture is Ecclesiastes 3:1-13 (NIV):

> *There is a time for everything,*
> *and a season for every activity under the heavens:*
> *a time to be born and a time to die,*
> *a time to plant and a time to uproot,*
> *a time to kill and a time to heal,*

a time to tear down and a time to build,
a time to weep and a time to laugh,
a time to mourn and a time to dance,
a time to scatter stones and a time to gather them,
a time to embrace and a time to refrain from embracing,
a time to search and a time to give up,
a time to keep and a time to throw away,
a time to tear and a time to mend,
a time to be silent and a time to speak,
a time to love and a time to hate,
a time for war and a time for peace.

What do workers gain from their toil? I have seen the burden God has laid on the human race. He has made everything beautiful in its time. He has also set eternity in the human heart; yet no one can fathom what God has done from beginning to end. I know that there is nothing better for people than to be happy and to do good while they live. That each of them may eat and drink, and find satisfaction in all their toil—this is the gift of God.

I remember loving this section of Scripture as a child and how it ministered to me. There is an appointed time for everything, and there is a time for every event under heaven . . . nothing escapes God. In my darkest times of grief, I had this assurance and buried it in my soul.

While it's true that time brings healing, I will always miss Frank, until the day I go Home to be with God.

Afterword

by Steven Wright, pitcher for the Boston Red Sox

I love the story that Gina Pastore just shared because she and Frank have had a tremendous effect on my life and what I do today—flinging knuckleballs for the Boston Red Sox.

I first started taking pitching lessons from Frank when I was nine years old, which would have been in 1995. My mom had to drive me forty-five minutes from our home in Moreno Valley to Frank's backyard in Upland for our thirty-minute private lesson, but the long commute was okay because my parents had been told that Frank was the best pitching instructor around.

We started with the mechanics—how to properly throw a fastball and curveball, and I progressed rapidly. But if you hung around Frank for any length of time, he wanted to teach you a lot more than the right release point—he wanted to talk about how to live the Christian life. He became a father figure to me in many ways.

I continued to take pitching lessons from Frank during my high school years, which earned me a scholarship to the University of Hawaii. I met a really cute girl my freshman year named Shannon. We were just friends for a couple of years, and then we started dating my junior year when I got picked in the second round of the major league draft by the Cleveland Indians.

I really wanted to marry Shannon, but I felt that Frank and Gina needed to meet her before I proposed. They hit it off, and Shannon would become very close to Gina as I kicked around the minor leagues, which was hard on us. Gina was "safe" for Shannon to talk to about the struggles of being the wife of a professional baseball player who hadn't progressed to the major leagues.

After the 2010 season was over, I still hadn't been called up. It looked like Triple A was my ceiling. I had a 90-mile-per-hour fastball—fast but not quite fast enough to get me to The Show. I was wondering if it was time to hang 'em up and go back to school or learn the carpentry trade from Shannon's father, who was a general contractor in Santa Cruz, California. At twenty-five years of age, I was at a crossroads.

I needed a swing-and-a-miss pitch, and that's when one of my coaches in the Indians organization suggested that I try using the knuckleball after seeing me throw a few while playing catch. I had been messing with the knuckleball for years and was intrigued on how you could throw the ball forward with no spin but still move like crazy.

Ever since I signed a pro contract, I continued to work with Frank in the off-season. I respected his experience and loved how he made pitching a baseball so much fun. When I told him about the Indians' suggestion that I try throwing the knuckleball, we spent about thirty minutes tossing each other knucklers back and forth. He had learned the pitch from Phil Niekro, one of the greatest knuckleball pitchers ever, but he never threw knuckleballs when he was on a major league mound.

Frank was impressed with how much my knuckler moved. "You've got a good one there," he said. "You never know. The knuckleball might come in handy for you."

With his encouragement ringing in my ears, I decided to turn to the knuckleball as my primary pitch. I wasn't an overnight success, however. In fact, I pitched for four different minor league teams in 2011. But I kept plugging away and continued to tutor with Frank during the off-season.

During the 2012 spring training, Frank and Gina drove out to Phoenix, where the Cleveland Indians and Frank's old team, the Cincinnati Reds, shared a spring training complex. Frank was in high spirits because he got to see a lot of his old teammates, like Tom Hume, who had become a coach in the Reds farm system.

Shannon and I shared some great news at spring training: we were pregnant with our first child. Gina just loved on Shannon, which was greatly encouraging. We were still hanging on to the dream of making it to the majors, but I was twenty-eight years old and wondering if it would ever happen.

In the middle of the 2012 season, I was traded to the Boston Red Sox and told to keep working on my knuckleball. I can't tell you the number of times I spoke with Frank on the phone. He told me to hang in there and that God had a plan for my life.

When the season was over, I went right into winter ball because I needed to pitch the knuckleball in live game situations. That fall, Shannon gave birth to our first child, a daughter we named Ella.

On November 17, 2012, Frank and I spoke on the phone, and he was his usual energetic self. "Man, I can't wait for you to get back!" he said. "I want to hold your daughter. I can't wait to meet her. I'm so excited for you and your family and your future."

Frank was always in my corner, telling me I could do it.

Three days later, on November 20, I learned that I had been added to the Red Sox 40-man roster, which was awesome news. The only way you can make it to the major leagues is to be on that 40-man roster, so this was huge.

I called Shannon to share the great news. Then I was going to call Frank.

"Babe, I just got put on the roster! Isn't that amazing?"

She had no reaction. Why wasn't she happy?

"Babe, that's exciting," she said flatly, "but you have to call your father."

"Why?"

"Because Frank's been in a motorcycle accident and it's not looking good."

I said goodbye and immediately called my father in Moreno Valley, who told me that Frank had been struck by a car while riding home the previous evening. He was in a coma, which was grim news.

The first thing I said to my father was, "I have to go see him."

"You should go," my father said.

I asked my team for permission to leave after my next start so that I could visit Frank in the hospital. We were at the end of the season anyway.

When I reached Gina to tell her I was coming, we both cried on the phone. So sad. She gave me his "Adam 32" alias to use when I arrived at the USC Medical Center.

My heart broke in little pieces seeing Frank in the ICU unit. I stayed several days in Los Angeles, visiting Frank each day. I told him how much he meant to me and how I tried to model my life and my marriage after his. I don't think he was able to hear me, but I wanted him to know how I felt.

I returned to Santa Cruz, where we were living with my wife's parents during the off-season. A couple of weeks later, we received the news that Frank had passed away.

We drove south for the memorial service. I'll admit that I gripped the steering wheel with anger. Why would God take somebody with such potential for getting the Gospel out? Since he was an atheist for so long, he could relate to anybody with his gift of speaking and communication. And then I realized that I was being selfish because Frank was my guy—the guy I went to for everything. And now I could never talk to him again.

But we still have Gina with us, and for that, Shannon and I are extremely grateful. Her ability to handle the struggles that she's gone through and relate the pain and sorrow that she's felt in a positive way is tremendous.

What I've learned through all this is that everybody is going to lose a loved one sooner or later. Whether it's your spouse, your mom or dad, or—God forbid—a child, we're not meant to live forever. Gina's desire to share her experiences with the platform that Frank created for her is something I tip my hat to.

When Gina told me she was writing a book, I had a one-word response—"Perfect!"

And after reading this highly enjoyable and yet poignant story of her fascinating life, I hope you'll join me in giving her a standing ovation.

Acknowledgments

To all of Frank's dedicated listeners, your notes, letters, comments, messages blessed me to no end. I can't even begin to express how your love and support during Frank's accident soothed me.

To Salem Broadcasting and the "KKLA Family," I have no words to describe your faithful support. Frank absolutely loved working for and with you each and every day. Special thanks to Terry Fahy, Bob Hastings, Richard Kennedy, and the entire KKLA team. To experience your steadfast love of my husband was beyond my expectations. I will always be indebted to all of you, as well as my broadcasting partner, David James Benzing, aka "Big Wave Dave." Thank you for your encouragement and for doing radio with me. I love you and Claire and thank you for your friendship.

My wonderful neighbors—Jeff and Terry Olsavsky, Mark and Judy Boroch, Jim and Diane Tucker, and Linda Ricci—thank you for being there for me.

To my pastor David Rosales and his wife, Marie, I love you more than words can express.

A special thank you to these pastors and friends who supported me during Frank's accident: Dudley Rutherford, Raul Ries, Ryan Ries, Steve Wilburn, Greg Laurie, and Dan Carroll.

A special hug to Frank and Erin Sontag—I love you both!

To my co-writer Mike Yorkey, I appreciate you for going on this journey with me. I loved working with you and I felt like you were present in each story I wrote. Thank you for making this collaboration a wonderful experience. I also greatly appreciate those who proofed my book for typos: Nadia Guy, Ionelee Brogna, Heidi Moss, Nicole Yorkey, Ross Mitchell, Jessica Snell, and former New York Yankee Bruce Robinson. Larry Weeden, Senior Book Producer at Focus on the

Family, gave me wise counsel and encouragement.

To Dr. Betsy Barber, thank you for guiding my "soul work" and helping me to become a more integrated woman. I would not be the woman I am today without you.

Dan Johnson, Robert Tyler, Jennifer Bursch, Tim Blied, and Greg Wood—thank you for your wisdom and expertise in helping me to move forward after Frank's death.

A special thank you to the wonderful people at American Vision Windows, Applied Financial Planning, and Econo Air who have helped me continue my husband's legacy.

To Frank's wonderful extended family in Birmingham, Alabama: Thank you for all your love and support over the years.

To my faithful close friends: Eldon and Pam Lahr; Joe and Veronica Roggemann; Walt and Marty Russell; Don and Kristina Kase; Bruce and Teresa Erickson; Mark and Cindy Stapleton; Steven and Shannon Wright; Tom and Susan Hume; Marcia and Jim Fisher; Roger and Diane Ingolia; Mike and Joanie Morrell; Allen and Donna Willshire; Brian and Patty Bird, Kim Borba, Debi Rooney Jaso, Debbie Siciliani, and Linda McDougal . . . I love each and every one of you.

To my family: my parents, John and Ann Pignotti; my sister Marina and her husband Don Gardner; my brother Johnny and his wife, Staci; my brother Nick and his wife, Janelle; my children's in-laws, Dennis and Cindy Dangerfield and Ron and Delia Smallwood; plus all my aunts and uncles, nieces and nephews, and many cousins, your love, strength, and support buoyed me. I am blessed beyond measure.

To my children, Frank and Christina and their spouses, Jessica and Josh: I am eternally grateful for all of your love and support as we weathered the most difficult storm of our lives. To my sweet grandchildren: Michael, William, and Finley, I love you all more than words could ever express.

To my beautiful husband, Frank: I will love you until I take my last breath . . . you are my heart and soul and I will love you forever.

Source Material

Chapter 16
"As it was, there were enough problems in Frank Pastore's life..." from "Red's Pastore Handles Crisis, Dodgers," by Mike Davis, *San Bernardino Sun*, May 31, 1981, and available at https://www.newspapers.com/image/63203763.

About the Authors

Gina Pastore, author of *Picking Up My Shattered Pieces*, is the co-host of *Real Life with Gina Pastore and David James*, a radio broadcast heard every Saturday evening from 7:30-8:00 p.m. throughout Southern California on KKLA 99.5 FM and through the web at kkla.com.

She grew up in Upland, California, thirty-five miles east of downtown Los Angeles, the third youngest of four children born to John and Ann Pignotti. Gina and Frank Pastore were childhood sweethearts and married in 1978 when Frank was a highly regarded pitcher in the Cincinnati Reds organization. Frank was elevated to the major leagues seven months after their wedding and enjoyed an eight-year career in the majors, pitching for the Reds except for one season as a reliever with the Minnesota Twins.

Gina and Frank, who lived in their hometown of Upland during the off-season, raised two children, Frank Jr. and Christina, who are both happily married to two wonderful spouses.

After Frank's baseball career ended, Frank pursued education and attained two master's degrees. In 2004, he became the host of *The Frank Pastore Show* heard daily on KKLA. On November 19, 2012, Frank was seriously injured on the 210 Freeway when he collided with a car while riding his Honda VTX 1800 motorcycle. He suffered serious head injuries and was hospitalized in critical condition. Frank died a month later at the age of fifty-five.

Following Frank's tragic death, Gina pursued radio and today enjoys encouraging people through her broadcasts and inspirational speaking events with a compelling message that God is always there during painful times.

She is currently attaining certification in Spiritual Direction at

Loyola Marymount University in Los Angeles. While Gina's life has taken a path she never expected, her greatest comfort comes from her three grandchildren. These days she says she enjoys the simple life: family, good friends, church, and taking long power walks.

Mike Yorkey is the author or co-author of one hundred books with more than 2 million copies in print. He has collaborated with Cyndy Feasel, an ex-NFL wife, in *After the Cheering Stops*; the Chicago Cubs' Ben Zobrist and his wife, Julianna, a Christian music artist, in *Double Play*; Washington Redskins quarterback Colt McCoy and his father, Brad, in *Growing Up Colt*; San Francisco Giants pitcher Dave Dravecky in *Called Up*; San Diego Chargers placekicker Rolf Benirschke in *Alive & Kicking*; tennis star Michael Chang in *Holding Serve*; and paralyzed Rutgers' defensive tackle Eric LeGrand in *Believe: My Faith and the Tackle That Changed My Life*. Mike is also the co-author of the internationally bestselling *Every Man's Battle* series with Steve Arterburn and Fred Stoeker. He has written several fiction books, including *The Swiss Courier* and *Chasing Mona Lisa*.

He and his wife, Nicole, are the parents of two adult children and make their home in Encinitas, California.

Mike's website is www.mikeyorkey.com.

Invite Gina Pastore
to Speak Today

G ina Pastore is a thoughtful speaker with a passion to talk about life's most important issues—loss, grief, and making it through tough times. She is available to speak at various events, including luncheons. Gina is also partnering with Debi Rooney Jaso and Debbie Siciliani to encourage other women during events and weekend retreats.

If you, your community group, women's ministry, or church would be interested in having Gina speak at your event, please contact her through her Facebook page: **Gina Pastore Radio.**

From the left, Debi Rooney Jaso, Gina Pastore, and Debbie Siciliani love speaking on how God has brought them through the most difficult times.